# Type 2 Diabetes
## Cookbook for Beginners

Easy-to-Cook Diabetes Recipes and Easy-to-Operate 1-Month
Diet Plan for Type 2 Diabetes Newly Diagnosed

Rosie Dobbins

# © Copyright 2023 – All Rights Reserved

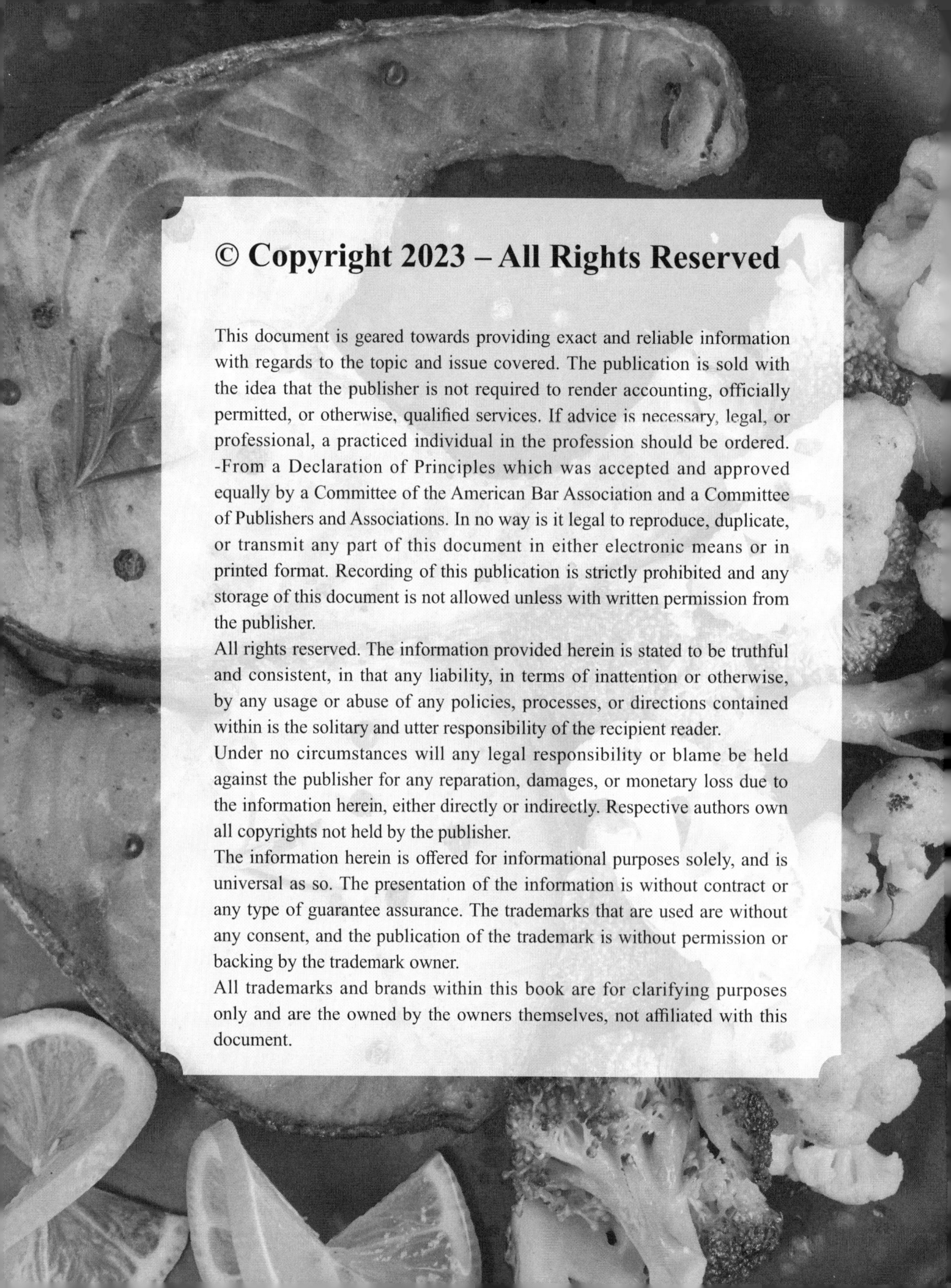

This document is geared towards providing exact and reliable information with regards to the topic and issue covered. The publication is sold with the idea that the publisher is not required to render accounting, officially permitted, or otherwise, qualified services. If advice is necessary, legal, or professional, a practiced individual in the profession should be ordered. -From a Declaration of Principles which was accepted and approved equally by a Committee of the American Bar Association and a Committee of Publishers and Associations. In no way is it legal to reproduce, duplicate, or transmit any part of this document in either electronic means or in printed format. Recording of this publication is strictly prohibited and any storage of this document is not allowed unless with written permission from the publisher.

All rights reserved. The information provided herein is stated to be truthful and consistent, in that any liability, in terms of inattention or otherwise, by any usage or abuse of any policies, processes, or directions contained within is the solitary and utter responsibility of the recipient reader.

Under no circumstances will any legal responsibility or blame be held against the publisher for any reparation, damages, or monetary loss due to the information herein, either directly or indirectly. Respective authors own all copyrights not held by the publisher.

The information herein is offered for informational purposes solely, and is universal as so. The presentation of the information is without contract or any type of guarantee assurance. The trademarks that are used are without any consent, and the publication of the trademark is without permission or backing by the trademark owner.

All trademarks and brands within this book are for clarifying purposes only and are the owned by the owners themselves, not affiliated with this document.

# CONTENTS

| | |
|---|---|
| 1 | Introduction |
| 2 | Fundamentals of Type 2 Diabetes Diet |
| 15 | 4-Week Meal Plan |
| 17 | Chapter 1 Breakfast Recipes |
| 30 | Chapter 2 Vegan and Vegetarian Recipes |
| 38 | Chapter 3 Fish and Seafood Recipes |
| 47 | Chapter 4 Chicken and Poultry Recipes |
| 54 | Chapter 5 Meat Recipes |
| 71 | Chapter 6 Stew, Soups, Salads, and Sandwiches Recipes |
| 87 | Chapter 7 Dessert and Snack Recipes |
| 95 | Chapter 8 Sauces, Dips, and Dressings Recipes |
| 100 | Conclusion |
| 101 | Appendix 1 Measurement Conversion Chart |
| 102 | Appendix 2 Recipes Index |

# Introduction

A worrying truth of our time is the exponential increase in diabetes incidences worldwide. The prevalence of diabetes, which affects one in every ten adults worldwide, necessitates significant dietary modifications, preventive interventions, and lifestyle changes to help everyone live better lives. Since it was created to keep patients' blood sugar levels regularly while also keeping them active and healthy, a diabetic-friendly diet has been shown to be beneficial over time. In order to provide a whole collection of recipes that are ideal for anyone who wants to prepare heart-healthy, low-carb, and sugar-free meals at home, I was able to successfully combine the concept of healthy cooking with a diabetic-friendly dietary approach. Thorough instruction on how to manage diabetes through dietary and lifestyle modifications is included in this diabetic cookbook, along with all the different types of diabetic-friendly recipes. So, are you prepared to begin working on it? Let's Do this!

# Fundamentals of Type 2 Diabetes Diet

## What is Diabetes?

Diabetes is a long-term and chronic illness that affects how your body turns food into energy. Most of the food you consume is converted by your body into sugar (glucose), which is then released into your bloodstream. When blood sugar levels rise, your pancreas releases insulin; for blood sugar to enter your body's cells and be used as energy, insulin functions like a key. When you have diabetes, your body either produces insufficient insulin or uses it improperly. Too much blood sugar remains in your bloodstream when there is insufficient insulin or when cells cease reacting to insulin. That can eventually lead to major health issues like renal disease, eyesight loss, and heart disease.

## Type 1 Diabetes

It is believed that an autoimmune reaction is what causes type 1 diabetes (the body attacks itself by mistake). Your body's production of insulin is stopped by this reaction. Type 1 diabetes affects between 5%–10% of those who have the disease. Type 1 diabetes symptoms frequently appear suddenly. Typically, it is discovered in kids, teenagers, and young adults. You must take insulin every day to stay alive if you have type 1 diabetes.

## Type 2 Diabetes

Your body struggles to properly utilize insulin in type 2 diabetes, making it not easy to maintain normal blood sugar levels. The majority of diabetics (90–95%) are type 2. It takes years to develop, and adults are typically diagnosed with it (but more and more in kids, teens, and young adults). If you are at risk, it is crucial to have your blood sugar tested because you might not exhibit any symptoms. By adopting healthy lifestyle adjustments like these, type 2 diabetes can be avoided or postponed.

## Gestational Diabetes

Women who have never had any type of diabetes before and who have become pregnant can acquire gestational diabetes. If you have gestational diabetes, your unborn child may be more susceptible to health issues. After your baby is born, gestational diabetes typically disappears. However, it raises your chance of developing type 2 diabetes in later life. Your child has a higher chance of being obese as a youngster or adolescent and going on to acquire type 2 diabetes.

## Prediabetes

Ninety-six million adults in the US, or more than one in three, have prediabetes. More than 80% of them are unaware of having it. Blood sugar levels are higher than normal in prediabetes but not high enough to be diagnosed as type 2. Your risk of having type 2 diabetes, heart disease, and stroke increases if you have prediabetes.

## What Causes Type 2 Diabetes?

The dip in the normal insulin levels in the body is not the actual cause of diabetes but the result of the damage caused to the cells producing the insulin. The actual causes of diabetes lie much deeper, and they gradually work to develop this condition. Here are some of the main causes of this condition:

### Obesity

Insulin resistance often develops because of obesity. When there is excess glucose left in the body, it is converted by the liver into glycogen, where it is then stored. That glycogen is then converted into fats. When a person is obese, the liver loses the ability to convert more glucose into glycogen and fats as there is already much accumulated around the organ. So it fails to convert the glucose and keep the blood sugar level normal, which ultimately leads to diabetes.

### Genetic History

If you have a family history of any type of diabetes, then you are twice as likely to develop diabetes as someone who does not have such a family history. There are a number of hereditary illnesses that are linked to insulin resistance or inadequate insulin production. We find people from one bloodline suffering from diabetes more than others. Cystic fibrosis and hemochromatosis are two diseases that affect the pancreas and cause diabetes. Diabetes can also be caused by a genetic abnormality.

### Poor Diet and Lifestyle

Poor diet and sedentary lifestyles are two major

causes of diabetes. Intake of high caloric diet, fatty, fried goods, and sugary meals can cause obesity, raise blood sugar levels and elevate blood cholesterol, which all are directly linked to diabetes. Any diet that is deficient in minerals, fibers, and vitamins while being heavy in fats and carbohydrates raises the risk of diabetes. To top it all, if such a diet is coupled with an inactive lifestyle with no exercise, that is going to exacerbate the condition.

## Difference Between Type 1 and Type 2

Type 1 diabetes is a genetic illness that frequently manifests in childhood, but type 2 diabetes is primarily connected to lifestyle choices and develops over time. The primary distinctions between type 1 and type 2 are outlined below.

**When you have both type 1 and type 2 diabetes, what happens?**

Diabetes, type 1 or type 2, is characterized by an excess of glucose (a form of sugar) in the blood. This holds for both kinds. However, how this occurs varies between them. Type 1 diabetes is an indication of an autoimmune disorder. This indicates that your body has attacked and killed the cells responsible for producing the hormone insulin. So you can no longer produce insulin. We all require insulin because it aids in transporting glucose from the blood into the cells of our bodies. After that, we use this glucose as fuel. Your blood glucose level rises too high if you don't have insulin. Diabetes type 2 is distinct. If you have type 2, either your body doesn't produce enough insulin, or your insulin is ineffective. Insulin resistance is the term for this. Similar to type 1, this denotes a very high blood glucose

|  | Type 1 | Type 2 |
| --- | --- | --- |
| What is happening? | Your pancreas cannot produce any insulin because your body is attacking its cells. | Insufficient insulin is produced by your body, or the insulin that is produced doesn't function effectively. |
| Risk factors | Type 1 diabetes has no known source at this time. | We are aware that factors like weight and ethnicity can increase your chance of developing type 2. |
| Symptoms | Type 1 symptoms emerge more quickly. | The slower onset of type 2 symptoms makes them potentially more difficult to detect. |
| Management | In order to manage type 1, you must take insulin to regulate your blood sugar. | Type 2 diabetes is more manageable than type 1 in many aspects. These include using medicine, physical activity, and food. Insulin can also be administered to people with type 2. |
| Prevention and cure | There is currently no treatment for type 1; however, research is ongoing. | Type 2 diabetes cannot be cured, although research suggests that it can often be prevented and put into remission. |

Fundamentals of Type 2 Diabetes Diet

level.

**Do type 1 and type 2 risk factors differ in any way?**

Type 1 and type 2 diabetes are not entirely preventable, but we are aware of the various risk factors. We now understand why you could be more likely to receive one type than the other. Even though we are aware of this, it's important to keep in mind that these aren't definite.

Type 1:

Type 1 differs greatly from type 2 in that your lifestyle has no bearing on it. Perhaps your weight. Thus, altering your lifestyle will not reduce your chance of type 1 diabetes. It is more common in those under the age of 40, particularly in children.

Type 2:

Type 2 diabetes differs. We are aware of various factors that increase your risk, including:
- If you're overweight or obese
- Age
- ethnic background
- Family history.

You can avoid type 2 by doing things like eating well, exercising, and maintaining a healthy weight. Being over 40 increases your risk of developing type 2 diabetes. Or if you are South Asian and older. However, type 2 is also spreading among younger individuals.

Symptoms of Diabetes

It is always important to detect the presence of disease at early stages to avoid maximum damage. The same is true for diabetes; far before going to a doctor, the following symptoms can be easily detected at home.

**Constant Thirst:** This symptom is somehow related to the next one. Frequent loss of salt and water from the body can cause increased thirst. And this thirst cannot be quenched with more water, as your body will be losing in eventually. It can be dealt with only by dealing with diabetes in a better way.

**Increased Urination:** A surge in blood glucose level affects the working of the kidneys and their over-function to, cause more urination than normal. This urination is not healthy as it makes the patient lose lots of water and salts the body. It is the unwanted removal of essential minerals from the body. So frequent urination should be taken seriously in any case. Else it will render the patient dehydrated.

**Abrupt Weight Loss:** Weight loss is a common symptom among patients with diabetes. They drastically lose several pounds if they are not on any sort of treatment. The excess of glucose makes the body metabolize excessively or more than the extent needed. Eventually, the body fails to absorb nutrients for its building process, and the muscles lose their energy and weight. The same happens with the bones and other organs.

**Affected Vision:** The sugar spike instantly affects vision by mingling with the optic nerves in the brain and weakening the eye muscles or affecting the lens or the retina. If you witness a sudden vision change, then consult a doctor. Carelessness can even cause impairment in extreme cases.

**Sudden Hunger:** The imbalance also causes hypoglycemia, which is the state of extreme hunger. This is mainly because of the fact that the body is incapable of harnessing the energy out of the food. It keeps the energy deficit and produces the sensation of extreme hunger. For this problem to deal with, it is suggested to take a small amount of meal after every 1 to 2 hours.

**Tiredness and Fatigue:** Fatigue is related to many chronic health disorders. It is also common among diabetic patients. They pretty much same the exhaustion all the time, even after rest. Get yourself to check if that is the case.

**Numbness of Limbs:** The sensation in the hands and feet is great lost when you are suffering from diabetes. This is the reason many diabetic patients don't even feel pain in most parts of the body when hurt. This numbness can get in the way of the normal function of the hands and feet.

**No Healing:** With diabetes, the body loses the normal function of healing. And it takes a longer duration of time to heal a sore or a wound. The infection may get serious if not treated properly in time. The use of additional medicines is prescribed for quick recovery. Nausea, stomach pain, and vomiting are a few of the additional symptoms that a patient may experience in the early or later stages of diabetes.

However, the way that the symptoms of type 1 and type 2 differ from one another. The 4Ts of type 1 diabetes are four prevalent symptoms that can frequently emerge rather suddenly. They are, therefore, more difficult to ignore. This is crucial since ignoring symptoms can result in diabetic ketoacidosis (DKA). However, type 2 diabetes may be simpler to overlook. This is because it develops more gradually, especially in the beginning. This makes identifying the symptoms more difficult. Because of this, it's critical to understand your risk of type 2 diabetes. Some people don't know they have diabetes. They may possess it secretly for up to ten years.

## How to Prevent Diabetes and Control Sugar Levels

If you haven't been taking your health seriously for most of your life, then after crossing 50, you have to change that attitude. Now your body needs extra care and attention to stay healthy.

Besides following a rich and balanced diet, you need major lifestyle changes, and the following suggestions can help:

**Use The "Plate" method:** The American Diabetes Association provides this simple and easy-to-follow meal-planning approach. Basically, it emphasizes eating more vegetables. Take the following actions to prepare your plate per meal:

1. Non-starchy veggies, such as spinach, carrots, and tomatoes, should make up half of your plate.
2. Give a protein, like tuna, lean pork, or chicken, a quarter of your dish.
3. Add a whole grain, such as brown rice, or a starchy vegetable, like green peas, to the last part of the plate.
4. Include "healthy" fats in moderation, such as those found in nuts or avocados.
5. Include a serving of dairy or fruit along with a glass of water, unsweetened tea, or coffee.

**Count Your Carbs:** Carbohydrates have the most effect on your blood glucose level since they break down into glucose. You might need to learn how to calculate the number of carbohydrates you consume so that you can change the insulin dosage to control your blood sugar. It's critical to monitor the carbohydrate content of each meal and snack. You can learn portion control techniques from a dietitian, who can also help you become a knowledgeable label reader. Additionally, you could learn from him or her how to pay close attention to portion size and carbohydrate content. A nutritionist can show you how to count the number of carbohydrates in each meal and snack if you are taking insulin and how to change your insulin dosage accordingly.

**Stay Physically Active:** It's time to get active if you aren't already. You can cross-train without joining a gym. Play some active video games, go for a stroll, or ride a bike. The majority of the week, you should aim for 30 minutes of exercise that causes you to perspire and breathe more laboriously. You can better manage your diabetes by leading an active lifestyle, which lowers your blood sugar. Additionally, it lessens your risk of developing heart disease. It can help in weight loss and stress reduction.

Monitor Your Physical Health: It is important to get yourself checked twice or thrice a year. Diabetes slowly progresses to damage other organs and their functions, and with regular checkups, you can manage your health as needed. The risk of developing heart disease is more likely if you have diabetes. Keep on checking your cholesterol, blood pressure, and A1c values after every 3 months. Since diabetes can affect your eyesight, so every year, go for a complete eye exam. To check for issues, including nerve damage and foot ulcers, see a foot doctor.

**Avoid Mental Stress:** Stress causes your blood

sugar levels to rise. Anxiety may affect how well you control your diabetes. You might neglect to take your medications, exercise, or eat properly. Find ways to relax, whether it be through yoga, deep breathing, or relaxing activities. Talk to an expert and share your feelings to release tension.

**Quit Smoking:** Diabetes increases your risk of developing conditions like nerve damage, heart disease, eye disease, kidney disease, blood vessel disease, stroke, and foot issues. Your likelihood of developing these issues is increased if you smoke while being diabetic.

**Treatment for Diabetes:** You can manage and treat your diabetes with a variety of treatments. Because each person is unique, the type of treatment you receive will depend on your needs. You will require the usage of insulin to manage your type 1 diabetes. You can use a pump or an injection to administer the insulin. Although you may initially be able to control Type 2 diabetes by eating healthily and moving more, you may eventually need to take insulin or medications.

**Insulin:** To control their blood glucose (sugar) levels, all individuals with type 1 diabetes and some individuals with type 2 diabetes must take insulin. It doesn't indicate that you have type 1 diabetes if you have type 2 and your medical team advises that you start taking insulin. Although you still have type 2, your medical care has altered. It's common for type 2 diabetics to require insulin therapy at some point, but it doesn't necessarily mean your diabetes has been poorly controlled. Simply said, insulin is a different type of drug that can support your continued good health.

## Additional Information on Nutritional Goals for Type 2 Diabetic Patients

A nutritious, well-balanced diet is an essential component of managing prediabetes and type 2 diabetes. One can manage the risks associated with diabetes by being aware of their carbohydrate intake, eating smaller meals more frequently, and making good, nutrient-dense food choices. People with type 2 diabetes can better manage their illness by making dietary choices that are satisfying, healthful, and fit their specific nutritional needs. People with diabetes should set the following three goals before creating a meal plan:

- Encourage healthy levels of blood sugar (glucose)
- Promote regular, daily eating choices that include a variety of foods.
- Keep a healthy weight. The initial step in managing diabetes is frequently losing 5–10 pounds. Healthy eating and regular exercise are effective weight-loss strategies.

## The Relationship Between

## Nutrients and Diabetes

The capacity of your body to use carbohydrates, protein, and fat as fuel is one of several factors that play into the interaction between diabetes and nutrition. Although insulin is necessary for all of them, it must be released more quickly after eating carbohydrates. The primary source of blood sugar, or glucose, which aids in the efficient operation of the brain and nervous system, is carbohydrates. In order to keep their blood glucose levels controlled, people with diabetes have to consume less refined carbs and more healthy fats, proteins, fibers, and vitamins.

In general, the diabetic diet is a nutritious one. The diet promotes a diverse eating approach that includes items from all the food groups, with a focus on fruits, vegetables, whole grains, lean protein sources, and low-fat dairy. The diet also promotes meal frequency and portion control. These healthy eating guidelines are similar to those offered to someone trying to lose weight. Losing even 10 pounds can be achieved if you have diabetes and you are overweight or obese.

## Role of Glycemic Index

The glycemic index divides foods that contain carbohydrates into groups based on the chances of likely they are to cause an increase in blood sugar. When compared to foods with a lower value, foods with a high GI are likely to cause your blood sugar to rise more quickly. The glycemic index (GI) indicates how quickly, moderately, or slowly a diet containing carbohydrates affects blood glucose levels. This implies that it may be helpful for you to control your diabetes.

Foods high in carbohydrates release glucose into circulation at varying rates. Low glycemic index (GI) foods are those that raise blood sugar levels more gradually and can be beneficial for controlling blood sugar levels. Some high-fiber bread and cereals (particularly grainy bread and oats), pasta, basmati or low GI rice, quinoa, barley, most fruits, legumes, and low-fat dairy products are examples of healthy carbohydrate foods.

## What to Eat?

Food that can elevate the blood sugar level is primarily damaging for diabetic patients. A diet specially designed to remove all the potentially dangerous ingredients for diabetic patients can prove to be effective in easing its effects. Following are the food items that can be freely consumed on a Diabetic Diet:

**Vegetables:**
Fresh vegetables never cause harm to anyone. So adding a meal full of vegetables is the best shot for all diabetic patients. But not all vegetables contain the same amount of macronutrients. Some vegetables contain a high amount of carbohydrates, so those are not suitable for a diabetic diet. We need to use vegetables that contain a low amount of carbohydrates.
1. Cauliflower
2. Spinach
3. Tomatoes
4. Broccoli
5. Lemons
6. Artichoke
7. Garlic
8. Asparagus
9. Spring onions
10. Onions
11. Ginger etc.

**Meat:**
Meat is not on the red list for the diabetic diet. It is fine to have some meat every now and then for diabetic patients. However, certain meat types are better than others. For instance, red meat is not a preferable option for such patients. They should consume white meat more often, whether it's seafood or poultry. Healthy options in meat are:
1. All fish, i.e., salmon, halibut, trout, cod, sardine, etc.
2. Scallops
3. Mussels
4. Shrimp
5. Oysters etc.

**Fruits:**
Not all fruits are good for diabetes. To know if the fruit is suitable for this diet, it is important to note its sugar content. Some fruits contain a high amount of sugar in the form of sucrose and fructose, and those should be readily avoided. Here is the list of popularly used fruits that can be taken on the diabetic diet:
1. Peaches
2. Nectarines
3. Avocados
4. Apples
5. Berries
6. Grapefruit
7. Kiwi Fruit
8. Bananas
9. Cherries
10. Grapes
11. Orange

12. Pears
13. Plums
14. Strawberries

**Nuts and Seeds:**
Nuts and seeds are perhaps the most enriched edibles, and they contain such a mix of macronutrients that can never harm anyone. So diabetic patients can take the nuts and seeds in their diet without any fear of glucose spikes.
1. Pistachios
2. Sunflower seeds
3. Walnuts
4. Peanuts
5. Pecans
6. Pumpkin seeds
7. Almonds
8. Sesame seeds etc.

**Grains:**
Diabetic patients should also be selective while choosing the right grains for their diet. The idea is to keep the amount of starch as minimum as possible. That is why you won't see any white rice on the list; rather, it is replaced with more fibrous brown rice.
1. Quinoa
2. Oats
3. Multigrain
4. Whole grains
5. Brown rice
6. Millet
7. Barley
8. Sorghum
9. Tapioca

**Fats:**
Fat intake is the most debated topic as far as the diabetic diet is concerned. Switching to unsaturated fats is a better option.
1. Sesame oil
2. Olive oil
3. Canola oil
4. Grapeseed oil
5. Other vegetable oils
6. Fats extracted from plant sources.

Diary:
Any dairy product which directly or indirectly causes a glucose rise in the blood should not be taken on this diet. Other than those, all products are good to use. These items include:
1. Skimmed milk
2. Low-fat cheese
3. Eggs
4. Yogurt
5. Trans fat-free margarine or butter

**Sugar Alternatives:**
Since ordinary sugars or sweeteners are strictly forbidden on a diabetic diet. There are artificial varieties that can add sweetness without raising the level of carbohydrates in the meal. These

substitutes are:
1. Stevia
2. Xylitol
3. Natvia
4. Swerve
5. Monk fruit
6. Erythritol

Make sure to substitute them with extra care. The sweetness of each sweetener is entirely different from the table sugar, so add each in accordance with the intensity of their flavor. Stevia is the sweetest of them, and it should be used with more care. In place of 1 cup of sugar, a teaspoon of stevia is enough. All other sweeteners are more or less similar to sugar in their intensity of sweetness.

## Food to Avoid

Following food items can cause a rise in blood sugar levels and can indirectly aggravate the diabetic condition of a patient. Therefore, the following ingredients should not be used in any amount on a Diabetic Diet.

**All Sugars:**
1. White sugar
2. Brown sugar
3. Confectionary sugar
4. Honey
5. Molasses
6. Granulated sugar

**High-Fat Products:**
When you are diabetic, you may get vulnerable to a number of fatal diseases like cardiovascular diseases. That is why doctors strictly forbid high-fat food products, especially those sourced from dairy items. The high amount of fat can cause insulin resistance.

**Saturated Fats:**
Saturated animal fats are never healthy for anyone, whether a diabetic patient or a normal individual. So, it is always better to completely. Whenever we are cooking meat, we should cut off all the excess fats. Cooking oils made out of saturated or trans fats should also be avoided. Distance yourself from all fat of animal origins.

**High Sodium Items:**
A high sodium diet can lead to hypertension and blood pressure. As diabetes is already caused by hormonal imbalance in the body, excess sodium can cause another imbalance- the fluid imbalance – which a diabetic body cannot bear. It further complicates the diseases. So, it is better to avoid using food that is high in sodium. Mainly packed and processed foods and salt contain a high dose

of sodium. Use only the food products marked as 'Unsalted,' whether it's margarine, nuts, butter, or other items.

**Sugar-Rich Beverages:**
Cola drinks or other beverages are full of sugars. These drinks can drastically increase the blood glucose level within 30-40 minutes of drinking. Luckily, there are other sugar-free varieties of drinks available which are suitable for diabetic patients

**High Cholesterol Items:**
Bad cholesterol or HDL - High-density Lipoprotein can deposit in different parts of the body and obstructs the flow of blood and the regulation of hormones. That is why food items having high bad cholesterol are not good for diabetes. Such items should be replaced with the ones with low cholesterol.

**Sugar Mixed Syrups and Toppings:**
There are several syrups available in the markets which are full of sugar, like Maple syrup, chocolate syrups, etc. A diabetic patient should avoid those sugary syrups and also stay away from the sugar-mixed toppings available in the stores.

**Chocolate and Candies:**
Diabetic patients should use sugar-free chocolates or candies. Other processed bars and candies are extremely hazardous for their health, and all of such items should be avoided. You can try homemade low-carb candies.

**No Alcohol:**
Alcohol can reduce the rate of metabolism and can negatively affect appetite, which can lead to a very life-threatening situation for a diabetic patient. Excessive use of alcohol is damaging for patients as it can excite the glucose levels in the blood.

## Frequently Asked Questions

**1. Is it okay for me to eat carbohydrates?**
Although carbohydrates boost blood sugar levels, it is advised that you don't have to exclude all carbohydrates from your diabetes diet. In general, people require four to five 15-gram carb servings per meal. Aim for 3-to 4 (15-grams) carb servings per meal. Depending on your degree of physical activity, weight, and height, you may need to change your carbohydrate consumption.

**2. What kinds of carbohydrates should I eat?**
Choose foods that are strong in nutritional content when restricting carbs. Eat whole grains and

fresh or frozen veggies and fruits to obtain the maximum nutrition for those calories, she advises. Non-starchy fresh veggies such as broccoli, lettuce, asparagus, carrots, and cucumber, for example, have roughly 5 grams of carbohydrates per cup.

**3. Do you think I'll ever be able to eat sweets?**
Sweets aren't entirely forbidden on a diabetes diet, but they must be swapped for other carbohydrates rather than consumed in addition to your meal. However, substituting sugary pleasures for healthier foods will rob you of essential nutrients. Foods with added sugar aren't useful when trying to reduce weight or maintain a healthy weight. When craving something sweet, she suggests going for natural sugar-free options like fresh or frozen fruit.

**4. Why am I permitted to consume fat? I was concerned that this might be detrimental to my health.**
Consuming harmful fats, such as saturated and trans fats, can raise your risk of heart disease, but other fats are beneficial and can help lower your LDL or bad cholesterol. Although items high in saturated fat, such as butter, cheese, and fatty cuts of meat, should be avoided, do add monounsaturated, polyunsaturated, and omega-3 fats in your diet, such as nuts and fish.

**5. Which foods are high in healthy fats?**
It is believed that the type of fat you consume is as important as the amount of fat. It's the fat quality that matters. I rely completely on the fats derived from plants as they are much healthy and unsaturated. Avocados, nuts and nut spreads, olives, olive oil, and canola oil are all good sources of healthy fats.

**6. What is the recommended amount of fat in my diet?**
Intake of total fat should be 20 to 35 percent of total calories in a healthy type 2 diabetic diet. Still, saturated fat intake should not exceed 7 percent of total calories. Trans fats or hydrogenated oils on food labels should be avoided at all costs. Even though nuts and plant-based oils are considered healthy fats, they are nevertheless high in calories and should be consumed in moderation, according to her.

**7. Why should I limit my alcohol consumption?**
Men can have no more than two drinks per day, and females can take no more than one. Aside from that, alcohol contains calories, and drinking on an empty stomach might result in a severe dip in blood sugar. It is recommended to test the blood sugar levels before and after drinking alcohol to observe how your body reacts.

# 4-Week Meal Plan

## Week 1

**Day 1:**
Breakfast: Raspberry, Ricotta, and Banana Smoothie
Lunch: Hearty Vegan Slow Cooker Chili with Yogurt
Snack: Healthy Berry Smoothie Pops
Dinner: Pot-Roasted Spiced Rabbit
Dessert: Roasted Spiced Pears with Cinnamon and Pistachios

**Day 2:**
Breakfast: Baked Spiced Seeds and Nuts Granola
Lunch: Quinoa and Vegetable Pilau
Snack: Almond Energy Balls
Dinner: Creamy Chicken Saltimbocca with Prosciutto
Dessert: Healthy Raspberry-Chocolate Chia Pudding

**Day 3:**
Breakfast: Tasty Strawberry and Ricotta Pancakes
Lunch: Easy Party-Time Beans
Snack: Easy Apple Crisp
Dinner: Slow Cooker Venison Roast
Dessert: Homemade Cream Cheese Swirl Brownies

**Day 4:**
Breakfast: Easy Shakshuka Eggs
Lunch: Slow Cooker Scandinavian Beans
Snack: Easy Stuffed Dates
Dinner: Tender Spiced Butter Chicken
Dessert: Healthy Dark Chocolate Almond Butter Cups

**Day 5:**
Breakfast: Apple, Kale and Cheddar Omelet
Lunch: Soft Pioneer Beans
Snack: Classic Dark Chocolate Baking Drops
Dinner: Easy Lemon Chicken Piccata
Dessert: Easy Buttermilk Pancakes

**Day 6:**
Breakfast: Breakfast Bruschetta with Cheese and Egg
Lunch: Slow Cooker Red Beans
Snack: Frozen Chocolate Peanut Butter Freezer Bites
Dinner: Main Dish Baked Beans and Beef
Dessert: Tasty Sweet Potato Cake

**Day 7:**
Breakfast: Baked Egg and Veggie Quesadillas
Lunch: Baked Beans with Raisin and Apple
Snack: Soft Oatmeal Cookies
Dinner: One-Pot Chicken and Brown Rice
Dessert: Homemade Carrot Cake

## Week 2

**Day 1:**
Breakfast: Simple Stir Fry Tofu
Lunch: Tempeh-Stuffed Peppers with Cheddar
Snack: Easy Pecan Sandies
Dinner: Calico Beans with Beef and Bacon
Dessert: Pear and Pecan Crumble Pie

**Day 2:**
Breakfast: Greek Yogurt Sundae with Mixed Berries
Lunch: Easy Barbecued Lentils
Snack: No-Bake Peanut Butter Energy Balls
Dinner: Easy Hoisin Chicken Lettuce Wraps
Dessert: Perfect Mango Smoothie

**Day 3:**
Breakfast: Easy Avocado and Goat Cheese Toast
Lunch: Herbed Chickpea Pasta
Snack: Classic Omega-3 Crackers
Dinner: Creamy Curried Shrimp
Dessert: Chocolate Covered Strawberries

**Day 4:**
Breakfast: Oat and Walnut Granola with Dried Cherries
Lunch: Slow Cooker Butter Macaroni with Cheese
Snack: Spiced Honey Roasted Almonds
Dinner: Herbed Lamb Stew with Peas
Dessert: Tasty Sweet Potato Cake

**Day 5:**
Breakfast: Baked Chocolate-Zucchini Muffins
Lunch: Bacon and Fruit Baked Bean Casserole
Snack: Authentic Green Goddess Dressing
Dinner: Seafood and Vegetable Gumbo
Dessert: Chocolate Covered Strawberries

**Day 6:**
Breakfast: Breakfast Egg Muffins
Lunch: Pizza Beans with Tomato and Sausage
Snack: Almond Energy Balls
Dinner: Venison Steak with Tomato Juice
Dessert: Low Calorie Avocado Chocolate Mousse

**Day 7:**
Breakfast: Crispy Breakfast Pita with Egg and Bacon
Lunch: Low-Fat Cajun Sausage and Beans
Snack: Easy Apple Crisp
Dinner: Daily Slow-Cooker Stew
Dessert: Low Carb Microwave Keto Bread

## Week 3

**Day 1:**
Breakfast: Brussels Sprout Hash with Fried Eggs
Lunch: Slow Cooker Four-Bean Medley
Snack: Easy Stuffed Dates
Dinner: Spaghetti with Shrimp Marinara
Dessert: Homemade Strawberry Yogurt Pops

**Day2:**
Breakfast: Egg White and Oatmeal Pancakes
Lunch: New Mexico - Style Pinto Beans
Snack: Simple Berry Sorbet
Dinner: Easy Hoisin Chicken Lettuce Wraps
Dessert: Creamy Minty Hot Chocolate

**Day3:**
Breakfast: Tasty Buckwheat Pancakes
Lunch: Cowboy Beans with Sliced Bacon
Snack: Classic Dark Chocolate Baking Drops
Dinner: Low Calorie Big Beef Stew
Dessert: Easy Pecan Sandies

**Day4:**
Breakfast: Shakshuka Eggs
Lunch: Spicy Asian-Style Tofu Salad
Snack: No Bake Apple Pie Parfait
Dinner: Baked Sesame Salmon with Bok Choy
Dessert: No-Bake Peanut Butter Energy Balls

**Day5:**
Breakfast: Easy Herby Egg Salad with Capers
Lunch: Simple Broccoli Slaw Crab Salad
Snack: Classic Omega-3 Crackers
Dinner: Easy Pot Roast
Dessert: Tasty Strawberry Cream Cheese Crepes

**Day6:**
Breakfast: Sliced Peach Muesli Bake
Lunch: Spicy Asian-Style Tofu Salad
Snack: Spiced Honey Roasted Almonds
Dinner: Tasty Garlic Beef Stroganoff
Dessert: Soft Oatmeal Cookies

**Day 7:**
Breakfast: Spinach Potato Cheese Quiche
Lunch: Fresh Herbed Tomato Salad
Snack: Simple Oatmeal-Cranberry Cookies
Dinner: Cheesy Tomato Tuna Melts
Dessert: Low Calorie Carrot Cake Bites

## Week 4

**Day 1:**
Breakfast: Healthy Egg and Veggie Breakfast Cups
Lunch: Nutritional Sweet Beet Grain Bowl
Snack: Soft Oatmeal Cookies
Dinner: Baked Cajun Shrimp Casserole with Quinoa
Dessert: Roasted Peach and Coconut Yogurt Bowls

**Day2:**
Breakfast: Potato, Zucchini and Sausage Breakfast Hash
Lunch: Simple Cauli-Lettuce Wraps
Snack: Soft Oatmeal Cookies
Dinner: Savory Sweet Crock Pot Roast
Dessert: Healthy Berry Smoothie Pops

**Day3:**
Breakfast: Whole-Grain Pancakes with Fresh Fruit
Lunch: Roasted Tomato Tartine with Ricotta Cheese
Snack: Simple Oatmeal-Cranberry Cookies
Dinner: Easy Lemon Chicken Piccata
Dessert: Homemade Carrot Cake

**Day4:**
Breakfast: Cinnamon Buckwheat Groats Breakfast Bowl
Lunch: Burger with Jicama Chips
Snack: Low Calorie Carrot Cake Bites
Dinner: Green Chili Stew with Pork
Dessert: Homemade Vanilla Bean Ice Cream

**Day5:**
Breakfast: Steel-Cut Oatmeal with Fruit and Nuts
Lunch: Lentil Sloppy Joes with Roasted Asparagus
Snack: Simple Oatmeal-Cranberry Cookies
Dinner: Blackened Tilapia with Mango Salsa
Dessert: Creamy Minty Hot Chocolate

**Day6:**
Breakfast: Baked Berry-Oat Breakfast Bars
Lunch: Cauliflower and Mushroom Soup
Snack: Tasty Strawberry Cream Cheese Crepes
Dinner: Turkey Cutlets with Zucchini
Dessert: Quick Chocolate Yogurt Granita

**Day 7:**
Breakfast: Healthy Tuna Salad Stuffed Avocado
Lunch: Miso Baked Tempeh and Carrot Wraps
Snack: No Bake Apple Pie Parfait
Dinner: Beef and Vegetables Stew
Dessert: Pear and Pecan Crumble Pie

# Chapter 1 Breakfast Recipes

| | | | |
|---|---|---|---|
| 18 | Strawberry, Spinach and Avocado Smoothie | 23 | Egg and Ham Slice Breakfast "Burritos" |
| 18 | Baked Spiced Seeds and Nuts Granola | 24 | Mixed Berry Vanilla Baked Oatmeal |
| 18 | Refrigerated Lemon-Blueberry Overnight Oats | 24 | Creamy Blueberry Crêpes |
| 18 | Tasty Strawberry and Ricotta Pancakes | 24 | Cheesy Breakfast Casserole with Red Pepper and Mushroom |
| 18 | Easy Shakshuka Eggs | | |
| 18 | Easy Avocado and Goat Cheese Toast | 24 | Whole-Wheat Blueberry Breakfast Cake |
| 19 | Raspberry, Ricotta, and Banana Smoothie | 25 | Potato, Zucchini and Sausage Breakfast Hash |
| 19 | Apple, Kale and Cheddar Omelet | 25 | Healthy Tuna Salad Stuffed Avocado |
| 19 | Oat and Walnut Granola with Dried Cherries | 25 | Baked Ricotta with Strawberry and Mint |
| 19 | Simple Stir Fry Tofu | 25 | Easy Yogurt Parfait with Nuts and Berries |
| 19 | Easy Buttermilk Pancakes | 25 | Easy Herby Egg Salad with Capers |
| 19 | Puff Pancakes with Berry Topping | 26 | Savory Cherry Tomato Cheese Salad |
| 20 | Brussels Sprout Hash with Fried Eggs | 26 | Avocado Toast with Egg and Black Pepper |
| 20 | Spinach Artichoke Breakfast Bake with Cheese | 26 | Pumpkin Pie Smoothie with Pecans |
| 20 | Homemade Turkey Breakfast Sausage Patties | 26 | Steel-Cut Oatmeal with Fruit and Nuts |
| 20 | Baked Chocolate-Zucchini Muffins | 26 | Whole-Grain Dutch Baby Pancake with Cinnamon |
| 20 | Cheesy Oat Pancakes with Carrot and Yogurt | | |
| 21 | Breakfast Egg Muffins | 26 | Healthy Overnight Oatmeal |
| 21 | Crispy Breakfast Pita with Egg and Bacon | 27 | Baked Berry-Oat Breakfast Bars |
| 21 | Egg White and Oatmeal Pancakes | 27 | Whole-Grain Breakfast Cookies with Cherries and Chocolate |
| 21 | Sweet Potato and Turkey Sausage Hash with Onion | | |
| | | 27 | Whole-Grain Pancakes with Fresh Fruit |
| 21 | Tasty Buckwheat Pancakes | 27 | Coconut, Berry and Leafy Greens Sunrise Smoothie |
| 21 | Creamy Almond Butter Pancakes | | |
| 22 | Sweet Potato Pancakes with Apple Sauce | 27 | Greek Yogurt Sundae with Mixed Berries |
| 22 | Country-Style Cheesy Vegetables Omelet | 28 | Cinnamon Buckwheat Groats Breakfast Bowl |
| 22 | Basic Fruit Smoothie | 28 | Sliced Peach Muesli Bake |
| 22 | Baked Egg and Veggie Quesadillas | 28 | Frozen Tofu and Fruit Smoothie |
| 22 | Breakfast Bruschetta with Cheese and Egg | 28 | Mushroom, Zucchini, and Onion Frittata with Feta Cheese |
| 23 | Yogurt and Fruit Smoothie | | |
| 23 | Creamed Egg Clouds on Toast | 28 | Healthy Egg and Veggie Breakfast Cups |
| 23 | Spinach Potato Cheese Quiche | 29 | Breakfast Tostada with Salsa |
| 23 | Cinnamon Quinoa Berry Breakfast | 29 | Shakshuka Eggs |
| 23 | Baked Lemon-Poppyseed Muffins | | |

## Strawberry, Spinach and Avocado Smoothie

**Prep time:** 5 minutes | **Cook time:** 0 minutes | **Serves:** 2

2 cups unsweetened non-dairy milk
2 cups baby spinach
1 cup frozen strawberries
½ avocado, peeled and pitted
2 scoops unsweetened vegan protein powder
2 teaspoons pure vanilla extract

1. Place the milk, spinach, strawberries, avocado, protein powder, and vanilla in a blender and blend until smooth. Serve.

**Per Serving:** Calories 309; Total Fat 11g; Saturated Fat 2g; Sodium 198mg; Carbs 25g; Fiber 7g; Sugar 6g; Protein 26g

## Baked Spiced Seeds and Nuts Granola

**Prep time:** 5 minutes | **Cook time:** 25 minutes | **Serves:** 8

2 cups gluten-free rolled oats
½ cup raw sunflower seeds
½ cup shredded unsweetened coconut
½ cup chopped pecans
½ cup slivered almonds
¼ cup maple syrup
2 tablespoons canola oil
½ teaspoon ground cinnamon
¼ teaspoon ground nutmeg
⅛ teaspoon sea salt

1. Preheat oven at 300°F and manage a baking sheet with parchment paper. Set it aside. 2. In a bowl, mix the oats, sunflower seeds, coconut, pecans, and almonds until mixed. 3. In a small bowl, whisk the maple syrup, oil, cinnamon, nutmeg, and salt until blended. 4. Add the maple syrup mixture to the oat mixture and mix until very well coated. 5. Spread the oat mix on the prepared baking sheet and bake for about 25 minutes, stirring frequently, until the granola is golden brown and crunchy. 6. Let the granola cool, break up the large pieces.

**Per Serving:** Calories 289; Total Fat 18g; Saturated Fat 3g; Sodium 43mg; Carbs 25g; Fiber 5g; Sugar 7g; Protein 7g

## Refrigerated Lemon-Blueberry Overnight Oats

**Prep time:** 5 minutes | **Cook time:** 0 minutes | **Serves:** 2

½ cup milk of choice
½ cup low-fat plain Greek yogurt
½ cup gluten-free rolled oats
2 tablespoons chia seeds
Juice and zest of 1 lemon
1 tablespoon maple syrup
1 teaspoon pure vanilla extract
Pinch sea salt
1 cup blueberries

1. In a medium bowl, whisk the milk, yogurt, oats, chia seeds, lemon juice, lemon zest, maple syrup, vanilla, and salt. 2. Fold in the blueberries, cover, and refrigerate for at least 4 hours or overnight.

**Per Serving:** Calories 283; Total Fat 6g; Saturated Fat 1g; Sodium 133mg; Carbs 42g; Fiber 10g; Sugar 17g; Protein 10g

## Tasty Strawberry and Ricotta Pancakes

**Prep time:** 10 minutes | **Cook time:** 20 minutes | **Serves:** 4

1¼ cups milk of choice
½ cup low-fat ricotta cheese
1 large egg
1 tablespoon canola oil
1 tablespoon freshly squeezed lemon juice
½ teaspoon pure vanilla extract
1¼ cups whole-wheat flour
1 tablespoon sugar
2 teaspoons baking powder
¼ teaspoon salt
Canola oil, for cooking
1 cup sliced strawberries

1. In a bowl, add the milk, ricotta, egg, oil, lemon juice, and vanilla until well blended. 2. Add in the flour along with sugar, baking powder, and salt until combined. 3. Heat a griddle or large skillet on medium heat and lightly grease it with oil. Reduce the heat to medium-low and, working in batches, add the batter in ¼-cup measures. 4. Cook until the pancakes are firm and golden, about 2 minutes, then scatter the strawberries on top of each, and flip. 5. Cook the pancakes for 1 minute more until cooked through. Repeat with the remaining batter and serve.

**Per Serving:** Calories 285; Total Fat 9g; Saturated Fat 2g; Sodium 220mg; Carbs 40g; Fiber 5g; Sugar 9g; Protein 12g

## Easy Shakshuka Eggs

**Prep time:** 10 minutes | **Cook time:** 20 minutes | **Serves:** 4

2 tablespoons olive oil
1 red bell pepper, seeded and chopped
1 onion, diced
1 tablespoon minced garlic
1 (28-ounce) can no-salt-added diced tomatoes, drained
1 teaspoon paprika
1 teaspoon ground cumin
½ teaspoon chili powder
8 large eggs
¼ cup chopped fresh parsley, for garnish

1. In a skillet, heat the oil. 2. Sauté the bell pepper, onion, and garlic for about 4 minutes, until softened. 3. Stir in the tomatoes, paprika, cumin, and chili powder and simmer for 10 minutes. 4. Use the back of a spoon to make 8 wells, then crack an egg into each well. Cover and let the eggs cook about 6 minutes, until the whites are no longer translucent. 5. Serve topped with parsley.

**Per Serving:** Calories 263; Total Fat 17g; Saturated Fat 4g; Sodium 178mg; Carbs 14g; Fiber 5g; Sugar 8g; Protein 15g

## Easy Avocado and Goat Cheese Toast

**Prep time:** 5 minutes | **Cook time:** 5 minutes | **Serves:** 2

2 slices whole-wheat thin-sliced bread
½ avocado
2 tablespoons crumbled goat cheese
Salt

1. In a toaster or broiler, toast the bread until browned. 2. Remove the flesh from the avocado. In a bowl, mash the avocado flesh. Spread it onto the toast. 3. Sprinkle with the goat cheese and season lightly with salt. 4. Add any toppings and serve.

**Per Serving:** Calories 137; Total Fat 6g; Saturated Fat 0.2g; Sodium 195mg; Carbs 18g; Fiber 5g; Sugar 0g; Protein 5g

## Raspberry, Ricotta, and Banana Smoothie

| Prep time: 5 minutes | Cook time: 0 minutes | Serves: 2 |

2 cups unsweetened non-dairy milk
1 cup low-fat ricotta cheese
1 cup frozen raspberries
1 cup chopped baby kale
½ banana
1 teaspoon pure vanilla extract
Pinch ground cinnamon

1. Place the milk, ricotta, raspberries, kale, banana, vanilla, and cinnamon in a blender and blend until smooth. Serve immediately.
Per Serving: Calories 324; Total Fat 14g; Saturated Fat 6g; Sodium 202mg; Carbs 26g; Fiber 7g; Sugar 8g; Protein 23g

## Apple, Kale and Cheddar Omelet

| Prep time: 10 minutes | Cook time: 10 minutes | Serves: 2 |

Nonstick cooking spray
4 large eggs
2 tablespoons milk of choice
¼ teaspoon chopped fresh thyme
Sea salt
Freshly ground black pepper
1 apple, cored and chopped
½ cup chopped kale
¼ cup shredded low-fat Cheddar cheese

1. Grease a skillet with oil and place it on medium-high heat. 2. In a small bowl, whisk the eggs, milk, and thyme and season with salt and pepper. 3. Pour the egg mix into the skillet, swirling it gently to move the eggs around. Cook until the eggs are mostly set, and then sprinkle the apple, kale, and Cheddar evenly over the surface. 4. When the Cheddar is melted, fold one side over the other, cut it in half, and serve.
Per Serving: Calories 259; Total Fat 13g; Saturated Fat 4g; Sodium 243mg; Carbs 15g; Fiber 2g; Sugar 11g; Protein 17g

## Oat and Walnut Granola with Dried Cherries

| Prep time: 10 minutes | Cook time: 30 minutes | Serves: 16 (⅓ cup each) |

4 cups rolled oats
1 cup walnut pieces
½ cup pepitas
¼ teaspoon salt
1 teaspoon ground cinnamon
1 teaspoon ground ginger
½ cup coconut oil, melted
½ cup unsweetened applesauce
1 teaspoon vanilla extract
½ cup dried cherries

1. Preheat the oven to 350°F and manage baking sheet with parchment paper. 2. In a bowl, toss the oats with walnuts, pepitas, salt, cinnamon, and ginger. 3. In a cup, combine the coconut oil with applesauce, and vanilla. Pour this sauce over the dry mixture and mix well. 4. Transfer the mix to the baking sheet and cook for 30 minutes, stirring twice. Remove and let sit until cool. Break the granola and mix in the dried cherries.
Per Serving: Calories 224; Total Fat 15g; Saturated Fat 3g; Sodium 30mg; Carbs 20g; Fiber 3g; Sugar 5g; Protein 5g

## Simple Stir Fry Tofu

| Prep time: 5 minutes | Cook time: 10 minutes | Serves: 2 |

1 (14-ounce) block extra-firm tofu, drained
2 teaspoons olive oil
½ onion, chopped
½ red bell pepper, seeded and chopped
1 teaspoon minced garlic
2 tablespoons nutritional yeast
¼ teaspoon ground turmeric
Freshly ground black pepper

1. Crumble the drained tofu into a small bowl. 2. In a skillet, heat the oil and sauté the onion, bell pepper, and garlic for about 3 minutes, until softened over medium heat. 3. Add the tofu and sauté for about 4 minutes, until heated through. Stir in the nutritional yeast and turmeric and toss until the tofu is well coated. 4. Season with pepper and serve.
Per Serving: Calories 243; Total Fat 16g; Saturated Fat 43g; Sodium 18mg; Carbs 9g; Fiber 2g; Sugar 3g; Protein 20g

## Easy Buttermilk Pancakes

| Prep time: 10 minutes | Cook time: 10 minutes | Serves: 2 |

1 cup all-purpose flour
2 tablespoons nonfat buttermilk powder
¼ teaspoon baking soda
½ teaspoon low-salt baking powder
1 cup water

1. In a bowl, blend all the ingredients, adding more water if necessary to get batter consistency desired. 2. Pour ¼ of batter into a medium nonstick skillet or a skillet treated with nonstick cooking spray. Cook until bubbles appear on the top half of pancake over medium heat. Flip and continue cooking until the center of the pancake is done, about 1–2 minutes each side. Repeat process with remaining batter.
Per Serving: Calories 143; Total Fat 2g; Saturated Fat 1g; Sodium 111mg; Carbs 26g; Fiber 1g; Sugar 4g; Protein 6g

## Puff Pancakes with Berry Topping

| Prep time: 5 minutes | Cook time: 10 minutes | Serves: 6 |

2 large whole eggs
1 large egg white
½ cup skim milk
½ cup all-purpose flour
1 tablespoon granulated sugar
⅛ teaspoon sea salt
2 cups berries such as raspberries, blackberries, boysenberries, blueberries, strawberries, or a combination
1 tablespoon powdered sugar

1. Preheat the oven to 450°F. Treat a 10" ovenproof skillet or deep pie pan with nonstick spray. Once oven is heated, place pan in the oven for a few minutes to get hot. 2. Add the eggs and egg white to medium bowl and beat until mixed. Whisk in milk. Slowly whisk in the flour, sugar, and salt. 3. Remove preheated pan from oven and pour the batter into it. Bake for 15 minutes, then lower the oven temp to 350°F and bake for an additional 10 minutes, or until batter is puffed and brown. Remove from oven and slide onto serving plate. 4. Cover with fruit and sift powdered sugar over top. Cut into 6 equal wedges and serve.
Per Serving: Calories 186; Total Fat 2g; Saturated Fat 1g; Sodium 89mg; Carbs 37g; Fiber 3g; Sugar 1g; Protein 5g

## Brussels Sprout Hash with Fried Eggs

**Prep time: 15 minutes | Cook time: 15 minutes | Serves: 4**

3 teaspoons extra-virgin olive oil, divided
1 pound Brussels sprouts, sliced
2 garlic cloves, thinly sliced
¼ teaspoon salt
Juice of 1 lemon
4 eggs

1. In a large skillet, heat 1½ teaspoons of oil over medium heat. Add the Brussels sprouts and toss. Cook, for 6-8 minutes until browned. Add and cook the garlic until fragrant, about 1 minute. Season with the salt and lemon juice. Transfer to a serving dish. 2. In the pan, heat the 1½ teaspoon s of oil over medium-high heat. Crack the eggs into the pan. Fry for 2 to 4 minutes, flip, and continue cooking to desired doneness. Serve over the bed of hash.
**Per Serving:** Calories 158; Total Fat 9g; Saturated Fat 0.1g; Sodium 234mg; Carbs 12g; Fiber 4g; Sugar 4g; Protein 10g

## Spinach Artichoke Breakfast Bake with Cheese

**Prep time: 10 minutes | Cook time: 35 minutes | Serves: 8**

Nonstick cooking spray
1 (10-ounce) package frozen spinach, thawed and drained
1 (14-ounce) can artichoke hearts, drained
¼ cup finely chopped red bell pepper
2 garlic cloves, minced
8 eggs, lightly beaten
¼ cup unsweetened plain almond milk
½ teaspoon salt
½ teaspoon freshly ground black pepper
½ cup crumbled goat cheese

1. Preheat the oven to 375°F. Grease an 8-by-8-inch baking pan with oil. 2. In a large mixing bowl, combine the spinach, artichoke hearts, bell pepper, garlic, eggs, almond milk, salt, and pepper. Stir well to combine. 3. Transfer the mixture to the baking dish. Sprinkle with the goat cheese.4. Bake for 35 minutes until set. Serve warm.
**Per Serving:** Calories 104; Total Fat 5g; Saturated Fat 0.3g; Sodium 488mg; Carbs 6g; Fiber 2g; Sugar 1g; Protein 9g

## Homemade Turkey Breakfast Sausage Patties

**Prep time: 10 minutes | Cook time: 10 minutes | Serves: 8**

1 pound lean ground turkey
½ teaspoon salt
½ teaspoon dried sage
½ teaspoon dried thyme
½ teaspoon freshly ground black pepper
¼ teaspoon ground fennel seeds
1 teaspoon extra-virgin olive oil

1. In a mixing bowl, mix the turkey, salt, sage, thyme, pepper, and fennel. Mix well. 2. Shape the meat into 8 small, round patties. 3. Heat the olive oil in a skillet and cook the patties for 3-4 minutes on each side until browned and cooked through. 4.Serve warm.
**Per Serving:** Calories 92; Total Fat 5g; Saturated Fat 0g; Sodium 156mg; Carbs 0g; Fiber 0g; Sugar 0g; Protein 11g

## Baked Chocolate-Zucchini Muffins

**Prep time: 15 minutes | Cook time: 20 minutes | Serves: 12**

1½ cups grated zucchini
1½ cups rolled oats
1 teaspoon ground cinnamon
2 teaspoons baking powder
¼ teaspoon salt
1 large egg
1 teaspoon vanilla extract
¼ cup coconut oil, melted
½ cup unsweetened applesauce
¼ cup honey
¼ cup dark chocolate chips

1. Preheat the oven to 350°F. Grease the 12-cup muffin tin or line with paper baking liners. Set aside. 2. Drain the zucchini. 3. In a blender jar, process the oats until they resemble flour. Place to a bowl and mix the cinnamon, baking powder, and salt. Mix well. 4. In mixing bowl, mix the egg, vanilla, coconut oil, applesauce, and honey. Stir to combine. 5. Press the zucchini into the colander, draining any liquids, and add to the wet mixture. 6. Mix the dry mix and the wet mix, and mix until no dry spots remain. Fold in the chocolate chips. 7. Transfer the batter to the greased muffin tin, filling each cup a little over halfway. Cook for 16 to 18 minutes until the muffins are lightly browned and a toothpick inserted in the center comes out clean. 8. Store in an airtight container, refrigerated, for up to 5 days.
**Per Serving:** Calories 121, Total Fat 7g; Saturated Fat 0.1g; Sodium 106mg; Carbs 16g; Fiber 2g; Sugar 7g; Protein 2g

## Cheesy Oat Pancakes with Carrot and Yogurt

**Prep time: 10 minutes | Cook time: 20 minutes | Serves: 4**

1 cup rolled oats
1 cup shredded carrots
1 cup low-fat cottage cheese
2 eggs
½ cup unsweetened plain almond milk
1 teaspoon baking powder
½ teaspoon ground cinnamon
2 tablespoons ground flaxseed
¼ cup plain nonfat Greek yogurt
1 tablespoon pure maple syrup
2 teaspoon s canola oil, divided

1. In a blender jar, process the oats until they resemble flour. Add the carrots, cottage cheese, eggs, almond milk, baking powder, cinnamon, and flaxseed to the jar. Process until smooth. 2. In a bowl, mix the yogurt with maple syrup and stir well. Set aside. 3. In a large skillet, heat 1 teaspoon of oil over medium heat. Using a measuring cup, add ¼ cup of batter per pancake to the skillet. Cook until bubbles on the surface about 2 minutes, and flip the pancakes. Cook for a minute until the pancakes are browned and cooked through. 4. Serve warm topped with the maple yogurt.
**Per Serving:** Calories 226; Total Fat 8g; Saturated Fat 3g; Sodium 403mg; Carbs 24g; Fiber 4g; Sugar 7g; Protein 15g

## Breakfast Egg Muffins

Prep time: 10 minutes | Cook time: 25 minutes | Serves: 8

Nonstick cooking spray
6 eggs, beaten
¼ cup unsweetened plain almond milk
1 red bell pepper, diced
1 cup chopped spinach
¼ cup crumbled goat cheese
½ cup sliced brown mushrooms
¼ cup sliced sun-dried tomatoes
Salt
Freshly ground black pepper

1. Preheat the oven to 350°F. Spray 8 muffin cups of a 12-cup muffin tin with nonstick cooking spray. Set aside. 2. In a bowl, combine the eggs, almond milk, bell pepper, spinach, goat cheese, mushrooms, and tomatoes. Season with salt and pepper. 3. Fill the muffin cups three-fourths with the egg mixture. Bake for 20-25 minutes until completely set. Let cool slightly and remove the egg bites from the muffin tin. 4. Serve warm, or store in an airtight container in the refrigerator for up to 5 days

Per Serving: Calories 67; Total Fat 4g; Saturated Fat 0.1g; Sodium 127mg; Carbs 3g; Fiber 1g; Sugar 2g; Protein 6g

## Crispy Breakfast Pita with Egg and Bacon

Prep time: 5 minutes | Cook time: 15 minutes | Serves: 2

1 (6-inch) whole-grain pita bread
3 teaspoons extra-virgin olive oil, divided
2 eggs
2 Canadian bacon slices
Juice of ½ lemon
1 cup microgreens
2 tablespoons crumbled goat cheese
Freshly ground black pepper

1. Heat a skillet over medium heat. Cut the pita bread in half and grease olive oil. Cook for 2 to 3 minutes until toasted. 2. In the skillet, Cook the eggs until they are set, 2 to 3 minutes. Remove from the skillet. 3. In the skillet, cook the bacon for 3 to 5 minutes. 4. In a bowl, mix the 1 teaspoon of oil and the lemon juice. Add the microgreens and toss to combine. 5. Top pita half with the microgreens, a bacon, 1 egg, and 1 tablespoon of goat cheese. Season with pepper and serve.
Per Serving: Calories 250; Total Fat 14g; Saturated Fat 2g; Sodium 398mg; Carbs 20g; Fiber 3g; Sugar 1g; Protein 13g

## Egg White and Oatmeal Pancakes

Prep time: 10 minutes | Cook time: 10 minutes | Serves: 2

4 egg whites
½ cup oatmeal
4 teaspoons reduced-calorie or low-sugar strawberry jam
1 teaspoon powdered sugar

1. Put all the ingredients, except powdered sugar, in blender and process until smooth. 2. Preheat a small nonstick pan treated with cooking spray over medium heat. Pour half of the mixture into pan. Cook for 4–5 minutes. 3. Flip the pancake and cook for another 4 minutes, until the inside is cooked. Repeat using remaining batter for second pancake. Dust each pancake with powdered sugar, if using.
Per Serving: Calories 197; Total Fat 3g; Saturated Fat 1g; Sodium 120mg; Carbs 31g; Fiber 4g; Sugar 2g; Protein 13g

## Sweet Potato and Turkey Sausage Hash with Onion

Prep time: 10 minutes | Cook time: 25 minutes | Serves: 4

1 tablespoon extra-virgin oil
2 medium sweet potatoes, cut into ½-inch dice
½ recipe Homemade Turkey Breakfast Sausage
1 small onion, chopped
½ red bell pepper, seeded and chopped
2 garlic cloves, minced
Chopped fresh parsley, for garnish

1. In a skillet, heat the oil over medium-high heat. Add the sweet potatoes and cook, stirring occasionally, for 12 to 15 minutes until they brown and begin to soften. 2. Add the turkey sausage in bulk, onion, bell pepper, and garlic. Cook for about 5 minutes until sausage are done and the vegetables soften. 3. Garnish with parsley and serve warm.
Per Serving: Calories 190; Total Fat 9g; Saturated Fat 2g; Sodium 197mg; Carbs 16g; Fiber 3g; Sugar 7g; Protein 12g

## Tasty Buckwheat Pancakes

Prep time: 10 minutes | Cook time: 15 minutes | Serves: 2

1 cup whole-wheat flour
½ cup buckwheat flour
1½ teaspoons baking powder
2 egg whites
¼ cup apple juice concentrate
1¼–1½ cups skim milk
Sift the flours and baking powder together.

1. In a bowl, add the egg whites with apple juice concentrate, and 1¼ cups milk and mix well. 2. Add the milk mix to dry mix and combine well, but do not overmix. Add remaining milk if necessary to reach desired consistency. 3. Cook pancakes in a nonstick skillet or on griddle treated with nonstick spray over medium heat, about 1–2 minutes on each side.
Per Serving: Calories 220; Total Fat 1g; Saturated Fat 0g; Sodium 200mg; Carbs 44g; Fiber 5g; Sugar 2g; Protein 11g

## Creamy Almond Butter Pancakes

Prep time: 5 minutes | Cook time: 15 minutes | Serves: 4

½ cup creamy almond butter (unsweetened)
2 large eggs
½ cup unsweetened almond milk
1 cup almond flour
1 teaspoon baking powder
Cooking spray, coconut oil, or butter

1. In a bowl, whisk the almond butter, eggs, and almond milk until smooth and creamy. Add in the almond flour with baking powder until smooth. If the batter is very thick, add additional almond milk 1 tablespoon at a time until pourable. 2. Heat a nonstick skillet and drizzle oil. Pour ¼ cup of the batter onto the hot skillet and cook for 4 to 5 minutes, until the edges begin to firm up. Flip the pancake and cook for 2 to 3 minutes on the second side. 3. You should get about 8 pancakes. Serve warm.
Per Serving: Calories 396; Total Fat 34g; Saturated Fat 3g; Sodium 180mg; Carbs 6g; Fiber 6g; Sugar 0g; Protein 16g

## Sweet Potato Pancakes with Apple Sauce

Prep time: 10 minutes | Cook time: 15 minutes | Serves: 4

2 medium sweet potatoes
¼ cup onions, grated
1 egg
3 tablespoons whole-wheat pastry flour
½ teaspoon cinnamon
½ teaspoon baking powder
½ cup egg whites
2 tablespoons canola oil

1. Scrub sweet potatoes; pierce skins with fork and microwave on high for 4–5 minutes. Scoop sweet potato out of skins; lightly mash with fork. 2. In a medium bowl, mix together the sweet potatoes, grated onion, and egg. Add in flour, cinnamon, and baking powder. 3. In separate small bowl, beat the egg whites until rounded peaks are formed. Gently fold egg whites into potato mixture. 4. Heat the oil until hot. Spoon batter onto skillet to form pancakes approximately 4" in diameter. Brown on both sides, about 3–4 minutes. 5. Serve hot with some unsweetened apple sauce.
Per Serving: Calories 168; Total Fat 7g; Saturated Fat 1g; Sodium 139mg; Carbs 25.87g; Fiber 3g; Sugar 3g; Protein 6g

## Country-Style Cheesy Vegetables Omelet

Prep time: 15 minutes | Cook time: 20 minutes | Serves: 2

2 teaspoons olive oil
1 cup diced zucchini
¼ cup diced red pepper
1 cup plum tomatoes, skinned and cubed
⅛ teaspoon pepper
4 eggs
1 tablespoon Parmesan cheese
1 teaspoon minced fresh basil

1. Heat the oil and add zucchini and red pepper and sauté for 5 minutes in a non-stick skillet. 2. Add tomatoes and pepper and cook uncovered for another 10 minutes, allowing fluid from tomatoes to cook down. 3. In a bowl, whisk the eggs, Parmesan cheese, and fresh basil; pour over the vegetables in skillet. 4. Cook over low heat until browned, approximately 10 minutes on each side.
Per Serving: Calories 253; Total Fat 17g; Saturated Fat 5g; Sodium 221mg; Carbs 7g; Fiber 2g; Sugar 1g; Protein 17g

## Basic Fruit Smoothie

Prep time: 5 minutes | Cook time: 0 minutes | Serves: 1

1 cup skim milk
2 exchange servings of any diced fruit
1 tablespoon honey
4 teaspoons toasted wheat germ
6 large ice cubes

Blend all ingredients until thick and smooth.
Per Serving: Calories 228; Total Fat 0.5g; Saturated Fat 0.1g; Sodium 308mg; Carbs 34g; Fiber 0.4g; Sugar 33g; Protein 21.6g

## Baked Egg and Veggie Quesadillas

Prep time: 10 minutes | Cook time: 15 minutes | Serves: 2

Nonstick cooking spray
4 large eggs
Sea salt
Freshly ground black pepper
1 teaspoon olive oil
1 red bell pepper, seeded and chopped
1 scallion (both white and green parts), chopped
2 (6-inch) whole-wheat tortillas
½ cup low-sodium canned white beans, drained and rinsed
¼ cup homemade or store-bought salsa (optional)
¼ cup shredded low-fat Cheddar cheese

1. Preheat oven to 400°F, grease a baking pan with oil. 2. In a bowl, beat the eggs and spice with salt and pepper. 3. Hot oil over medium heat and sauté the bell pepper and scallion for about 2 minutes, until softened. Spread in the eggs mix and scramble for about 3 minutes, until they are fluffy curds. 4. Place the tortillas on the baking pan and evenly divide the eggs between them, placing them on one-half of each. Top the eggs with the beans, salsa (if using), and Cheddar, and fold the other side of the tortilla over the filling. 5. Lightly grease the top of the tortilla with cooking spray and bake for about 10 minutes, until the cheese melts and toasted browned. Serve.
Per Serving: Calories 419; Total Fat 18g; Saturated Fat 6g; Sodium 567mg; Carbs 33g; Fiber 8g; Sugar 5g; Protein 23g

## Breakfast Bruschetta with Cheese and Egg

Prep time: 10 minutes | Cook time: 15 minutes | Serves: 4

2 large tomatoes, chopped
¼ red onion, finely chopped
2 tablespoons finely chopped fresh basil
2 tablespoons olive oil
½ teaspoon minced garlic
Sea salt
Freshly ground black pepper
4 whole-wheat English muffins, split
6 large eggs
Nonstick cooking spray
¼ cup shredded Parmesan cheese

1. Preheat the oven to 400°F and manage a baking sheet with parchment paper. 2. In a small bowl, mix the tomatoes, red onion, basil, oil, and garlic. Season with salt and pepper. 3. Place the English muffins on the baking sheet and evenly top the halves with the bruschetta mixture. Bake for 10 minutes, until toasted. 4. While the bruschetta is cooking, in a small bowl, whisk the eggs and season them lightly with salt and pepper. 5. Lightly grease a skillet with oil and place it on medium-high heat. 6. Pour in the eggs and scramble them for about 2 minutes, until fluffy curds form. 7. Top the English muffins with the eggs, sprinkle with Parmesan cheese, and serve.
Per Serving: Calories 347; Total Fat 17g; Saturated Fat 4g; Sodium 487mg; Carbs 32g; Fiber 6g; Sugar 8g; Protein 18g

## Yogurt and Fruit Smoothie

**Prep time: 5 minutes | Cook time: 0 minutes | Serves: 2**

1 cup plain low-fat yogurt
½ cup sliced strawberries
½ cup orange juice
½ cup nectarines, peeled and sliced
2 tablespoons ground flax seed

Blend all ingredients until thick and smooth.
Per Serving: Calories 149; Total Fat 1g; Saturated Fat 0g; Sodium 96mg; Carbs 26g; Fiber 2g; Sugar 6g; Protein 10g

## Creamed Egg Clouds on Toast

**Prep time: 10 minutes | Cook time: 10 minutes | Serves: 1**

2 egg whites
½ teaspoon sugar
1 cup water
1 tablespoon frozen apple juice concentrate
1 slice reduced-calorie oat-bran bread, lightly toasted

1. In a copper bowl, beat the egg whites until thickened. Add sugar in and beat until stiff peaks form. 2. In a small saucepan, heat water and apple juice over medium heat until it just begins to boil. Reduce heat and allow mixture to simmer. 3. Drop egg whites by teaspoon full into the simmering water. Simmer for 3 minutes; turn over and simmer for an additional 3 minutes. 4. Ladle "clouds" over bread and serve immediately.
Per Serving: Calories 57; Total Fat 1g; Saturated Fat 0g; Sodium 101mg; Carbs 9g; Fiber 0g; Sugar 3g; Protein 4g

## Spinach Potato Cheese Quiche

**Prep time: 10 minutes | Cook time: 50 minutes | Serves: 4-6**

Nonstick cooking spray
8 ounces Yukon Gold potatoes, shredded
1 tablespoon plus 2 teaspoons extra-virgin olive oil, divided
1 teaspoon salt, divided
Freshly ground black pepper
1 onion, finely chopped
1 (10-ounce) bag fresh spinach
4 large eggs
½ cup skim milk
1 ounce Gruyère cheese, shredded

1. Preheat the oven to 350°F. Spray a 9-inch pie dish with cooking spray. Set aside. 2. In a bowl, add the potatoes with olive oil, ½ teaspoon of salt, and season with pepper and toss well. Press the potatoes like a crust on the pie dish to form a thin, even layer. Bake for 20 minutes, until golden brown. Once cooked, set aside to cool. 3. In a large skillet over medium-high heat, heat the remaining 1 tablespoon of olive oil. 4. Add the onion, and sauté for 3 to 5 minutes, until softened. 5. By handfuls, add the spinach, stirring between each addition, until it just starts to wilt before adding more. Cook for about 1 minute, until it cooks down. 6. In a bowl, mix the eggs and milk. Add the Gruyère, and season with the remaining ½ teaspoon of salt and some pepper. Fold the eggs into the spinach. Pour the egg mixture into the pie dish and bake for 25 minutes, until the eggs are set. 7. Let rest for 10 minutes before serving.
Per Serving: Calories 445; Total Fat 14g; Saturated Fat 4g; Sodium 773mg; Carbs 68g; Fiber 7g; Sugar 6g; Protein 19g

## Cinnamon Quinoa Berry Breakfast

**Prep time: 10 minutes | Cook time: 15 minutes | Serves: 4**

1 cup quinoa
2 cups water
¼ cup walnuts
1 teaspoon cinnamon
2 cups berries

1. Rinse the quinoa before cooking. Place the quinoa, water, walnuts, and cinnamon in a 1½-quart saucepan and bring to a boil. 2. Lower the heat; cover and cook for 15 minutes, or until all water has been absorbed. 3. Add the berries and serve with milk, soy milk, or sweetener if desired.
Per Serving: Calories 228; Total Fat 5g; Saturated Fat 0g; Sodium 2mg; Carbs 41g; Fiber 5g; Sugar 3g; Protein 7g

## Baked Lemon-Poppyseed Muffins

**Prep time: 15 minutes | Cook time: 20 minutes | Serves: 12**

½ cup extra-virgin olive oil
½ cup sour cream
3 large eggs
1 teaspoon vanilla extract
Zest of 1 lemon
½ cup granulated sugar-free sweetener, such as Swerve
1¾ cups almond flour
1½ teaspoons baking powder
1 teaspoon xanthan gum
1½ teaspoons poppy seeds

1. Preheat the oven to 350°F. Line a 12-cup muffin tin with liners. 2. In a large bowl, whisk together the olive oil, sour cream, eggs, vanilla, lemon zest, and granulated sweetener. Add the almond flour, baking powder, xanthan gum (if using), and poppy seeds, and mix until well incorporated. 3. Divide the batter evenly to the prepared muffin cups, filling each about three-quarters full. Bake until a toothpick inserted in the center of a muffin comes out clean, 16 to 18 minutes.
Per Serving: Calories 215; Total Fat 21g; Saturated Fat 3g; Sodium 82mg; Carbs 12g; Fiber 2g; Sugar 8g; Protein 5g

## Egg and Ham Slice Breakfast "Burritos"

**Prep time: 5 minutes | Cook time: 5 minutes | Serves: 2**

4 large eggs
¼ cup jarred pesto (preferably made with olive oil)
½ teaspoon salt
¼ teaspoon freshly ground black pepper
2 tablespoons extra-virgin olive oil
4 large slices thick-cut uncured ham or turkey

1. In a bowl, whisk the eggs, pesto, salt, and pepper. 2. Heat the olive oil in a medium skillet over medium heat. Spread the egg mix in the pan, lower the heat to low, and cook, stirring frequently, to scramble the eggs until just set, 3 to 4 minutes. Remove them from the heat. 3. Put the ham slices on a microwave-safe plate and microwave on high for 15 seconds, or until heated through. 4. Place one-quarter of the egg mixture along one edge of each ham slice and roll like a burrito around the eggs. Secure with a toothpick if needed, and serve warm.
Per Serving: Calories 537; Total Fat 40g; Saturated Fat 8g; Sodium 2054mg; Carbs 5g; Fiber 0.4g; Sugar 0g; Protein 39g

## Mixed Berry Vanilla Baked Oatmeal

Prep time: 5 minutes | Cook time: 40 minutes | Serves: 4

1 tablespoon coconut oil or cooking spray
1 cup unsweetened almond milk
½ cup hemp hearts
1 teaspoon cinnamon
1 teaspoon vanilla extract
4 large eggs
¼ cup ground flaxseed
1 teaspoon baking powder
½ cup berries (such as blueberries, raspberries, blackberries, or chopped strawberries)

1. Preheat the oven to 375°F. Grease an 8½-by-4½-inch loaf pan with coconut oil or cooking spray. 2. In a saucepan over boil the milk, add hemp hearts, then reduce the heat to low and simmer, stirring occasionally, until thickened and the hemp seeds are soft, 8 to 10 minutes. Remove and add in cinnamon and vanilla. 3. In a bowl, whisk the eggs, flaxseed, and baking powder. Add in the warm hemp mixture, whisking constantly so that the heat does not scramble the eggs. Stir in the berries and transfer the mixture to the prepared pan. 4. Bake for 20 to 25 minutes, until fully set in the middle and golden brown on top.
**Per Serving:** Calories 278; Total Fat 22g; Saturated Fat 6g; Sodium 230mg; Carbs 6g; Fiber 3g; Sugar 0g; Protein 15g

## Creamy Blueberry Crêpes

Prep time: 15 minutes | Cook time: 15 minutes | Serves: 2

½ cup heavy (whipping) cream, very chilled
2 to 4 teaspoons granulated sugar-free sweetener, such as Swerve, divided
1 teaspoon vanilla extract, divided
½ cup fresh or frozen blueberries
2 tablespoons orange juice
2 ounces full-fat cream cheese
2 large eggs
4 teaspoons unsalted butter, divided

1. In a bowl, mix the heavy cream, 1 to 2 teaspoons of sweetener (if using), and ½ teaspoon of vanilla. Whisk vigorously until thickened and whipped. Set aside. 2. In a saucepan, heat the blueberries, water, ¼ teaspoon of vanilla, and the remaining 1 to 2 teaspoons of sweetener over medium-high heat for 5 to 6 minutes, until bubbly. Using a fork, mash the berries and whisk until smooth. 3. Put the cream cheese in a medium microwave-safe bowl, and microwave on high for 20 to 30 seconds or until warm and melted. Add the eggs and remaining vanilla and whisk until smooth. 4. Working in batches, make the crêpes. Melt little butter in a skillet over medium heat and swirl to coat the bottom of the skillet. Pour one-quarter of the batter (about 2 tablespoons) into the skillet and swirl to spread thinly and evenly. Cook for 2 minutes until just bubbly. Using a spatula, flip to cook another 30 to 60 seconds on the second side. 5. To assemble, spoon 1 tablespoon of warm berry sauce along one side of each crêpe and roll like a burrito. Serve topped with the whipped cream.
**Per Serving:** Calories 474; Total Fat 44g; Saturated Fat 26g; Sodium 169mg; Carbs 8g; Fiber 1g; Sugar 0g; Protein 10g

## Cheesy Breakfast Casserole with Red Pepper and Mushroom

Prep time: 10 minutes | Cook time: 45 minutes | Serves: 4

4 tablespoons extra-virgin olive oil, divided
1 red bell pepper, thinly sliced
4 ounces sliced baby bella or shiitake mushrooms
1 teaspoon salt, divided
½ teaspoon freshly ground black pepper, divided
8 large eggs
1 teaspoon onion powder
4 ounces goat cheese, crumbled

1. Preheat the oven to 350°F. Pour 2 tablespoons of olive oil into a medium 8-by-8-inch glass casserole dish and swirl to coat the bottom and sides. 2. Heat the remaining 2 tablespoons of olive oil in a medium skillet. Once oil is hot, cook the bell pepper and mushrooms, season with ½ teaspoon of salt and ¼ teaspoon of black pepper, until soft and tender, 5 to 8 minutes. Remove the skillet from the heat. 3. In a bowl, whisk the eggs, remaining ½ teaspoon of salt and ¼ teaspoon of black pepper, and onion powder until well blended. Add the cooked peppers and mushrooms and goat cheese, and stir to combine. 4. Transfer the egg mixture to the prepared casserole dish and bake until set, 30 to 35 minutes.
**Per Serving:** Calories 374; Total Fat 30g; Saturated Fat 9g; Sodium 804mg; Carbs 4g; Fiber 1g; Sugar 0g; Protein 19g

## Whole-Wheat Blueberry Breakfast Cake

Prep time: 15 minutes | Cook time: 45 minutes | Serves: 12

**For the Topping**
¼ cup finely chopped walnuts
½ teaspoon ground cinnamon
2 tablespoons butter, chopped into small pieces
2 tablespoons sugar
**For the Cake**
Nonstick cooking spray
1 cup whole-wheat pastry flour
1 cup oat flour
¼ cup sugar
2 teaspoons baking powder
1 large egg, beaten
½ cup skim milk
2 tablespoons butter, melted
1 teaspoon grated lemon peel
2 cups fresh or frozen blueberries

**To make the topping**
In a bowl, stir the walnuts, cinnamon, butter, and sugar. Set aside.
**To make the cake**
1. Preheat the oven to 350°F. Spray a 9-inch square pan with cooking spray. Set aside. 2. In a large bowl, stir together the pastry flour, oat flour, sugar, and baking powder. 3. Add the egg, milk, butter, and lemon peel, and stir until there are no dry spots. 4. Stir in the blueberries, and gently mix until incorporated. Press the batter into the prepared pan, using a spoon to flatten it into the dish. 5. Sprinkle the topping over the cake. 6. Bake for 40 -45 minutes and serve.
**Per Serving:** Calories 177; Total Fat 7g; Saturated Fat 3g; Sodium 39mg; Carbs 26g; Fiber 3g; Sugar 9g; Protein 4g

## Potato, Zucchini and Sausage Breakfast Hash

**Prep time: 20 minutes | Cook time: 20 minutes | Serves: 4**

½ cup shredded potato (from 1 medium yellow waxy potato or 2 small red potatoes)
1½ cups shredded zucchini (from 1 large or 2 smaller zucchini)
1 teaspoon salt
1 pound ground Italian pork sausage
¼ cup extra-virgin olive oil
1 teaspoon garlic powder
¼ teaspoon freshly ground black pepper

1. Combine the shredded potato and zucchini in a colander or on several layers of paper towels. Spread the salt to it and let sit for 10 minutes. Using another paper towel, press on the vegetables to release any excess moisture. 2. While the vegetables are draining, cook the sausage. Heat a deep skillet and cook the sausage, break up the meat and render the fat, until browned and cooked;8 to 10 minutes. Place cooked sausage to a bowl, reserving the rendered fat in the pan. 3. To the rendered fat, add the olive oil, add the drained potato and zucchini. Sprinkle with the garlic powder and pepper, and fry, without stirring, for 2 minutes. Using a spatula, stir the vegetables in the oil, continuing to fry for another 2 to 3 minutes until crispy and cooked .4. Return back the cooked sausage to the pot and fry for another 1 to 2 minutes, or until reheated. Serve warm.
**Per Serving:** Calories 533; Total Fat 40g; Saturated Fat 11g; Sodium 1507mg Carbs 18g; Fiber 2g; Sugar 0g; Protein 23g

## Healthy Tuna Salad Stuffed Avocado

**Prep time: 10 minutes | Cook time: 0 minutes | Serves: 2**

1 large ripe avocado
2 tablespoons mayonnaise
2 tablespoons stone-ground mustard
2 tablespoons finely diced red onion
1 teaspoon salt
½ teaspoon garlic powder
¼ teaspoon freshly ground black pepper
1 (4-ounce) can tuna, packed in olive oil (preferably wild-caught), drained

1. Halve the avocado lengthwise and remove the pit. Using a spoon, scoop out about 1 tablespoon from the center of each avocado to create a larger opening. Transfer the scooped-out flesh to a medium bowl and mash with a fork. 2. To the mashed avocado, add the mayonnaise, mustard, red onion, salt, garlic powder, and pepper, and whisk until smooth. Add the tuna to the mayonnaise mixture and, using a fork to break up any clumps, mash until well combined. 3. Divide the tuna salad evenly between the two avocado halves, saving any salad mixture that will not fit into the avocados to be served alongside them. Enjoy immediately.
**Per Serving:** Calories 387; Total Fat 30g; Saturated Fat 5g; Sodium 1739mg; Carbs 3g; Fiber 7g; Sugar 0g; Protein 17g

## Baked Ricotta with Strawberry and Mint

**Prep time: 10 minutes | Cook time: 40 minutes | Serves: 4**

2 tablespoons coconut oil, melted
16 ounces whole-milk ricotta cheese
2 large eggs
1 teaspoon vanilla extract
1 teaspoon baking powder
2 to 4 teaspoons granulated sugar-free sweetener
1 cup coarsely chopped strawberries
2 tablespoons chopped fresh mint

1. Preheat the oven to 350°F. 2. Pour the coconut oil into an 8-by-8-inch glass baking dish or9-inch round pie pan, and swirl to coat the bottom and sides. 3. In a medium bowl, whisk together the ricotta, eggs, vanilla, baking powder, and sweetener (if using, to taste). Add the chopped strawberries and mint (if using), and stir until well combined. 4. Pour the mixture into the prepared baking dish and bake until lightly browned and set in the middle, 35 to 40 minutes.
**Per Serving:** Calories 285; Total Fat 21g; Saturated Fat 14g; Sodium 278mg; Carbs 12g; Fiber 1g; Sugar 0g; Protein 12g

## Easy Yogurt Parfait with Nuts and Berries

**Prep time: 5 minutes | Cook time: 0 minutes | Serves: 1**

½ cup plain whole-milk (4 or 5 percent milk fat) Greek yogurt
1 tablespoon unsweetened almond or peanut butter
½ teaspoon vanilla extract
½ teaspoon cinnamon
2 tablespoons chopped walnuts (or other nuts such as almonds, pecans, or macadamia nuts)
¼ cup fresh berries such as blueberries, raspberries, blackberries, or strawberries

In a bowl, whisk the yogurt, almond butter, vanilla (if using), and cinnamon (if using). Top with the chopped nuts and berries, and serve immediately.
**Per Serving:** Calories 316; Total Fat 23g; Saturated Fat 5g; Sodium 48mg; Carbs 14g; Fiber 4g; Sugar 0g; Protein 17g

## Easy Herby Egg Salad with Capers

**Prep time: 10 minutes | Cook time: 0 minutes | Serves: 2**

2 tablespoons mayonnaise
3 tablespoons store-bought basil pesto
1 tablespoon capers or chopped green olives
¼ teaspoon freshly ground black pepper
4 large hard-boiled eggs, peeled

1. In a bowl, mix the mayonnaise, pesto, capers (if using), and pepper, and whisk until smooth. 2. Using a box grater, grate the hard-boiled eggs into the pesto mixture. Alternatively, you can coarsely chop the eggs and add to the sauce. Stir to combine well, and serve immediately.
**Per Serving:** Calories 344; Total Fat 31g; Saturated Fat 6g; Sodium 440mg; Carbs 2g; Fiber 0.9g; Sugar 0g; Protein 14g

## Savory Cherry Tomato Cheese Salad

**Prep time: 5 minutes | Cook time: 0 minutes | Serves: 2**

1 cup full-fat cottage cheese
1 medium ripe avocado, pitted, peeled, and cut into ½-inch cubes
8 cherry tomatoes, quartered
¼ cup chopped fresh cilantro
1 to 2 teaspoons hot sauce
4 cups baby spinach or arugula
2 tablespoons roasted pumpkin seeds (pepitas)

1. Combine the cottage cheese, avocado cubes, quartered tomatoes, cilantro, and hot sauce to taste in a bowl, and combine. 2. Put 2 cups spinach or arugula in each of 2 large salad bowls. Top each with one-half of the cottage cheese mixture and sprinkle with 1 tablespoon of pumpkin seeds. Serve immediately.

**Per Serving:** Calories 285; Total Fat 19g; Saturated Fat 4g; Sodium 389mg; Carbs 15g; Fiber 7g; Sugar 0g; Protein 18g

## Avocado Toast with Egg and Black Pepper

**Prep time: 10 minutes | Cook time: 15 minutes | Serves: 2**

1 recipe Microwave Keto Bread
1 medium ripe avocado, pitted, peeled, and thinly sliced
1 tablespoon plus 2 teaspoons extra-virgin olive oil, divided
2 large eggs
½ teaspoon freshly ground black pepper

1. Slice the keto bread in half lengthwise and toast the slices. 2. Place avocado slices on the bread slices and set aside. 3. Heat olive oil in a medium nonstick skillet over medium-high heat. Crack the eggs into the hot oil, keeping them separated. Fry the eggs to your desired level of doneness, flipping halfway through. It should take 1 to 2 minutes per side for a runny egg and 3 to 4 minutes per side for a more cooked yolk. 4. Place 1 fried egg atop the avocado slices on each of the bread slices. Sprinkle each with ¼ teaspoon pepper and drizzle with 1 teaspoon of olive oil. Serve warm.

**Per Serving:** Calories 451; Total Fat 42g; Saturated Fat 7g; Sodium 456mg; Carbs 9g; Fiber 6g; Sugar 0g; Protein 13g

## Pumpkin Pie Smoothie with Pecans

**Prep time: 10 minutes | Cook time: 0 minutes | Serves: 2**

1 cup whole-milk plain Greek yogurt
¼ cup heavy (whipping) cream
2 cups unsweetened almond milk, plus additional if needed
¼ cup unsweetened canned pumpkin puree
2 teaspoons pumpkin pie spice (no-sugar-added)
1 to 2 teaspoons liquid or granular sugar-free sweetener
1 teaspoon vanilla extract
2 tablespoons coarsely chopped pecans

1. In a blender, combine the yogurt, cream, almond milk, pumpkin puree, pumpkin pie spice, sweetener (if using), and vanilla, and blend until smooth, adding additional almond milk as needed for your desired consistency. 2. Divide the mixture between two glasses and sprinkle each with 1 tablespoon of pecans.

**Per Serving:** Calories 312; Total Fat 23g; Saturated Fat 11g; Sodium 229mg; Carbs 13g; Fiber 2g; Sugar 0g; Protein 14g

## Steel-Cut Oatmeal with Fruit and Nuts

**Prep time: 5 minutes | Cook time: 20 minutes | Serves: 4**

1 cup steel-cut oats
2 cups almond milk
¾ cup water
1 teaspoon ground cinnamon
¼ teaspoon salt
2 cups chopped fresh fruit, such as blueberries, strawberries, raspberries, or peaches
½ cup chopped walnuts
¼ cup chia seeds

1. In a saucepan combine the oats, almond milk, water, cinnamon, and salt over medium-high heat. boil, low the heat, and simmer for 15 to 20 minutes, until the oats are softened and thickened. 2. Top each bowl with ½ cup of fresh fruit, 2 tablespoons of walnuts, and 1 tablespoon of chia seeds before serving.

**Per Serving:** Calories 288; Total Fat 11g; Saturated Fat 1g; Sodium 329mg; Carbs 38g; Fiber 10g; Sugar 7g; Protein 10g

## Whole-Grain Dutch Baby Pancake with Cinnamon

**Prep time: 5 minutes | Cook time: 25 minutes | Serves: 4**

2 tablespoons coconut oil
½ cup whole-wheat flour
¼ cup skim milk
3 large eggs
1 teaspoon vanilla extract
½ teaspoon baking powder
¼ teaspoon salt
¼ teaspoon ground cinnamon
Powdered sugar, for dusting

1. Preheat the oven to 400°F. 2. Put the coconut oil in a medium oven-safe skillet, and place the skillet in the oven to melt the oil while it preheats. 3. In a blender, Add the flour with milk, eggs, vanilla, baking powder, salt, and cinnamon. Process until smooth. 4. Tilt the hot skillet to spread the oil around evenly. 5. Pour the pancake batter into it and return it to the oven for 23 to 25 minutes, until the pancake puffs and lightly browns.6. Remove, dust lightly with powdered sugar, cut into 4 wedges, and serve.

**Per Serving:** Calories 195; Total Fat 11g; Saturated Fat 7g; Sodium 209mg; Carbs 16g; Fiber 2g; Sugar 1g; Protein 8g

## Healthy Overnight Oatmeal

**Prep time: 15 minutes | Cook time: 15 minutes | Serves: 4**

1 cup steel-cut oats
14 dried apricot halves
1 dried fig
2 tablespoons golden raisins
4 cups water
½ cup Mock Cream

1.Add all ingredients in a slow cooker with a ceramic interior. 2.Set to low heat. Cover and cook overnight (8–9 hours).

**Per Serving:** Calories 221; Total Fat 3g; Saturated Fat 1g; Sodium 25mg; Carbs 42g; Fiber 6g; Sugar 3g; Protein 9g

## Baked Berry-Oat Breakfast Bars

Prep time: 10 minutes | Cook time: 25 minutes | Serves: 12

2 cups fresh raspberries or blueberries
2 tablespoons sugar
2 tablespoons freshly squeezed lemon juice
1 tablespoon cornstarch
1½ cups rolled oats
½ cup whole-wheat flour
½ cup walnuts
¼ cup chia seeds
¼ cup extra-virgin olive oil
¼ cup honey
1 large egg

1. Preheat the oven to 350°F. 2. In a small saucepan over medium heat, stir together the berries, sugar, lemon juice, and cornstarch. Bring to a simmer. Simmer on low;2 to 3 minutes, until the mixture thickens. 3. In a food processor, combine the oats, flour, walnuts, and chia seeds. Process until powdered. Add the olive oil, honey, and egg. Pulse until well combined. Press half mixture into a 9-inch square baking dish. 4. Spread the berry filling over the oat mixture. Place the remaining oats mixture on the berries. Bake for 25 minutes, until browned. 5. Cut into pieces, and serve.
**Per Serving:** Calories 201; Total Fat 10g; Saturated Fat 1g; Sodium 8mg; Carbs 26g; Fiber 5g; Sugar 9g; Protein 5g

## Whole-Grain Breakfast Cookies with Cherries and Chocolate

Prep time: 20 minutes | Cook time: 10 minutes | Serves: 18

2 cups rolled oats
½ cup whole-wheat flour
¼ cup ground flaxseed
1 teaspoon baking powder
1 cup unsweetened applesauce
2 large eggs
2 tablespoons vegetable oil
2 teaspoons vanilla extract
1 teaspoon ground cinnamon
½ cup dried cherries
¼ cup unsweetened shredded coconut
2 ounces dark chocolate, chopped

1. Preheat the oven to 350°F. 2. In a large bowl, combine the oats, flour, flaxseed, and baking powder. Stir well to mix. 3. In a bowl, whisk the applesauce with eggs, vegetable oil, vanilla, and cinnamon. Pour the wet mixture into the dry mixture, and stir until just combined. 4. Fold in the cherries, coconut, and chocolate. Drop small size dough balls onto a baking sheet. Bake for 10-12 minutes, until browned and cooked. 5. Let cool for about 3 minutes, remove from the baking sheet, and cool completely before serving.
**Per Serving:** Calories 136; Total Fat 7g; Saturated Fat 3g; Sodium 11mg; Carbs 14g; Fiber 3g; Sugar 4g; Protein 4g

## Whole-Grain Pancakes with Fresh Fruit

Prep time: 10 minutes | Cook time: 15 minutes | Serves: 4-6

2 cups whole-wheat pastry flour
4 teaspoons baking powder
2 teaspoons ground cinnamon
½ teaspoon salt
2 cups skim milk, plus more as needed
2 large eggs
1 tablespoon honey
Nonstick cooking spray
Maple syrup, for serving
Fresh fruit, for serving

1. In a bowl, stir the flour, baking powder, cinnamon, and salt. 2. Add the milk, eggs, and honey, and stir well combine. 3. Heat a skillet and grease with oil. 4. Using a ¼-cup measuring cup, scoop 2 or 3 pancakes into the skillet at a time. Cook until bubbly surface of the pancakes, flip, and cook for 1-2 minutes more, until golden brown and cooked through. Repeat with the remaining batter. 5. Serve topped with maple syrup or fresh fruit.
**Per Serving:** Calories 392; Total Fat 4g; Saturated Fat 1g; Sodium 396mg; Carbs 71g; Fiber 9g; Sugar 11g; Protein 15g

## Coconut, Berry and Leafy Greens Sunrise Smoothie

Prep time: 5 minutes | Cook time: 30 minutes or less Serves: 2

½ cup mixed berries
 (blueberries, strawberries, blackberries)
1 tablespoon ground flaxseed
2 tablespoons unsweetened coconut flakes
½ cup unsweetened plain coconut milk
½ cup leafy greens (kale, spinach)
¼ cup unsweetened vanilla nonfat yogurt
½ cup ice

1. In a blender jar, combine the berries, flaxseed, coconut flakes, coconut milk, greens, yogurt, and ice. 2. Process until smooth. Serve.
**Per Serving:** Calories 181; Total Fat 15g; Saturated Fat 2g; Sodium 24mg; Carbs 8g; Fiber 4g; Sugar 3g; Protein 6g

## Greek Yogurt Sundae with Mixed Berries

Prep time: 5 minutes | Cook time: 30 minutes or less Serves: 1

¾ cup plain nonfat Greek yogurt
¼ cup mixed berries
 (blueberries, strawberries, blackberries)
2 tablespoons cashew, walnut, or almond pieces
1 tablespoon ground flaxseed
2 fresh mint leaves, shredded

1. Spoon the yogurt into a bowl. Top with the berries, nuts, and flaxseed. 2. Garnish with the mint and serve.
**Per Serving:** Calories 237; Total Fat 11g; Saturated Fat 2g; Sodium 64mg; Carbs 16g; Fiber 4g; Sugar 9g; Protein 21g

## Cinnamon Buckwheat Groats Breakfast Bowl

**Prep time: 5 minutes | Cook time: 10-12 minutes | Serves: 4**

3 cups skim milk
1 cup buckwheat groats
¼ cup chia seeds
2 teaspoons vanilla extract
½ teaspoon ground cinnamon
Pinch salt
1 cup water
½ cup unsalted pistachios
2 cups sliced fresh strawberries
¼ cup cacao nibs

1. In a bowl, stir the milk, groats, chia seeds, vanilla, cinnamon, and salt. Cover and refrigerate overnight. 2. The next morning, transfer the soaked mixture to a medium pot and add the water. Boil it, lower the heat to maintain a simmer, and cook for 10-12 minutes, until the buckwheat is tender and thickened. 3. Transfer to bowls and serve, topped with the pistachios, strawberries, and cacao nibs (if using).
**Per Serving:** Calories 340; Total Fat 8g; Saturated Fat 1g; Sodium 140mg; Carbs 52g; Fiber 10g; Sugar 14g; Protein 15g

## Sliced Peach Muesli Bake

**Prep time: 10 minutes | Cook time: 40 minutes | Serves: 8**

Nonstick cooking spray
2 cups skim milk
1½ cups rolled oats
½ cup chopped walnuts
1 large egg
2 tablespoons maple syrup
1 teaspoon ground cinnamon
1 teaspoon baking powder
½ teaspoon salt
2 to 3 peaches, sliced

1. Preheat the oven to 375°F Spray a 9-inch square baking dish with cooking spray. Set aside. 2. In a bowl, stir the milk, oats, walnuts, egg, maple syrup, cinnamon, baking powder, and salt. Spread half mixture in the baking dish. 3. Place half the peaches in a single layer across the oat mixture. 4. Spread the remaining oat mixture over the top. Add the remaining peaches in a thin layer over the oats. Bake for 35-40 minutes, uncovered, until thickened and browned. 5. Cut into 8 squares and serve warm.
**Per Serving:** Calories 138; Total Fat 3g; Saturated Fat 1g; Sodium 191mg; Carbs 22g; Fiber 3g; Sugar 10g; Protein 6g

## Frozen Tofu and Fruit Smoothie

**Prep time: 10 minutes | Cook time: 0 minutes | Serves: 1**

1⅓ cups frozen unsweetened strawberries
½ banana
½ cup (4 ounces) silken tofu

Blend all ingredients until thick and smooth. Add a little chilled water for thinner smoothies if desired.
**Per Serving:** Calories 319; Total Fat 11g; Saturated Fat 2g; Sodium 19mg; Carbs 35g; Fiber 8g; Sugar 4g; Protein 20g

## Mushroom, Zucchini, and Onion Frittata with Feta Cheese

**Prep time: 10 minutes | Cook time: 20 minutes | Serves: 4**

1 tablespoon extra-virgin olive oil
½ onion, chopped
1 medium zucchini, chopped
1½ cups sliced mushrooms
6 large eggs, beaten
2 tablespoons skim milk
Salt
Freshly ground black pepper
1 ounce feta cheese, crumbled

1. Preheat the oven to 400°F. 2. In a medium oven-safe skillet over medium-high heat, heat the olive oil. 3. Add the onion, and sauté for 3 to 5 minutes, until translucent. 4. Add the zucchini and mushrooms, and cook for 3 to 5 more minutes, until the vegetables are tender. 5. Meanwhile, in a bowl, whisk the eggs, milk, salt, and pepper. Pour the mixture into the skillet, stirring to combine, and transfer the skillet to the oven. Cook for 7-9 minutes, until set. 6. Sprinkle with the feta cheese, and cook for 1 to 2 minutes more, until heated through. 7. Remove, cut into 4 wedges, and serve.
**Per Serving:** Calories 178; Total Fat 13g; Saturated Fat 4g; Sodium 234mg; Carbs 5g; Fiber 1g; Sugar 3g; Protein 12g

## Healthy Egg and Veggie Breakfast Cups

**Prep time: 10 minutes | Cook time: 25 minutes | Serves: 8**

Nonstick cooking spray
1 tablespoon extra-virgin olive oil
1 onion, finely chopped
½ green bell pepper, finely chopped
½ red bell pepper, finely chopped
2 garlic cloves, minced
8 large eggs
Salt
Freshly ground black pepper
¼ cup sun-dried tomatoes, finely chopped

1. Preheat the oven to 350°F. Spray 8 wells of a muffin tin with cooking spray. Set aside. 2. In a skillet, heat the olive oil over medium heat. 3. Add the onion and green and red bell peppers, and sauté for 4 to 5 minutes, until they begin to soften. Cook the garlic for 30 seconds until fragrant. Remove from the heat. 4. In a bowl, mix the eggs and spice with salt and pepper. Stir in the vegetable mixture and the sun-dried tomatoes. Divide the egg mixture among the 8 prepared muffin cups. Bake for 16 to 20 minutes, until the eggs are set. 5. Remove and serve.
**Per Serving:** Calories 102; Total Fat 7g; Saturated Fat 2g; Sodium 126mg; Carbs 4g; Fiber 1g; Sugar 2g; Protein 7g

## Breakfast Tostada with Salsa

**Prep time: 5 minutes | Cook time: 20 minutes | Serves: 4**

Nonstick cooking spray
4 corn tortillas
½ cup fat-free refried beans
1 tablespoon extra-virgin olive oil
4 large eggs
Salt
Freshly ground black pepper
1 avocado, peeled, pitted, and sliced
½ cup salsa
¼ cup crumbled feta cheese

1. Preheat the oven to 350°F. Spray a baking sheet with nonstick cooking spray. 2. Place the tortillas on the baking sheet, overlapping the edges if needed. Bake for 12 to 15 minutes until crisp. Once cooked, set aside. 3. In a small pot over medium heat, warm the refried beans. 4. In a skillet heat the olive oil over medium-high heat, .5. Crack the eggs into the skillet. Fry for 3 to 5 minutes, depending on preferred doneness. Season lightly with salt and pepper. 6. Assemble the tostadas with a layer of beans on each tortilla, topping each with 1 egg, a couple of avocado slices, 2 tablespoons of salsa, and 1 tablespoon of feta cheese.
**Per Serving:** Calories 290; Total Fat 18g; Saturated Fat 5g; Sodium 549mg; Carbs 23g; Fiber 7g; Sugar 2g; Protein 12g

## Shakshuka Eggs

**Prep time: 5 minutes | Cook time: 20 minutes | Serves: 4**

1 (24-ounce) jar no-sugar-added marinara sauce, such as Rao's
¼ cup extra-virgin olive oil
½ to 1 teaspoon crushed red pepper flakes
6 ounces frozen spinach, thawed and drained of excess liquid (about 1½ cups)
4 large eggs
4 ounces shredded mozzarella cheese

1. In a medium, deep skillet with a lid, combine the marinara sauce, olive oil, red pepper flakes to taste (if using), and spinach, and stir until well combined. 2. Bring the mixture to a boil over medium-high heat, then reduce the heat to low, cover, and simmer for 2 to 3 minutes. 3. Uncover the skillet and gently crack each egg into the simmering sauce, allowing the egg to create a crater and being careful not to let the eggs touch. Return the lid and cook, poaching the eggs until the yolks are just set, 8 to 10 minutes. 4. Uncover and sprinkle with the cheese. Cook for 3 minutes until the cheese is melted and the eggs are fully cooked, another 3 to 5 minutes. Serve warm.
**Per Serving:** Calories 395; Total Fat 32g; Saturated Fat 8g; Sodium 825mg; Carbs 9g; Fiber 3g; Sugar 0g; Protein 17g

# Chapter 2 Vegan and Vegetarian Recipes

31 Crisp Vegetable and Quinoa Bowl
31 Broccoli-Almond-Sesame Soba Noodles
31 Pasta with Sun-Dried Tomatoes, Feta Cheese, and Arugula
31 Crispy Sage-Roasted Root Vegetables
31 Black-Eyed Peas and Kale Salad
32 Old-Fashioned Sweet Potato Bake with Pecans
32 Baked Beans with Raisin and Apple
32 Wheat Berry and Tabbouleh Salad
32 Sweet Potato Fries
32 Mediterranean Oven-Roasted Potatoes and Vegetables with Herbs
32 Mashed Cauliflower and Potatoes
33 Wild Rice Pilaf with Broccoli and Carrots
33 Quinoa and Vegetable Pilau
33 Roasted Broccoli and Parmesan Millet Bake
33 Easy, Cheesy Quinoa Fritters
34 Macaroni and Cheese with Mixed Vegetables
34 Broccoli, Chard, and Cheddar Bread Pudding
34 New England Baked Beans
34 Famous Baked Beans
34 Crock-O-Beans
35 Barbecued Lima Beans
35 Refried Beans with Bacon
35 Red Beans and Sausage
35 Red Beans and Pasta
35 Easy Party-Time Beans
35 Soft Pioneer Beans
36 Slow Cooker Scandinavian Beans
36 Easy Barbecued Lentils
36 Slow Cooker Red Beans
36 Herbed Chickpea Pasta
36 Slow Cooker Butter Macaroni with Cheese
36 Tempeh-Stuffed Peppers with Cheddar
37 Hearty Vegan Slow Cooker Chili with Yogurt
37 Mushroom Burgers
37 Creamy Pesto Zoodles
37 Cheesy Garlic Pasta Salad

## Crisp Vegetable and Quinoa Bowl

**Prep time: 15 minutes | Cook time: 12 minutes | Serves: 4**

¾ cup plain 2% Greek yogurt
¼ cup freshly squeezed lemon juice
2 tablespoons extra-virgin olive oil
6 garlic cloves, minced
½ teaspoon salt
1 cup quinoa
2 cups water
1 pound asparagus, cut into 2-inch pieces
1 cup fresh or frozen green peas
1 cucumber, peeled, thinly sliced crosswise
8 cups baby spinach
½ cup walnut pieces

1. In a bowl, mix the yogurt along with lemon juice, olive oil, garlic, and salt. Set aside. 2. In a pot, mix the quinoa and water. Boil over medium-high heat, reduce the heat, cover, and simmer until tender, about 10 minutes. Drain any remaining water and spread out the quinoa on a baking sheet to cool. 3. Boil water over medium-high heat. Boil the asparagus with peas until they are crisp-tender, about 2 minutes. Drain and soak the vegetables under cold water to stop them from cooking. 4. Divide the quinoa among four bowls. Top each bowl with equal amounts of asparagus, peas, cucumber, spinach, and walnuts. Drizzle the dressing over the bowls and serve.
**Per Serving:** Calories 462; Total Fat 25g; Saturated Fat 4g; Sodium 420mg; Carbs 47g; Fiber 10g; Sugar 6g; Protein 19g

## Broccoli-Almond-Sesame Soba Noodles

**Prep time: 10 minutes | Cook time: 15 minutes | Serves: 4**

¼ cup sliced almonds
6-ounces dried buckwheat soba noodles
1 cup fresh or frozen broccoli florets
2 tablespoons low-sodium soy sauce
1 tablespoon rice vinegar
2 teaspoons honey
2 teaspoons toasted sesame oil
½ cup sliced sugar snap or snow peas
1 bunch scallions, finely chopped
1 red bell pepper, seeded and sliced

1. Heat a skillet and toast the almonds, shaking the pan continuously, until just browned, 2 to 3 minutes. 2. Boil water over high heat. Add the noodles. Cook according to the package directions. Transfer to a large bowl. 3. Meanwhile, fill another large pot with a couple of inches of water and a steaming basket. Boil water over high heat and add the broccoli. Cover and steam the broccoli until fork-tender yet still bright green, 3 to 5 minutes. Remove the broccoli from the basket and run it under cold water until cool. Transfer to the bowl with the noodles. 4. In a bowl, Add the rice vinegar, honey, and sesame oil and soy sauce. 5. Add the peas, scallions, bell pepper, almonds, and soy sauce mixture to the noodles and broccoli. Toss well to combine.
**Per Serving:** Calories 247; Total Fat 6g; Saturated Fat 1g; Sodium 749mg; Carbs 10g; Fiber 3g; Sugar 6g; Protein 7g

## Pasta with Sun-Dried Tomatoes, Feta Cheese, and Arugula

**Prep time: 5 minutes | Cook time: 10 minutes | Serves: 4**

½ pound whole-wheat penne pasta
2 tablespoons extra-virgin olive oil
3 garlic cloves, minced
½ cup sun-dried tomatoes
½ cup reduced-fat feta cheese, crumbled
¼ teaspoon salt
¼ teaspoon freshly ground black pepper
3 cups arugula

1. Boil water over high heat. Cook the pasta. Drain. 2. In a skillet, heat the olive oil, and cook the garlic and sauté until just fragrant in medium high heat. Add the sun-dried tomatoes and cook for 1 additional minute, stirring constantly. 3. Add the cooked pasta noodles to it sprinkle with the feta cheese, salt, and pepper. Stir to combine. Add the arugula, toss, and serve.
**Per Serving:** Calories 217; Total Fat 7g; Saturated Fat 1g; Sodium 352mg; Carbs 31g; Fiber 5g; Sugar 3g; Protein 9g

## Crispy Sage-Roasted Root Vegetables

**Prep time: 5 minutes | Cook time: 35 minutes | Serves: 4**

1 medium sweet potato, peeled and diced
2 new potatoes, diced
2 beets, diced
3 carrots, peeled and cut into pieces
1 tablespoon extra-virgin olive oil
15 fresh sage leaves
1 teaspoon garlic powder

1. Preheat the oven to 400°F. Line a baking sheet with parchment paper. 2. Toss together all the ingredients on the lined baking sheet. Roast, tossing once halfway through, until the sweet potatoes are slightly browned and the beets are soft inside, 25 to 35 minutes. Remove the sage leaves prior to serving.
**Per Serving:** Calories 110; Total Fat 4g; Saturated Fat 1g; Sodium 85mg; Carbs 19g; Fiber 4g; Sugar 7g; Protein 2g

## Black-Eyed Peas and Kale Salad

**Prep time: 10 minutes | Cook time: 1 hour | Serves: 8**

1 pound dried black-eyed peas, soaked in water overnight
1 bunch kale, stemmed, leaves cut into bite-size pieces
3 tablespoons extra-virgin olive oil
10 garlic cloves, minced
1 teaspoon salt

1. In a pot, cook the beans until are tender, 40 to 50 minutes. Drain and place to a bowl. 2. Boil water on high heat. Add the kale in it and cook until tender yet still bright green, 2 to 3 minutes. 3. Remove the kale from hot water and transfer it to the bowl with the beans. 4. Add the olive oil, garlic, and salt and mix well. Serve hot or cold.
**Per Serving:** Calories 251; Total Fat 6g; Saturated Fat 1g; Sodium 310mg; Carbs 37g; Fiber 7g; Sugar 4g; Protein 14g

## Old-Fashioned Sweet Potato Bake with Pecans

**Prep time: 10 minutes | Cook time: 1 hour 15 minutes | Serves: 8**

Nonstick cooking spray
2 pounds sweet potatoes (about 4 medium potatoes)
½ teaspoon ground cinnamon
2 tablespoons freshly squeezed orange juice
2 large eggs
¼ cup chopped pecans

1. Preheat the oven to 350°F. Lightly coat an 8-inch square baking dish with nonstick cooking spray. 2. Boil water over high heat. Add the sweet potatoes, reduce the heat, and slow-boil the potatoes until a fork can be inserted in each potato easily, about 30 minutes. Drain the potatoes and cool. Peel the potatoes. 3. Transfer the potatoes to the electric mixer bowl and lightly beat them. Add the cinnamon, orange juice, and eggs. Whip on high until all the ingredients are incorporated and the mixture is slightly fluffy, about 45 seconds. 4. Pour the mix into the baking dish. Bake for 40 minutes. Sprinkle the pecans evenly across the top and bake for another 5 minutes.
**Per Serving:** Calories 97; Total Fat 4g; Saturated Fat 1g; Sodium 41mg; Carbs 13g; Fiber 2g; Sugar 4g; Protein 3g

## Baked Beans with Raisin and Apple

**Prep time: 20 minutes | Cook time: 6-8 hours | Serves: 20**

1 cup raisins
2 small onions, diced
2 tart apples, unpeeled, diced
1 cup chili sauce
1 cup chopped extra-lean, reduced-sodium ham
1 can baked beans, 1 pound to 15 ounce
2 (14.8-ounce) cans no-added-salt baked beans
3 teaspoons dry mustard
½ cup sweet pickle relish

1. Mix together all ingredients. 2. Cover. Cook on low 6-8 hours.
**Per Serving:** Calories 148; Total Fat 1g; Saturated Fat 0.1g; Sodium 443mg; Carbs 32g; Fiber 6g; Sugar 16g; Protein 6g

## Wheat Berry and Tabbouleh Salad

**Prep time: 10 minutes | Cook time: 1 hour | Serves: 6**

1 cup wheat berries
3 cups water
1 cup chopped tomato
1 cup chopped cucumber
¼ cup sliced scallions
½ cup chopped fresh parsley
1 tablespoon chopped fresh mint
3 tablespoons extra-virgin olive oil
3 tablespoons freshly squeezed lemon juice
¼ teaspoon salt

1. In a small pot, combine the wheat berries and water. Cook the berries for about 60 minutes until tender. 2. In a bowl, combine the wheat berries, tomato, cucumber, scallions, parsley, and mint. Toss to combine. 3. In a bowl, Add the olive oil with lemon juice, and salt and mix. Pour over the salad and toss to combine. Serve immediately.
**Per Serving:** Calories 172; Total Fat 7g; Saturated Fat 1g; Sodium 103mg; Carbs 24g; Fiber 5g; Sugar 1g; Protein 5g

## Sweet Potato Fries

**Prep time: 10 minutes | Cook time: 40 minutes | Serves: 4**

4 medium sweet potatoes
1 tablespoon extra-virgin olive oil
1 teaspoon ground cinnamon
¼ teaspoon salt
¼ teaspoon cayenne pepper

1. Preheat the oven to 425°F. 2. Cut the sweet potatoes lengthwise into disks, then stack the disks into piles and cut the disks into strips. 3. In a bowl, add the potatoes with the olive oil until lightly coated. Add the cinnamon, salt, and cayenne pepper and toss again. 4. Place the potatoes on a dark baking sheet. Bake, flipping once about halfway through cooking, until crisp and browned, 30 to 40 minutes. Serve hot.
**Per Serving:** Calories 134; Total Fat 4g; Saturated Fat 1g; Sodium 187mg; Carbs 24g; Fiber 4g; Sugar 7g; Protein 2g

## Mediterranean Oven-Roasted Potatoes and Vegetables with Herbs

**Prep time: 10 minutes | Cook time: 25 minutes | Serves: 6**

8 ounces fingerling potatoes, quartered
8 ounces miniature red bell peppers, halved lengthwise and seeded
8 ounces mushrooms, sliced
1 cup cauliflower florets
1 onion, sliced
2 tablespoons extra-virgin olive oil
½ teaspoon salt
½ teaspoon freshly ground black pepper
1 tablespoon chopped fresh rosemary
1 tablespoon chopped fresh oregano
1 tablespoon chopped fresh parsley

1. Preheat the oven to 425°F. 2. In a large bowl, combine the potatoes, peppers, mushrooms, cauliflower, and onion. Drizzle the olive oil spice with salt, and pepper and toss to combine. 3. Arrange the vegetables on a baking sheet. Bake for 25 minutes, stirring once. Remove and toss with the rosemary, oregano, and parsley. Serve.
**Per Serving:** Calories 108; Total Fat 5g; Saturated Fat 1g; Sodium 209mg; Carbs 14g; Fiber 3g; Sugar 4g; Protein 3g

## Mashed Cauliflower and Potatoes

**Prep time: 10 minutes | Cook time: 10 minutes | Serves: 6**

1 pound new potatoes, cut into 1-inch cubes
1 large head cauliflower
¼ cup unsweetened almond milk
1 tablespoon unsalted butter
½ teaspoon salt
¼ teaspoon freshly ground black pepper
2 tablespoons chopped fresh chives

1. Boil potatoes over medium-high heat until tender when pierced with a fork, about 10 minutes. Drain and return to the pot. 2. Meanwhile, fill another large pot with a couple of inches of water and a steaming basket. Boil water over high heat. Cook cauliflower until tender, 6 to 8 minutes. Drain and add to the pot with the potatoes. 3. Mash the potatoes and cauliflower together to the desired consistency. Add the almond milk, butter, salt, pepper, and chives and mix well. Serve hot.
**Per Serving:** Calories 125; Total Fat 3g; Saturated Fat 1g; Sodium 247mg; Carbs 23g; Fiber 4g; Sugar 4g; Protein 4g

## Wild Rice Pilaf with Broccoli and Carrots

**Prep time: 10 minutes | Cook time: 1 hour 30 minutes | Serves: 8**

Nonstick cooking spray
4 cups low-sodium chicken broth
¾ cup wild rice
¾ cup long-grain brown rice
¼ cup extra-virgin olive oil
1 large onion, chopped
2 carrots, peeled and chopped
½ teaspoon dried thyme
2 garlic cloves, minced
3 cups broccoli florets
1 teaspoon salt
½ teaspoon freshly ground black pepper

1. Preheat the oven to 350°F. Lightly coat a 2-quart casserole dish with nonstick cooking spray. 2. In a large pot, combine the broth, wild rice, and brown rice. Bring to a boil over high heat, then reduce the heat to medium. Cover it, cook until the rice is tender and the water is absorbed, about 45 minutes. Let stand for 10 minutes, covered. 3. In a skillet, heat the oil, add the onion, carrots, and thyme, and sauté until the onion becomes translucent, 5 to 7 minutes. Add the garlic and sauté for 1 additional minute. Remove the skillet from the heat. 4. Stir in the broccoli, rice, salt, and pepper. Place the mix to the casserole dish, cover, and bake until the broccoli is tender, about 30 minutes.
**Per Serving:** Calories 210; Total Fat 8g; Saturated Fat 1g; Sodium 340mg; Carbs 29g; Fiber 2g; Sugar 2g; Protein 6g

## Quinoa and Vegetable Pilau

**Prep time: 10 minutes | Cook time: 30 minutes | Serves: 6**

1 teaspoon organic canola oil
1 medium onion, sliced
2 garlic cloves, crushed
4 cardamom pods
1 cinnamon stick
2 whole cloves
1 dried red chili
1 leek, thinly sliced on the bias
½ red bell pepper, sliced
½ yellow bell pepper, sliced
1 cup quinoa
2 cups water
1 teaspoon coriander seeds
½ teaspoon salt
1 small zucchini, sliced

1. In a pot, cook the onion in hot over medium heat until it begins to soften, 3 to 4 minutes. Sauté the garlic for a minute. Add the cardamom pods, cinnamon stick, cloves, and chili and sauté for 1 minute. Add the leek and bell peppers and sauté for 2 minutes. 2. Add the quinoa and water. Boil it and add the coriander seeds and salt. Reduce the heat to low, cover, and simmer for 15 minutes. Add the zucchini, and continue to cook until the quinoa is tender and the liquid has evaporated, about 5 minutes. Fluff with a fork, remove the whole spices if desired, and serve.
**Per Serving:** Calories 146; Total Fat 3g; Saturated Fat 0g; Sodium 203mg; Carbs 26g; Fiber 4g; Sugar 2g; Protein 5g

## Roasted Broccoli and Parmesan Millet Bake

**Prep time: 10 minutes | Cook time: 40 minutes | Serves: 8**

8 cups broccoli florets
2 tablespoons extra-virgin olive oil, divided
½ teaspoon freshly ground black pepper
Nonstick cooking spray
1½ cups millet
3 cups water
3 garlic cloves, minced
1 cup unsweetened almond milk
1 teaspoon dried thyme
¾ teaspoon salt, divided
8 ounces grated Parmesan cheese

1. Preheat the oven to 450°F. 2. In a large mixing bowl, toss the broccoli with 1 tablespoon of olive oil and the pepper. Spread out the broccoli on a large baking sheet and roast for 20 minutes, stirring once about halfway through. Remove and set aside. 3. Reduce the oven heat to 400°F. Lightly coat a 2-quart casserole dish with nonstick cooking spray. 4. While the broccoli is cooking, in a small pot, combine the millet and water. Boil water, then simmer on low. Cook until millet is tender and all the water is absorbed, about 15 minutes. Fluff with a fork. 5. In a skillet, Sauté the garlic for 1 minute in hot olive oil. Add the almond milk, thyme, and ¼ teaspoon of salt. Add the Parmesan cheese, stirring until it melts. Turn off the heat. 6. Transfer the millet to the casserole dish and toss with the remaining ½ teaspoon of salt. Fold in the broccoli, pour the cheese mixture over the casserole, and stir to combine. Bake the casserole, uncovered, until warmed through, about 15 minutes.
**Per Serving:** Calories 332; Total Fat 14g; Saturated Fat 6g; Sodium 561mg; Carbs 35g; Fiber 6g; Sugar 2g; Protein 18g

## Easy, Cheesy Quinoa Fritters

**Prep time: 10 minutes | Cook time: 10 minutes | Serves: 5**

1 cup cooked quinoa
1 large egg, beaten
¼ cup shredded nonfat mozzarella cheese
¼ cup whole-wheat bread crumbs
¼ cup finely chopped spinach
2 tablespoons finely chopped yellow onion
2 tablespoons finely chopped scallion
3 fresh basil leaves, minced
1 tablespoon garlic powder
¼ teaspoon freshly ground black pepper
⅛ teaspoon salt
1 tablespoon extra-virgin olive oil

1. Mix all ingredients instead of olive oil in a bowl. 2. Heat the olive oil in a skillet and place heaping spoonfuls of the quinoa mixture into the hot skillet. Cook until browned, 3-4 minutes each side. Serve warm.
**Per Serving:** Calories 142; Total Fat 6g; Saturated Fat 2g; Sodium 138mg; Carbs 15g; Fiber 2g; Sugar 1g; Protein 7g

## Macaroni and Cheese with Mixed Vegetables

**Prep time: 10 minutes | Cook time: 1 hour | Serves: 8**

Nonstick cooking spray
1½ cups whole-wheat elbow noodles
4 cups frozen broccoli and cauliflower mix, thawed in a colander
1 cup shredded sharp Cheddar cheese, divided
2 large eggs, beaten
2 cups unsweetened almond milk
1 teaspoon onion powder
½ teaspoon mustard powder
½ teaspoon salt
½ teaspoon freshly ground black pepper

1. Preheat the oven to 350°F. Coat a 9-inch square baking dish with nonstick cooking spray. 2. Boil water over high heat. Cook the noodles until just tender. Drain. 3. Squeeze any excess moisture from the cauliflower and broccoli and transfer them to the baking dish. Add the noodles and the vegetables and toss them together. Add ¾ cup of cheese and toss to combine. 4. In a bowl, whisk the eggs, almond milk, onion powder, mustard powder, salt, and pepper. Pour egg mix over the noodles and vegetables evenly, and top with the remaining ¼ cup of cheese. 5. Cover and bake for about 40 minutes. Uncover it and bake again until the top is browned, another 5 to 10 minutes. Let rest for 10 minutes before serving.
**Per Serving:** Calories 176; Total Fat 7g; Saturated Fat 3g; Sodium 326mg; Carbs 20g; Fiber 4g; Sugar 1g; Protein 11g

## Broccoli, Chard, and Cheddar Bread Pudding

**Prep time: 10 minutes | Cook time: 1 hour 10 minutes | Serves: 6**

Nonstick cooking spray
1½ tablespoons extra-virgin olive oil
1 large onion, chopped
2 bunches Swiss chard, stemmed and leaves chopped
3 large eggs, beaten
1¼ cups unsweetened almond milk
2 tablespoons Dijon or whole-grain mustard
2 teaspoons dried sage
1 teaspoon ground nutmeg
¼ teaspoon freshly ground black pepper
5 cups chopped broccoli florets
3 slices whole-grain bread, cut into ½-inch cubes
6 ounces Cheddar cheese, cut into ½-inch cubes

1. Preheat the oven to 375°F. Lightly coat an 8-by-11-inch baking dish with nonstick cooking spray. 2. In a skillet, Add the onion in hot oil and sauté until softened, about 5 minutes. Add the chard and sauté until wilted and softened. Set aside. 3. In a bowl, whisk the eggs, almond milk, mustard, sage, nutmeg, and pepper. 4. In a bowl, toss the broccoli, bread, and cheese. Transfer half of this mixture to the prepared baking dish. Top with the chard. Add the remaining broccoli mixture to the dish. Pour the egg mix evenly over the casserole, making sure to wet all the bread pieces. 5. Bake for 1 hour, rotating the dish about halfway through. Let rest for 10 minutes before serving.
**Per Serving:** Calories 290; Total Fat 17g; Saturated Fat 8g; Sodium 721mg; Carbs 21g; Fiber 6g; Sugar 4g; Protein 17g

## New England Baked Beans

**Prep time: 20 minutes | Cook time: 14-16 hours | Serves: 8**

1 lb. dried Great Northern, pea, or navy beans
2 oz. salt pork, sliced
1 qt. water
1 teaspoon salt
1 tablespoon brown sugar
½ cup molasses
½ teaspoon dry mustard
½ teaspoon baking soda
1 onion, coarsely chopped
5 cups water

1. Wash beans and remove any stones or shriveled beans. 2. Meanwhile, simmer salt pork in 1 quart water in a saucepan for 10 minutes. Drain. Do not reserve liquid. 3. Mix all ingredients in a slow cooker. 4. Cook on high until contents come to boil. Turn to low. Cook 14-16 hours, or until beans are tender.
**Per Serving:** Calories 269; Total Fat 5g; Saturated Fat 1.6g; Sodium 444mg; Carbs 47g; Fiber 10g; Sugar 18g; Protein 12g

## Famous Baked Beans

**Prep time: 20 minutes | Cook time: 3-6 hours | Serves: 15**

1 lb. ground beef
¼ cup minced onions
1 cup no-salt-added ketchup
4 15-oz. cans pork and beans
⅓ cup brown sugar
brown sugar substitute to equal ¼ cup sugar
2 tablespoons liquid smoke
1 tablespoon Worcestershire sauce

1. Brown beef and onions in skillet. Drain. Spoon meat and onions into slow cooker. 2. Add remaining ingredients and stir well. 3. Cover. Cook on high temp setting for 3 hours or on low for 5-6 hours.
**Per Serving:** Calories 207; Total Fat 5g; Saturated Fat 1.2g; Sodium 539mg; Carbs 32g; Fiber 5g; Sugar 17g; Protein 10g

## Crock-O-Beans

**Prep time: 15 minutes | Cook time: 6 hours | Serves: 12**

15-oz. can tomato purée
1 medium onion, chopped
2 cloves garlic, chopped
1 tablespoon chili powder
1 tablespoon dried oregano
1 tablespoon ground cumin
1 tablespoon dried parsley
1-2 teaspoons hot sauce, to taste
15-oz. can black beans, drained and rinsed
15-oz. can kidney beans, drained and rinsed
15-oz. can garbanzo beans, drained and rinsed
2 15-oz. cans vegetarian baked beans
15-oz. can whole-kernel corn

1. Place tomato purée, onion, garlic, and seasonings in slow cooker. Stir together well. 2. Add each can of beans, stirring well after each addition. Stir in corn. 3. Cover and cook on low 6 hours.
**Per Serving:** Calories 220; Total Fat 2g; Saturated Fat 0g; Sodium 270mg; Carbs 41g; Fiber 11g; Sugar 8g; Protein 12g

## Barbecued Lima Beans

**Prep time: 15 minutes | Cook time: 5-11 hours | Serves: 20**

1½ lbs. dried lima beans
6 cups water
2¼ cups chopped onions
½ cup brown sugar
Brown sugar substitute to equal 6 tablespoon sugar
1½ cups ketchup
13 drops Tabasco sauce
½ cup dark corn syrup
1 teaspoon salt
¼ lb. bacon, diced

1. Boil the soaked beans. 2. Add onion in it and cook, Simmer 30-60 minutes, or until beans are tender. Drain beans, reserving liquid. 3. Combine all ingredients except bean liquid in the slow cooker. Mix well. half cover with water. 4. Cover. Cook on low temp setting for 10 hours. Stir occasionally.
Per Serving: Calories 195; Total Fat 3g; Saturated Fat 0.9g; Sodium 393mg; Carbs 36g; Fiber 36g; Sugar 15g; Protein 8g

## Refried Beans with Bacon

**Prep time: 20 minutes | Cook time: 5 ½ hours | Serves: 8**

2 cups dried red, or pinto, beans
6 cups water
2 garlic cloves, minced
1 large tomato, peeled, seeded, and chopped
1 teaspoon salt
2 oz. bacon

1. Combine beans, water, garlic, tomato, and salt in a slow cooker. 2. Cover. Cook on high temp setting for 5 hours, stirring occasionally. When the beans are soft, drain off liquid. 3. While the beans cook, brown bacon in a skillet. Drain, reserving drippings. Crumble bacon. Add half of bacon and 1½ Tablespoon drippings to beans. Stir. 4. Mash or purée beans. Fry the mashed bean mix in the bacon drippings. Add salt to taste. 5. Serve, with the bacon.
Per Serving: Calories 171; Total Fat 4g; Saturated Fat 1.2g; Sodium 354mg; Carbs 26g; Fiber 9g; Sugar 3g; Protein 9g

## Red Beans and Sausage

**Prep time: 20 minutes | Cook time: 10-12 hours | Serves: 10**

1-lb. pkg. dried red beans
water
4 oz. smoked sausage
½ teaspoon salt
1 teaspoon pepper
3-4 cups water
6-oz. can tomato paste
8-oz. can tomato sauce
4 garlic cloves, minced

1. Soak beans for 8 hours. Drain. Discard soaking water. 2. Mix together all ingredients in a slow cooker. 3. Cover. Cook on low for 10-12 hours, or until beans are soft.
Per Serving: Calories 198; Total Fat 4g; Saturated Fat 1.2g; Sodium 370mg; Carbs 30g; Fiber 8g; Sugar 4g; Protein 12g

## Red Beans and Pasta

**Prep time: 20 minutes | Cook time: 3- hours | Serves: 8**

3 14.5-oz. cans fat-free, reduced-sodium chicken broth
½ teaspoon ground cumin
1 tablespoon chili powder
1 garlic clove, minced
8 oz. uncooked spiral pasta
Half a large green pepper, diced
Half a large red pepper, diced
1 medium onion, diced
15-oz. can red beans, rinsed and drained
Chopped fresh parsley
Chopped fresh cilantro

1. Combine broth, cumin, chili powder, and garlic in slow cooker. 2. Cover. Cook on high temp setting until mixture comes to boil. 3. Add pasta, vegetables, and beans. Stir together well. 4. Cover. Cook on low 3-4 hours. 5. Add parsley or cilantro before serving.
Per Serving: Calories 180; Total Fat 1g; Saturated Fat 0.0g; Sodium 448mg; Carbs 34g; Fiber 4g; Sugar 4g; Protein 9g

## Easy Party-Time Beans

**Prep time: 30 minutes | Cook time: 5-7 hours | Serves: 14**

1½ cups ketchup
1 onion, chopped
1 green pepper, chopped
1 red pepper, chopped
½ cup water
¼ cup packed brown sugar
Brown sugar substitute to equal 2 tablespoons sugar
2 bay leaves
2-3 teaspoons cider vinegar
1 teaspoon ground mustard
⅛ teaspoon pepper
16-oz. can kidney beans, rinsed and drained
15½-oz. can Great Northern beans, rinsed and drained
15-oz. can lima beans, rinsed and drained
15-oz. can black beans, rinsed and drained
15½-oz. can black-eyed peas, rinsed and drained

1. Combine first 10 ingredients in the slow cooker. Mix well. 2. Add remaining ingredients. Mix well. 3. Cover. Cook on low temp setting for 5-7 hours, or until onion and peppers are tender. 4. Remove bay leaves before serving.
Per Serving: Calories 172; Total Fat 1g; Saturated Fat 0.1g; Sodium 493mg; Carbs 35g; Fiber 8g; Sugar 11g; Protein 9g

## Soft Pioneer Beans

**Prep time: 10 minutes | Cook time: 8-9 hours | Serves: 8**

1 lb. dry lima beans
1 bunch green onions, chopped
3 teaspoons salt-free beef bouillon powder
6 cups water
1 lb. low-fat smoked sausage
½ teaspoon garlic powder
¾ teaspoon Tabasco sauce

1. Combine all ingredients in slow cooker. Mix well. 2. Cover. Cook on high 8-9 hours, or until beans are soft but not mushy.
Per Serving: Calories 252; Total Fat 3g; Saturated Fat 1.1g; Sodium 487mg; Carbs 38g; Fiber 10g; Sugar 7g; Protein 18g

Chapter 2 Vegan and Vegetarian Recipes | 35

## Slow Cooker Scandinavian Beans

**Prep time: 10 minutes | Cook time: 6-8 hours | Serves: 8**

1 lb. dried pinto beans
6 cups water
¼ lb. bacon, or 1 ham hock
1 onion, chopped
2-3 garlic cloves, minced
¼ teaspoon pepper
¼ teaspoon salt
2 tablespoons molasses
1 cup ketchup
Tabasco to taste
1 teaspoon Worcestershire sauce
¼ cup brown sugar
Brown sugar substitute to equal ¼ cup sugar
⅓ cup cider vinegar
¼ teaspoon dry mustard

1. Soak beans in water in a soup pot for 8 hours. Bring beans to boil and cook 1½–2 hours, or until soft. Drain, reserving liquid. 2. Combine all ingredients in the slow cooker, using just enough bean liquid to cover everything. 3. Cook on low for 5-6 hours.
**Per Serving:** Calories 305; Total Fat 7g; Saturated Fat 2.2g; Sodium 564mg; Carbs 51g; Fiber 11g; Sugar 18g; Protein 12g

## Easy Barbecued Lentils

**Prep time: 10 minutes | Cook time: 6-8 hours | Serves: 8**

2 cups Phyllis' Homemade Barbecue Sauce
3½ cups water
1 lb. dry lentils
9.7-oz. pkg. vegetarian hot dogs, sliced

1. Add all ingredients in a slow cooker pot. 2. Cover. Cook on low 6-8 hours.
**Per Serving:** Calories 270; Total Fat 1g; Saturated Fat 0.1g; Sodium 464mg; Carbs 43g; Fiber 15g; Sugar 12g; Protein 23g

## Slow Cooker Red Beans

**Prep time: 25 minutes | Cook time: 14-17 hours | Serves: 8**

3 cups dried small red beans
8 cups water
3 garlic cloves, minced
1 large onion, chopped
8 cups fresh water
1 ham hock
½ cup ketchup
½ teaspoon salt
Pinch of pepper
1½-2 teaspoons ground cumin
1 tablespoon parsley
1-2 bay leaves

1. Place soaked beans in slow cooker with garlic, onion, 8 cups fresh water, and ham hock. 2. Cover. Cook on high 12-14 hours. 3. Take ham hocks out of cooker and allow to cool. Remove meat from bones. Remove and discard visible fat and skin. Cut up and return to slow cooker. Add remaining ingredients. 4. Cover. Cook on high 2-3 hours.
**Per Serving:** Calories 148; Total Fat 3g; Saturated Fat 0.8g; Sodium 382mg; Carbs 24g; Fiber 6g; Sugar 5g; Protein 8g

## Herbed Chickpea Pasta

**Prep time: 20 minutes | Cook time: 5-6 hours | Serves: 8**

1 lb. dry chickpeas
1 sprig fresh rosemary
10 leaves fresh sage
1 tablespoon salt
1-2 large garlic cloves, minced
1 teaspoon olive oil
1 cup small dry pasta, your choice of shape

1. Wash chickpeas. Place in slow cooker. Soak for 8 hours in a full pot of water, along with rosemary, sage, and salt. 2. Drain water. Remove herbs. 3. Refill slow cooker with water to 1" above peas. 4. Cover. Cook on low 5 hours. 5. Sauté garlic in olive oil in skillet until clear. 6. Purée half of peas, along with several cups of broth from cooker, in blender. Return purée to slow cooker. Add garlic and oil. 7. Boil pasta in saucepan until al dente, about 5 minutes. Drain. Add to beans. 8. Cover. Cook on high temp setting for 30-60 minutes, or until pasta is tender and heated through, but not mushy.
**Per Serving:** Calories 236; Total Fat 4g; Saturated Fat 0.4g; Sodium 445mg; Carbs 40g; Fiber 9g; Sugar 7g; Protein 12g

## Slow Cooker Butter Macaroni with Cheese

**Prep time: 10 minutes | Cook time: 3-4 hours | Serves: 6**

1½ cups dry macaroni
1½ tablespoons light, soft tub margarine
6 oz. light Velveeta cheese, sliced
2 cups fat-free milk
1 cup fat-free half-and-half

1. Combine macaroni, and butter. 2. Layer cheese over top. 3. Pour in milk and half-and-half. 4. Cover. Cook on high 3-4 hours, or until macaroni is soft.
**Per Serving:** Calories 208; Total Fat 5g; Saturated Fat 2.5g; Sodium 555mg; Carbs 27g; Fiber 0g; Sugar 12g; Protein 14g

## Tempeh-Stuffed Peppers with Cheddar

**Prep time: 35 minutes | Cook time: 3-8 hours | Serves: 4**

4 oz. tempeh, cubed
1 garlic clove, minced
2 14½-oz. cans diced no-salt-added tomatoes
2 teaspoons soy sauce
¼ cup chopped onions
1½ cups cooked rice
1 cup shredded fat-free cheddar cheese
Tabasco sauce, optional
4 green, red, or yellow, bell peppers, with tops sliced off and seeds removed
¼ cup shredded fat-free cheddar cheese

1. Steam tempeh 10 minutes in saucepan. Mash in bowl with the garlic, half the tomatoes, and soy sauce. 2. Stir in onions, rice, ½ cup cheese, and Tabasco sauce. Stuff into peppers. 3. Place peppers in slow cooker. Pour remaining half of tomatoes over peppers. 4. Cover. Cook on low temp setting 6-8 hours, or high 3-4 hours. Top with remaining cheese in last 30 minutes.
**Per Serving:** Calories 266; Total Fat 3g; Saturated Fat 0.1g; Sodium 510mg; Carbs 42g; Fiber 6g; Sugar 17g; Protein 21gv

## Hearty Vegan Slow Cooker Chili with Yogurt

**Prep time: 10 minutes | Cook time: 3 to 4 hours | Serves: 4**

1 (15-ounce) can no-salt-added red kidney beans, rinsed and drained
1 (14.5-ounce) can no-salt-added diced tomatoes, undrained
1 medium sweet potato, peeled and diced
1 cup water
3 celery stalks, diced
1 yellow bell pepper, diced
1 small onion, diced
2 or 3 garlic cloves, minced
2 tablespoons chili powder
1 tablespoon dried oregano
2 teaspoons ground cumin
Pinch cayenne pepper
2 teaspoons chopped fresh cilantro, for garnish
Dollop plain 2% Greek yogurt, for garnish

In a slow cooker, combine all the ingredients except the garnishes. Cook on high temp setting for 3 to 4 hours. Serve garnished with cilantro and Greek yogurt (if using).
**Per Serving:** Calories 205; Total Fat 1g; Saturated Fat 0.9g; Sodium 275mg; Carbs 40g; Fiber 13g; Sugar 10g; Protein 10g

## Mushroom Burgers

**Prep time: 10 minutes + 30 minutes to marinate | Cook time: 6-8 minutes | Serves: 2**

2 tablespoons balsamic vinegar
1 tablespoon extra-virgin olive oil
2 teaspoons Dijon mustard, plus 1 teaspoon for the buns
Freshly ground black pepper
2 portobello mushrooms, stemmed
1 red bell pepper, cut into ¼-inch-thick rings
2 whole-wheat buns
2 provolone cheese slices
½ cup baby spinach
2 red onion slices
2 tomato slices

1. In a zip-top bag, combine the vinegar, olive oil, mustard, and a pinch of black pepper. Add the mushrooms and bell pepper. Marinate for about 30 minutes. 2. Heat a skillet over medium-high heat. Add the mushrooms, bell pepper, and remaining marinade to the skillet. Cook the veggies for 3 -4 minutes on each side. 3. Divide the vegetables between the buns. Add the provolone cheese. Top with the spinach, onion, and tomato. Add additional Dijon mustard to the buns.
**Per Serving:** Calories 365; Total Fat 17g; Saturated Fat 6g; Sodium 697mg; Carbs 37g; Fiber 7g; Sugar 8g; Protein 17g

## Creamy Pesto Zoodles

**Prep time: 15 minutes | Cook time: 15 minutes | Serves: 4**

4 small zucchini
2 cups packed fresh basil leaves
2 garlic cloves, peeled
¼ cup walnuts
¼ cup extra-virgin olive oil
½ teaspoon salt
¼ teaspoon freshly ground black pepper
¼ cup grated Parmesan cheese
1 cup cherry tomatoes, halved

1. Using a spiralizer, cut the zucchini into noodles 4 to 6 inches long. 2. In a food processor, add the basil with garlic, walnuts, olive oil, salt, and pepper. Process until smooth. Add in Parmesan cheese and pulse once or twice to mix. 3. Transfer the pesto to a large bowl and add the zoodles. Toss to combine. Add the tomatoes and toss again. Serve.
**Per Serving:** Calories 240; Total Fat 21g; Saturated Fat 4g; Sodium 405mg; Carbs 10g; Fiber 3g; Sugar 6g; Protein 7g

## Cheesy Garlic Pasta Salad

**Prep time: 10 minutes | Cook time: 5 minutes | Serves: 4**

6 asparagus spears, trimmed and cut into 1-inch pieces
1 teaspoon extra-virgin olive oil
Freshly ground black pepper
3 cups cooked whole-wheat penne pasta
3 ounces goat cheese
¾ cup cherry tomatoes, quartered
½ cup diced yellow bell pepper
2 garlic cloves, minced
1 cup chopped arugula
3 large basil leaves, minced
Pinch salt

1. Preheat the broiler on high. Manage a baking sheet with foil. 2. Put the asparagus on the lined baking sheet. Drizzle the olive oil and spice with black pepper. Broil for 5 minutes. 3. If the pasta is not already warm, heat in the microwave for about 30 seconds. Put the pasta in a bowl. Add the goat cheese, tomatoes, bell pepper, garlic, arugula, and basil. Stir to combine well. 4. Add the asparagus to the pasta mixture. Spice with salt and freshly ground pepper.
**Per Serving:** Calories 212; Total Fat 7g; Saturated Fat 4g; Sodium 158mg; Carbs 30g; Fiber 4g; Sugar 3g; Protein 11g

# Chapter 3 Fish and Seafood Recipes

| | | | |
|---|---|---|---|
| 39 | Spicy Tuna Barbecue | 42 | Fish Tacos with Avocado Salsa and Lettuce |
| 39 | Cheesy Herbed Potato Fish Bake | 42 | Ceviche with Vegetable |
| 39 | Creamy Seafood Pasta | 43 | Roasted Salmon with Honey-Mustard Sauce |
| 39 | Seafood Medley with Milk Butter Soup | 43 | Baked Ginger-Glazed Salmon and Broccoli |
| 39 | Creamy Curried Shrimp | 43 | Roasted Spiced Salmon with Salsa Verde |
| 39 | Baked Caprese Fish and Bean | 43 | Homemade Fish Stock |
| 40 | Tropical Shrimp Cocktail with Sweet and Sour Sauce | 44 | Roasted Whole Veggie-Stuffed Trout |
| 40 | Shrimp and Vegetable Creole | 44 | Ginger-Garlic Cod with Bell Pepper |
| 40 | Seafood and Vegetable Gumbo | 44 | Spaghetti with Shrimp Marinara |
| 40 | Baked Almond Shrimp with Grapefruit Salsa | 44 | Speedy Vegetable Broth and Tomato Fish Stew |
| 41 | Baked Tilapia and Quinoa | 45 | Roasted Halibut with Red Peppers and Green Beans |
| 41 | Salmon Cheese Mushroom Casserole | 45 | Blackened Tilapia with Mango Salsa |
| 41 | Lemon Trout with Potato Hash Browns | 45 | Butter Scallops and Asparagus Skillet |
| 41 | Salmon and Vegetables Po'boy | 45 | Baked Oysters and Vegetable |
| 41 | Cheesy Tomato Tuna Melts | 46 | Baked Cajun Shrimp Casserole with Quinoa |
| 41 | Peppercorn-Crusted Baked Spiced Salmon | 46 | Shrimp Burgers with Fruity Salsa and Salad |
| 42 | Baked Sesame Salmon with Bok Choy | | |
| 42 | Shrimp and Ham Jambalaya | | |

## Spicy Tuna Barbecue

**Prep time: 20 minutes | Cook time: 4-10 hours | Serves: 4**

12-oz. can tuna, packed in water, drained
2 cups no-salt-added tomato juice
1 medium green bell pepper, finely chopped
2 tablespoons onion flakes
2 tablespoons Worcestershire sauce
3 tablespoons vinegar
2 tablespoons sugar
1 tablespoon prepared mustard
1 rib celery, chopped
Dash chili powder
½ teaspoon cinnamon
Dash hot sauce, optional

1. Add all ingredients in a slow cooker pot. 2. Cover. Cook on low 8-10 hours, or high 4-5 hours. 3. Serve on buns.
Per Serving: Calories 162; Total Fat 1g; Saturated Fat 0.2g; Sodium 423mg; Carbs 18g; Fiber 2g; Sugar 14g; Protein 21g

## Cheesy Herbed Potato Fish Bake

**Prep time: 25 minutes | Cook time: 1-2 hours | Serves: 4**

10¾-oz. can cream of celery soup
½ cup water
1-lb. perch fillet, fresh or thawed
2 cups cooked, diced potatoes
¼ cup freshly grated Parmesan cheese
1 tablespoon chopped parsley
½ teaspoon dried basil
¼ teaspoon dried oregano

1. Combine soup and water. Pour half in slow cooker. 2. Lay fillet on top. Place potatoes on fillet. Pour remaining soup mix over top. 3. Combine cheese and herbs. Sprinkle over ingredients in slow cooker. 4. Cover. Cook on high temp setting for 1-2 hours.
Per Serving: Calories 269; Total Fat 8g; Saturated Fat 2.8g; Sodium 696mg; Carbs 22g; Fiber 2g; Sugar 2g; Protein 26g

## Creamy Seafood Pasta

**Prep time: 35 minutes | Cook time: 1-2 hours | Serves: 8**

2 cups fat-free sour cream
1¼ cups shredded reduced-fat Monterey Jack cheese
1 tablespoon light, soft tub margarine, melted
½ lb. fresh crab meat
⅛ teaspoon pepper
½ lb. bay scallops, lightly cooked
1 lb. medium shrimp, cooked and peeled
4 cups cooked linguine
Fresh parsley, for garnish

1. Combine sour cream, cheese and margarine in slow cooker. 2. Stir in remaining ingredients, except linguine. 3. Cover. Cook on low 1-2 hours. 4. Serve immediately over linguine. Garnish with fresh parsley.
Per Serving: Calories 308; Total Fat 7g; Saturated Fat 3.1g; Sodium 449mg; Carbs 31g; Fiber 1g; Sugar 5g; Protein 29g

## Seafood Medley with Milk Butter Soup

**Prep time: 10 minutes | Cook time: 3-4 hours | Serves: 12**

1 lb. peeled and deveined shrimp
1 lb. crabmeat
1 lb. bay scallops
2 10¾-oz. cans cream of celery soup
2 soup cans fat-free milk
3 teaspoons margarine
1 teaspoon Old Bay seasoning
¼ teaspoon pepper

1. Layer shrimp, crab, and scallops in a slow cooker. 2. Combine soup and milk. Pour over seafood. 3. Mix together margarine and spices and pour over top. 4. Cover. Cook on low 3-4 hours.
Per Serving: Calories 168; Total Fat 6g; Saturated Fat 1.6g; Sodium 679mg; Carbs 7g; Fiber 0g; Sugar 3g; Protein 20g

## Creamy Curried Shrimp

**Prep time: 10 minutes | Cook time: 4-6 hours | Serves: 5**

1 small onion, chopped
2 cups cooked shrimp
1½ teaspoons curry powder
10¾-oz. can 98% fat-free, lower-sodium cream of mushroom soup
1 cup sour cream

1. Add all ingredients instead of cream in a slow cooker. 2. Cover. Cook on low 4-6 hours. 3. Before serving, stir in sour cream and enjoy.
Per Serving: Calories 130; Total Fat 2g; Saturated Fat 0.6g; Sodium 390mg; Carbs 15g; Fiber 1g; Sugar 5g; Protein 12g

## Baked Caprese Fish and Bean

**Prep time: 10 minutes | Cook time: 20 minutes | Serves: 4**

1 (15-ounce) can low-sodium white beans, drained and rinsed
1 cup baby spinach leaves
1 cup chopped Swiss chard
12 medium tomatoes, chopped
4 (4-ounce) halibut fillets
Sea salt
Freshly ground black pepper
2 teaspoons olive oil
1 tablespoon chopped fresh basil

1. Preheat the oven to 400°F. Grease a 10-inch square baking dish with cooking spray. 2. Layer the beans, spinach, Swiss chard, and tomatoes in the bottom of the baking dish. Place the fish in the dish, spice with salt and pepper, and drizzle with the olive oil. 3. Foil cover and bake for about 20 minutes, until the fish flakes easily. 4. Serve topped with basil.
Per Serving: Calories 290; Total Fat 5g; Saturated Fat 1g; Sodium 164mg; Carbs 33g; Fiber 9g; Sugar 10g; Protein 31g

## Tropical Shrimp Cocktail with Sweet and Sour Sauce

**Prep time: 15 minutes | Cook time: 3 minutes | Serves: 4**

1 pound medium shrimp, peeled and deveined
1 cup diced mango
2 ripe avocados, diced
¼ cup finely diced red onion
2 Roma tomatoes, diced
¼ cup chopped fresh cilantro
2 tablespoons Low-Carb No-Cook Tomato Ketchup (here)
Juice of 1 lime
Juice of 1 orange
1 tablespoon extra-virgin olive oil
1 jalapeño pepper, seeded and minced
Lime wedges, for serving

1. Boil water in a pot. Meanwhile, fill a large bowl ⅔ of the way with ice and about 1 cup of cold water. 2. Cook shrimps in a boiling water for 3 minutes until they are opaque and firm. Drain and transfer to the ice water for 3 minutes to stop the cooking and cool them. Drain and pat the shrimp dry with a clean paper towel. 3. In a large bowl, mix together the shrimp, mango, avocado, red onion, tomatoes, and cilantro. 4. In a bowl, mix the ketchup with lime juice, orange juice, oil, and jalapeño. Mix well and gently fold the sauce into the shrimp mixture. 5. Divide among 4 glasses or small dishes, with a lime wedge on the rim of each.
**Per Serving:** Calories 279; Total Fat 16g; Saturated Fat 3g; Sodium 676mg; Carbs 20g; Fiber 6g; Sugar 10g; Protein 18g

## Shrimp and Vegetable Creole

**Prep time: 30 minutes | Cook time: 6-8 hours | Serves: 10**

¼ cup canola oil
⅓ cup flour
1¾ cups sliced onions
1 cup diced green bell peppers
1 cup diced celery
1½ large carrots, shredded
2¾-lb. can tomatoes
¾ cup water
½ teaspoon dried thyme
1 garlic clove, minced
Pinch of rosemary
1 tablespoon sugar
3 bay leaves
1 tablespoon Worcestershire sauce
¾ teaspoon salt
⅛ teaspoon dried oregano
2 lbs. shelled shrimp, deveined

1. Combine canola oil and flour in a skillet. Brown, stirring constantly. Add onions, green peppers, celery, and carrots. Cook 5-10 minutes. Transfer to slow cooker. 2. Add remaining ingredients, except shrimp, and stir well. 3. Cover. Cook on low 6-8 hours. 4. Add shrimp during last hour.
**Per Serving:** Calories 187; Total Fat 7g; Saturated Fat 0.6g; Sodium 563mg; Carbs 15g; Fiber 3g; Sugar 8g; Protein 17g

## Seafood and Vegetable Gumbo

**Prep time: 40 minutes | Cook time: 2-3 hours | Serves: 6**

3 tablespoons canola oil, divided
1 lb. okra, sliced
¼ cup flour
1 bunch green onions, sliced
½ cup chopped celery
2 garlic cloves, minced
16-oz. can tomatoes and juice
1 bay leaf
1 tablespoon chopped fresh parsley
1 fresh thyme sprig
½ teaspoon salt
½-1 teaspoon red pepper
3-5 cups water, depending upon the consistency you like
1 lb. peeled, deveined fresh shrimp
½ lb. fresh crab meat

1. Sauté okra in 1 tablespoon canola oil until okra is lightly browned. Transfer to slow cooker. 2. Combine remaining 2 tablespoons canola oil and flour in skillet. Cook over medium heat, stirring constantly until roux is the color of chocolate, 20-25 minutes. 3. Stir in green onions, celery, and garlic. Cook until vegetables are tender. Add to slow cooker. 4. Gently stir in tomatoes with juice, bay leaf, parsley, thyme, salt, red pepper, and water. 5. Cover. Cook on high 2 hours. 6. Add shrimp, crab, and additional water if you wish. Cover. Cook for another 30-60 minutes on high temp setting, until shrimp is cooked and crab is heated.
**Per Serving:** Calories 221; Total Fat 8g; Saturated Fat 0.7g; Sodium 548mg; Carbs 15g; Fiber 3g; Sugar 5g; Protein 22

## Baked Almond Shrimp with Grapefruit Salsa

**Prep time: 20 minutes | Cook time: 10 minutes | Serves: 4**

**For the Salsa**
2 ruby red grapefruits, peeled and chopped
½ cucumber, chopped
½ yellow bell pepper, seeded and chopped
1 teaspoon chopped fresh cilantro
Sea salt
**For the Shrimp**
Nonstick cooking spray
1 pound (21 to 25 count) raw shrimp, peeled and deveined
2 large eggs, beaten
1 cup almond flour

To make the salsa 1. In a small bowl, mix the grapefruit, cucumber, bell pepper, and cilantro. Season with salt and set it aside.
To make the shrimp
2. Preheat the oven to 450°F. Oil a baking sheet with cooking spray. 3. Dredge the shrimp in the egg and then the almond flour until well coated. 4. Arrange the shrimp on the sheet and cook for about 10 minutes, until cooked through and the coating is golden brown. 5. Serve the shrimp with grapefruit salsa.
**Per Serving:** Calories 232; Total Fat 8g; Saturated Fat 1g; Sodium 193mg; Carbs 16g; Fiber 4g; Sugar 1g; Protein 28g

## Baked Tilapia and Quinoa

**Prep time: 5 minutes | Cook time: 25 minutes | Serves: 4**

1 cup quinoa, rinsed
1 cup low-sodium chicken broth
1 cup light coconut milk
1 tomato, chopped
2 teaspoons minced garlic
1 teaspoon ground turmeric
⅛ teaspoon freshly ground black pepper
1 pound tilapia fillets

2 tablespoons chopped fresh cilantro, for garnish
1. Preheat your oven at 400°F temp setting. 2. Combine the quinoa, chicken broth, coconut milk, tomato, garlic, turmeric, and pepper in a deep 9-inch square baking or casserole dish. 3. Nestle the fish in the quinoa mixture and cover the baking dish with foil. 4. Bake for about 25 minutes, until the quinoa is tender and the fish is cooked through. Top with cilantro and serve.
Per Serving: Calories 343; Total Fat 11g; Saturated Fat 6g; Sodium 86mg; Carbs 31g; Fiber 5g; Sugar 1g; Protein 31g

## Salmon Cheese Mushroom Casserole

**Prep time: 15 minutes | Cook time: 3-4 hours | Serves: 6**

14¾-oz. can salmon, no added salt, liquid reserved
1(4-oz.) can mushroom, drained
1½ cups bread crumbs
2 eggs, beaten
½ cup grated reduced-fat cheddar cheese
1 tablespoon lemon juice
1 tablespoon minced onion

1. Flake fish in bowl, removing bones. 2. Stir in remaining ingredients. Pour into lightly greased slow cooker. 3. Cover. Cook on low 3-4 hours.
Per Serving: Calories 257; Total Fat 9g; Saturated Fat 2.9g; Sodium 442mg; Carbs 21g; Fiber 1g; Sugar 2g; Protein 23g

## Lemon Trout with Potato Hash Browns

**Prep time: 10 minutes | Cook time: 20 minutes | Serves: 4**

2 large russet potatoes, chopped
¼ onion, chopped
2 teaspoons minced garlic
½ teaspoon smoked paprika
2 tablespoons olive oil, divided
Sea salt
Freshly ground black pepper
4 (4-ounce) boneless, skinless trout fillets
1 tablespoon chopped fresh parsley
1 lemon, quartered

1. Preheat the oven to 400°F. Manage a baking sheet with parchment paper. 2. In a large bowl, toss the potatoes, onion, garlic, paprika, and 1 tablespoon of the oil. Spread the potatoes on half the baking sheet and season lightly with salt and pepper. 3. Place the fish on the other half of the baking sheet, brush with 1 tablespoon of oil, and spice with salt and pepper. 4. Bake for about 20 minutes, tossing halfway through, until the potatoes are golden and lightly crispy and the fish is flaky. 5. Serve topped with parsley and lemon wedges.
Per Serving: Calories 349; Total Fat 10g; Saturated Fat 2g; Sodium 85mg; Carbs 35g; Fiber 3g; Sugar 2g; Protein 27g

## Salmon and Vegetables Po'boy

**Prep time: 20 minutes | Cook time: 10 minutes | Serves: 4**

4 (4-ounce) skinless salmon fillets
2 teaspoons Cajun seasoning
2 teaspoons olive oil
1 cup finely shredded cabbage
1 large carrot, shredded
1 scallion, sliced
¼ cup low-fat plain Greek yogurt
1 tablespoon apple cider vinegar
1 teaspoon maple syrup
4 crusty whole-wheat rolls, halved

1. Preheat your oven at 400°F temp setting. 2. Season the salmon fillets with the Cajun seasoning. 3. In an ovenproof skillet, sear the salmon for 2 minutes per side, then place the skillet in the oven. Roast salmon for about 6 minutes. Place the cooked salmon in plate and set it aside. 4. In a bowl, toss the cabbage, carrot, scallion, yogurt, vinegar, and maple syrup until well combined. 5. Place a salmon fillet on each roll and top with of the cabbage mixture. Serve.
Per Serving: Calories 326; Total Fat 11g; Saturated Fat 3g; Sodium 276mg; Carbs 25g; Fiber 3g; Sugar 5g; Protein 30g

## Cheesy Tomato Tuna Melts

**Prep time: 5 minutes | Cook time: 5 minutes | Serves: 2**

1 (5-ounce) can chunk light tuna packed in water, drained
2 tablespoons plain nonfat Greek yogurt
2 teaspoons freshly squeezed lemon juice
2 tablespoons finely chopped celery
1 tablespoon finely chopped red onion
Pinch cayenne pepper
1 large tomato, cut into ¾-inch-thick rounds
½ cup shredded cheddar cheese

1. Preheat the broiler to high. 2. In a bowl, mix the tuna, yogurt, lemon juice, celery, red onion, and cayenne pepper. Stir well. 3. Arrange the tomato on a baking sheet. Top each with some tuna salad and cheddar cheese. 4. Broil the tomatoes for 3- 4 minutes until the cheese is melted and bubbly. Serve.
Per Serving: Calories 243; Total Fat 10g; Saturated Fat 2g; Sodium 444mg; Carbs 7g; Fiber 1g; Sugar 2g; Protein 30g

## Peppercorn-Crusted Baked Spiced Salmon

**Prep time: 5 minutes | Cook time: 20 minutes | Serves: 4**

Nonstick cooking spray
½ teaspoon freshly ground black pepper
¼ teaspoon salt
Zest and juice of ½ lemon
¼ teaspoon dried thyme
1 pound salmon fillet

1. Preheat your oven at 425°F. Manage a baking sheet with cooking spray. 2. In a small bowl, combine the pepper, salt, lemon zest and juice, and thyme. Stir to combine. 3. Place the spiced salmon on the baking sheet, skin-side down. Spread the seasoning mixture evenly over the fillet. 4. Bake it for 15-20 minutes, until the flesh flakes easily.
Per Serving: Calories 163; Total Fat 7g; Saturated Fat 0.8g; Sodium 167mg; Carbs 1g; Fiber 0g; Sugar 0g; Protein 23g

## Baked Sesame Salmon with Bok Choy

Prep time: 12 minutes | Cook time: 18 minutes | Serves: 4

4 (4-ounce) salmon fillets
Sea salt
Freshly ground black pepper
4 teaspoons olive oil, divided
¼ cup maple syrup
¼ cup sesame seeds
16 baby bok choy, quartered
Juice of 1 lemon

1. Preheat the oven to 400°F. Manage a baking sheet with parchment paper and set aside. 2. Season the salmon with salt and pepper. 3. In a skillet, Pan-sear the salmon on both sides for about 3 minutes in total, turning halfway through. Place the fish on one-third of the baking sheet. Spread maple syrup on each fillet and top with sesame seeds. 4. In a large bowl, toss the bok choy, remaining 3 teaspoons of oil, and lemon juice. Spice with salt and pepper and place on the remaining two-thirds of the baking sheet. 5. Bake until the fish easily flakes and the bok choy is tender-crisp, about 15 minutes. Serve.
Per Serving: Calories 329; Total Fat 17g; Saturated Fat 3g; Sodium 108mg; Carbs 19g; Fiber 5g; Sugar 12g; Protein 25g

## Shrimp and Ham Jambalaya

Prep time: 25 minutes | Cook time: 1½ hours | Serves: 8

2 tablespoons margarine
2 medium onions, chopped
2 green bell peppers, chopped
3 ribs celery, chopped
1 cup chopped extra-lean, lower-sodium cooked ham
2 garlic cloves, chopped
1½ cups minute rice
1½ cups 99% fat-free, lower-sodium beef broth
1 (28-oz.) can chopped tomatoes
2 tablespoons chopped parsley
1 teaspoon dried basil
½ teaspoon dried thyme
¼ teaspoon pepper
⅛ teaspoon cayenne pepper
1 lb. shelled, deveined, medium-size shrimp
1 tablespoon chopped parsley

1. Melt margarine in slow cooker set on high. Add onions, peppers, celery, ham, and garlic. Cook 30 minutes. 2. Add rice. Cover and cook 15 minutes. 3. Add broth, tomatoes, 2 tablespoons parsley, and seasonings. Cover and cook on high temp setting for 1 hour. 4. Add shrimp. Cook on high temp setting 30 minutes, or until liquid is absorbed. 5. Garnish with parsley.
Per Serving: Calories 205; Total Fat 4g; Saturated Fat 0.8g; Sodium 529mg; Carbs 26g; Fiber 3g; Sugar 7g; Protein 16g

## Fish Tacos with Avocado Salsa and Lettuce

Prep time: 20 minutes | Cook time: 10 minutes | Serves: 4

1 teaspoon blackening spice
4 (4-ounce) haddock fillets
1 teaspoon olive oil
1 avocado, pitted and diced
1 tomato, chopped
1 scallion, finely chopped
1 tablespoon chopped fresh cilantro
Juice of 1 lime
8 (4-inch) corn tortillas, at room temperature
1 cup finely shredded lettuce

1. Rub the blackening spice all over the fish. 2. In a skillet, Pan-sear the fish for about 10 minutes in total, turning halfway through, until just cooked through and golden. Transfer the fish to a plate and, using a fork, break the fish into large chunks. 3. In a bowl, combine the avocado, tomato, scallion, cilantro, and lime juice. 4. Divide the fish on tortillas and top with the salsa and lettuce. Fold the tortillas over and serve 2 per person.
Per Serving: Calories 259; Total Fat 10g; Saturated Fat 1g; Sodium 252mg; Carbs 23g; Fiber 6g; Sugar 2g; Protein 22g

## Ceviche with Vegetable

Prep time: 10 minutes | Cook time: 0 minutes | Serves: 4

½ pound fresh skinless, white, ocean fish fillet (halibut, Mahi Mahi, etc.), diced
1 cup freshly squeezed lime juice, divided
2 tablespoons chopped fresh cilantro, divided
1 serrano pepper, sliced
1 garlic clove, crushed
¾ teaspoon salt, divided
½ red onion, thinly sliced
2 tomatoes, diced
1 red bell pepper, seeded and diced
1 tablespoon extra-virgin olive oil

1. In a mixing bowl, mix the fish, ¾ cup of lime juice, 1 tablespoon of cilantro, serrano pepper, garlic, and ½ teaspoon of salt. The fish should be covered or nearly covered in lime juice. Refrigerate; covered for 4 hours. 2. Sprinkle the salt over the onion in a bowl, and let sit for 10 minutes. Drain and rinse well. 3. In a bowl, add the tomatoes, bell pepper, olive oil, remaining ¼ cup of lime juice, and onion. If desired, remove the serrano pepper and garlic. 4. Add the vegetables to the fish, and stir gently. Taste, and add some of the reserved lime juice to the ceviche as desired. Serve topped with cilantro.
Per Serving: Calories 121; Total Fat 4g; Saturated Fat 0.9g; Sodium 405mg; Carbs 11g; Fiber 2g; Sugar 5g; Protein 12g

## Roasted Salmon with Honey-Mustard Sauce

**Prep time: 5 minutes | Cook time: 20 minutes | Serves: 4**

Nonstick cooking spray
2 tablespoons whole-grain mustard
1 tablespoon honey
2 garlic cloves, minced
¼ teaspoon salt
¼ teaspoon freshly ground black pepper
1 pound salmon fillet

1. Preheat your oven at 425°F. manage a baking sheet with cooking spray. 2. In a small bowl, whisk together the mustard, honey, garlic, salt, and pepper. 3. Place the fillet on the baking sheet, skin-side down. Spoon the sauce onto the salmon and spread evenly. 4. Roast it for 15-20 minutes, depending on the thickness of the fillet, until the flesh flakes easily.

**Per Serving:** Calories 186; Total Fat 7g; Saturated Fat 0.4g; Sodium 312mg; Carbs 6g; Fiber 0g; Sugar g; Protein 23g

## Baked Ginger-Glazed Salmon and Broccoli

**Prep time: 10 minutes | Cook time: 15 minutes | Serves: 4**

Nonstick cooking spray
1 tablespoon low-sodium tamari or gluten-free soy sauce
Juice of 1 lemon
1 tablespoon honey
1 (1-inch) piece fresh ginger, grated
1 garlic clove, minced
1 pound salmon fillet
¼ teaspoon salt, divided
⅛ teaspoon freshly ground black pepper
2 broccoli heads, cut into florets
1 tablespoon extra-virgin olive oil

1. Preheat the oven to 400°F. Manage a baking sheet with cooking spray. 2. In a small bowl, mix the tamari, lemon juice, honey, ginger, and garlic. Set aside. 3. Place the spiced salmon on the baking sheet; skin-side down. Season with ⅛ teaspoon of salt and the pepper. 4. In a mixing bowl, toss the broccoli and olive oil. Season with the remaining ⅛ teaspoon of salt. Arrange in the baking sheet next to the salmon. Bake for 15 to 20 minutes until the salmon flakes easily with a fork and the broccoli is fork-tender. 5. In a pan, bring the tamari-ginger mixture to a simmer and cook for 1-2 minutes until thicken. 6. Drizzle the sauce and serve.

**Per Serving:** Calories 238; Total Fat 11g; Saturated Fat 0.8g; Sodium 334mg; Carbs 11g; Fiber 2g; Sugar 6g; Protein 25g

## Roasted Spiced Salmon with Salsa Verde

**Prep time: 5 minutes | Cook time: 25 minutes | Serves: 4**

Nonstick cooking spray
8 ounces tomatillos, husks removed
½ onion, quartered
1 jalapeño or serrano pepper, seeded
1 garlic clove, unpeeled
1 teaspoon extra-virgin olive oil
½ teaspoon salt, divided
4 (4-ounce) wild-caught salmon fillets
¼ teaspoon freshly ground black pepper
¼ cup chopped fresh cilantro
Juice of 1 lime

1. Preheat your oven at 425°F. Manage a baking sheet with cooking spray. 2. In a large bowl, toss the tomatillos, onion, jalapeño, garlic, olive oil, and ¼ teaspoon of salt to coat. Arrange them on baking sheet, and roast for about 10 minutes until just softened. Transfer to a dish or plate and set aside. 3. Arrange the Spiced salmon fillets skin-side down on the same baking sheet, and season with the remaining ¼ teaspoon of salt and the pepper. Bake it for 12-15 minutes until the fish flakes easily. 4. Meanwhile, peel the roasted garlic and place it and the roasted vegetables in a blender or food processor. Add a scant ¼ cup water to the jar, and process until smooth. 5. Add the cilantro and lime juice and process until smooth. Serve the salmon topped with the salsa verde.

**Per Serving:** Calories 199; Total Fat 9g; Saturated Fat 1g; Sodium 295mg; Carbs 6g; Fiber 2g; Sugar 3g; Protein 23g

## Homemade Fish Stock

**Prep time: 10 minutes | Cook time: 20 minutes | Serves: 4**

4 cups fish heads, bones, and trimmings (approx. 1 pound)
2 stalks celery and leaves, chopped
1 onion, chopped
1 carrot, peeled and chopped
1 bay leaf
4 sprigs fresh parsley
Sea salt and pepper, to taste (optional)

1. Use your own fish trimmings (saved in a bag in the freezer) or ask the butcher at your local fish market or supermarket for fish trimmings. Wash the trimmings well. 2. In a stockpot, combine all the ingredients. add water and boil, then reduce heat to low. Cover and simmer for 20 minutes. 3. Remove from heat and strain through a sieve, discarding all solids. Refrigerate or freeze.

**Per Serving:** Calories 40; Total Fat 2g; Saturated Fat 1g; Sodium 2mg; Carbs 0g; Fiber 0g; Sugar 0g; Protein 5g

## Roasted Whole Veggie-Stuffed Trout

**Prep time: 10 minutes | Cook time: 25 minutes | Serves: 2**

Nonstick cooking spray
2 (8-ounce) whole trout fillets, dressed (cleaned but with bones and skin intact)
1 tablespoon extra-virgin olive oil
¼ teaspoon salt
⅛ teaspoon freshly ground black pepper
½ red bell pepper, seeded and thinly sliced
1 small onion, thinly sliced
2 or 3 shiitake mushrooms, sliced
1 poblano pepper, seeded and thinly sliced
1 lemon, sliced

1. Preheat your oven at 425°F. Manage a baking sheet with cooking spray. 2. Rub both trout, inside and out, with the olive oil, then season with the salt and pepper. 3. In a bowl, add the bell pepper along with onion, mushrooms, and poblano pepper. Stuff half of this mixture into the cavity of each fish. Top the mixture with 2 or 3 lemon slices inside each fish. 4. Arrange the fish on the prepared baking sheet side by side and roast for 25 minutes until the fish is cooked and vegetables are tender.
**Per Serving:** Calories 452; Total Fat 22g; Saturated Fat 6g; Sodium 357mg; Carbs 14g; Fiber 3g; Sugar 5g; Protein 49g

## Ginger-Garlic Cod with Bell Pepper

**Prep time: 10 minutes | Cook time: 15 minutes | Serves: 4**

1 chard bunch, stemmed, leaves and stems cut into thin strips
1 red bell pepper, cut into strips
1 pound cod fillets, divide into 4 pieces
1 tablespoon grated fresh ginger
3 garlic cloves, minced
2 tablespoons white wine vinegar
2 tablespoons low-sodium tamari or gluten-free soy sauce
1 tablespoon honey

1. Preheat oven at 425°F. 2. Lay the four pieces out on a large workspace. 3. On each piece of paper, arrange a small pile of chard leaves and stems, topped by several strips of bell pepper. Top with a piece of cod. 4. In a bowl, mix the ginger and garlic, vinegar, tamari, and honey. Top each piece of fish with one-fourth of the mixture. 5. Fold the parchment paper over so the edges overlap. Fold the edges over several times to secure the fish in the packets. Carefully place the packets on a large baking sheet. 6. Bake for 12 minutes. Carefully open the packets, allowing steam to escape, and serve.
**Per Serving:** Calories 118; Total Fat 1g; Saturated Fat 0g; Sodium 715mg; Carbs 9g; Fiber 1g; Sugar 6g; Protein 19g

## Spaghetti with Shrimp Marinara

**Prep time: 10-15 minutes | Cook time: 6-7 hours | Serves: 6**

1 (6-oz.) can no-salt-added tomato paste
2 tablespoons dried parsley
1 cloves garlic, minced
¼ teaspoon pepper
½ teaspoon dried basil
1 teaspoon dried oregano
scant ½ teaspoon garlic salt
2 14½-oz. cans no-salt-added diced tomatoes
1 lb. cooked shrimp, peeled
Cooked spaghetti
Grated Parmesan cheese, optional

1. In slow-cooker combine tomato paste, parsley, garlic, pepper, basil, oregano, salt, garlic salt, and 1 can of diced tomatoes. 2. Cook on low 6-7 hours. 3. Turn to high and add shrimp. 4. If you'd like the sauce to have more tomatoes, stir in remaining can of tomatoes. 5. Cover and cook an additional 15-20 minutes. 6. Serve over cooked spaghetti. Garnish with grated Parmesan cheese if you wish.
**Per Serving:** Calories 95; Total Fat 1g; Saturated Fat 0g; Sodium 550mg; Carbs 12g; Fiber 3g; Sugar 7g; Protein 11g

## Speedy Vegetable Broth and Tomato Fish Stew

**Prep time: 10 minutes | Cook time: 20 minutes | Serves: 4**

1 tablespoon olive oil
1 red bell pepper, seeded and chopped
1 onion, chopped
3 celery stalks, chopped
1 tablespoon minced garlic
2 teaspoons ground cumin
6 cups low-sodium vegetable broth
1 (15-ounce) can no-salt-added diced tomatoes
1 (15-ounce) can low-sodium lentils, drained and rinsed
12 ounces salmon, cubed
Freshly ground black pepper

1. In a stockpot, heat the oil over medium-high heat. 2. Sauté the bell pepper, onion, celery, garlic, and cumin for about 4 minutes until softened. 3. Stir in the broth, tomatoes and their juices, and lentils and bring to a boil. lower the heat and simmer stew for 10 minutes. 4. Add the fish and simmer for about 6 minutes, until just cooked through. Season with pepper and serve.
**Per Serving:** Calories 396; Total Fat 16g; Saturated Fat 3g; Sodium 357mg; Carbs 40g; Fiber 12g; Sugar 16g; Protein 24g

## Roasted Halibut with Red Peppers and Green Beans

**Prep time:** 10 minutes | **Cook time:** 15 minutes | **Serves:** 4

1 pound green beans, trimmed
2 red bell peppers, seeded and cut into strips
1 onion, sliced
Zest and juice of 2 lemons
3 garlic cloves, minced
2 tablespoons extra-virgin olive oil
1 teaspoon dried dill
1 teaspoon dried oregano
4 (4-ounce) halibut fillets
½ teaspoon salt
¼ teaspoon freshly ground black pepper

1. Preheat your oven to 400°F temp setting. Manage a baking sheet with parchment paper. 2. In a bowl, add the green beans, bell peppers, onion, lemon zest and juice, garlic, olive oil, dill, and oregano and toss well. 3. Transfer the spiced veggies to the baking sheet, leaving the juice behind in the bowl. 4. Gently place the halibut fillets in the bowl, and coat in the juice. Transfer the fillets to the baking sheet, nestled between the vegetables, and drizzle them with any juice left in the bowl. Sprinkle the vegetables and halibut with the salt and pepper. 5. Bake them for 15-20 minutes until the vegetables are just tender and the fish flakes apart easily.

**Per Serving:** Calories 234; Total Fat 9g; Saturated Fat 0.5g; Sodium 349mg; Carbs 16g; Fiber 5g; Sugar 8g; Protein 24g

## Blackened Tilapia with Mango Salsa

**Prep time:** 15 minutes | **Cook time:** 10 minutes | **Serves:** 2

**For the Salsa**
1 cup chopped mango
2 tablespoons chopped red onion
2 tablespoons chopped fresh cilantro
2 tablespoons freshly squeezed lime juice
½ jalapeño pepper, seeded and minced
Pinch salt

**For the Tilapia**
1 tablespoon paprika
1 teaspoon onion powder
½ teaspoon freshly ground black pepper
½ teaspoon dried thyme
½ teaspoon garlic powder
¼ teaspoon cayenne pepper
¼ teaspoon salt
½ pound boneless tilapia fillets
2 teaspoons extra-virgin olive oil
1 lime, cut into wedges, for serving

To make the salsa
In a bowl, toss the mango, onion, cilantro, lime juice, jalapeño, and salt. Set aside.
To make the tilapia
1. In a bowl, add the paprika, onion powder, pepper, thyme, garlic powder, cayenne, and salt and mix. Rub the spices on the tilapia fillets. 2. In a skillet, cook the fish for 3 to 5 minutes on each side until the outer is crisp and cooked through. 3. Spoon half of the salsa over each fillet and serve with lime wedges on the side.

**Per Serving:** Calories 240; Total Fat 8g; Saturated Fat 0.4g; Sodium 417mg; Carbs 22g; Fiber 4g; Sugar 13g; Protein 25g

## Butter Scallops and Asparagus Skillet

**Prep time:** 10 minutes | **Cook time:** 15 minutes | **Serves:** 4

3 teaspoons extra-virgin olive oil, divided
1 pound asparagus, cut into 2-inch segments
1 tablespoon butter
1 pound sea scallops
¼ cup dry white wine
Juice of 1 lemon
2 garlic cloves, minced
¼ teaspoon freshly ground black pepper

1. In a large skillet, heat 1½ teaspoons of oil over medium heat. 2. Add the asparagus and sauté for 5 to 6 minutes until just tender, stirring regularly. Remove from the skillet and cover with aluminum foil to keep warm. 3. Add the remaining 1½ teaspoons of oil and the butter to the skillet. In hot sizzling butter, place the scallops in the skillet. Cook for 3 minutes each side until nicely browned. Use tongs to gently loosen and flip the scallops, and cook on the other side for another 3 minutes until browned and cooked through. Remove and cover with foil to keep warm. 4. In the same skillet, combine the wine, lemon juice, garlic, and pepper. Manage simmer for 1-2 minutes, stirring to mix in any browned pieces left in the pan. 5. Return the asparagus and the cooked scallops to the skillet to coat with the sauce. Serve warm.

**Per Serving:** Calories 252; Total Fat 7g; Saturated Fat 0.4g; Sodium 493mg; Carbs 15g; Fiber 2g; Sugar 3g; Protein 26g

## Baked Oysters and Vegetable

**Prep time:** 30 minutes | **Cook time:** 15 minutes | **Serves:** 2

2 cups coarse salt, for holding the oysters
1 dozen fresh oysters, scrubbed
1 tablespoon butter
½ cup finely chopped artichoke hearts
¼ cup finely chopped scallions, both white and green parts
¼ cup finely chopped red bell pepper
1 garlic clove, minced
1 tablespoon finely chopped fresh parsley
Zest and juice of ½ lemon
Pinch salt
Freshly ground black pepper

1. Pour the coarse salt into an 8-by-8-inch baking dish and spread to evenly fill the bottom of the dish. 2. Prepare a clean surface to shuck the oysters. Using a shucking knife, insert the blade at the joint of the shell, where it hinges open and shut. Firmly apply pressure to pop the blade in, and work the knife around the shell to open. Discard the empty half of the shell. Use the knife to gently loosen the oyster, and remove any shell particles. Set the oysters in their shells on the salt, being careful not to spill the juices. 3. Preheat the oven to 425°F. 4. Melt butter and cook the artichoke hearts, scallions, and bell pepper, and cook for 5 to 7 minutes. Add the garlic in it and cook a minute. Remove from the heat and mix in the parsley, lemon zest and juice, and season with salt and pepper. 5. Divide the vegetable mixture evenly among the oysters and bake for 10 to 12 minutes until the vegetables are lightly browned.

**Per Serving:** Calories 134; Total Fat 7g; Saturated Fat 0.7g; Sodium 281mg; Carbs 11g; Fiber 2g; Sugar 7g; Protein 6g

## Baked Cajun Shrimp Casserole with Quinoa

**Prep time: 15 minutes | Cook time: 30 minutes | Serves: 6**

½ cup quinoa
1 cup water
1 pound shrimp, peeled and deveined
1½ teaspoons Cajun seasoning, divided
4 tomatoes, diced
3 tablespoons extra-virgin olive oil, divided
½ onion, diced
1 jalapeño pepper, seeded and minced
3 garlic cloves, minced
1 tablespoon tomato paste
¼ teaspoon freshly ground black pepper
½ cup shredded pepper jack cheese

1. In a pot, combine the quinoa and water. Boil while cover and simmer on low for 10 to 15 minutes until all the water is absorbed. Fluff with a fork. 2. Preheat the oven to 350°F. 3. In a mixing bowl, toss the shrimp and ¾ teaspoon of Cajun seasoning. 4. In another bowl, toss the remaining ¾ teaspoon of Cajun seasoning with the tomatoes and 1½ teaspoons of olive oil. 5. In an oven-safe skillet, heat olive oil. Cook the shrimps for 2 to 3 minutes per side until they are opaque and firm. 6. In the skillet, add the onion, jalapeño, and garlic, and cook until the onion softens, 3 to 5 minutes. 7. Add the seasoned tomatoes, tomato paste, cooked quinoa, and pepper. Stir well to combine. 8. Return the shrimp to the skillet, placing them in a single layer on top of the quinoa. Sprinkle the cheese over the top. 9. Transfer the skillet to the oven and bake for 15 minutes. Broil to brown the cheese. Serve.

**Per Serving:** Calories 255; Total Fat 12g; Saturated Fat 2g; Sodium 469mg; Carbs 15g; Fiber 2g; Sugar 1g; Protein 18g

## Shrimp Burgers with Fruity Salsa and Salad

**Prep time: 15 minutes | Cook time: 10 minutes | Serves: 4**

**For the Salsa**
1 cup diced mango
1 avocado, diced
1 scallion, finely chopped
1 tablespoon chopped fresh cilantro
Juice of 1 lime
¼ teaspoon freshly ground black pepper
**For the Burgers**
1 pound shrimp, peeled and deveined
1 large egg
½ red bell pepper, seeded and coarsely chopped
¼ cup chopped scallions
2 tablespoons fresh chopped cilantro
2 garlic cloves
¼ teaspoon freshly ground black pepper
1 tablespoon extra-virgin olive oil
4 cups mixed salad greens

To make the salsa
In a small bowl, toss the mango, avocado, scallion, and cilantro. Sprinkle with the lime juice and pepper. Mix gently to combine and set aside.
To make the burgers
1. In the food processor bowl, add half the shrimp and process until coarsely puréed. Add the egg, bell pepper, scallions, cilantro, and garlic, and process until uniformly chopped. Transfer to a large mixing bowl. 2. Using a sharp knife, chop the remaining half pound of shrimp into small pieces. Add to the puréed mixture and stir well to combine. Add the pepper and stir well. Make 4 equal size patties. 3. In a skillet, cook the burgers for 3 minutes on each side until browned and cooked through. 4. Arrange 1 cup of salad greens, and top with a scoop of salsa and a shrimp burger on all serving plates.

**Per Serving:** Calories 229; Total Fat 11g; Saturated Fat 4g; Sodium 200mg; Carbs 14g; Fiber 4g; Sugar 7g; Protein 19g

# Chapter 4 Chicken and Poultry Recipes

| | | | |
|---|---|---|---|
| 48 | Easy Lemon Chicken Piccata | 50 | Flavored Roast Chicken with Collards |
| 48 | Chicken Cacciatore with Red Wine Sauce | 51 | Turkey Cutlets with Zucchini |
| 48 | Easy Turkey Bolognese with Mushroom and Cheese | 51 | Chicken and Shrimp Jambalaya |
| 48 | One-Pot Chicken and Brown Rice | 51 | West African–Style Chicken Stew with Potatoes |
| 48 | Easy Hoisin Chicken Lettuce Wraps | 51 | Sun-Dried Tomato Stuffed Grilled Chicken Breasts |
| 49 | Tasty Manhattan Chicken Salad | 52 | Creamy Mushroom and Kale Sliced Chicken |
| 49 | Homemade Shirataki Noodles with Vegetables and Turkey | 52 | Greek-Inspired Turkey Sauté with vegetables |
| 49 | Whole Spatchcock Chicken with Roasted Vegetable Medley | 52 | Homemade Chicken Satay with Peach Fennel Salad |
| 49 | Tropical Chicken Salad Sandwiches | 53 | Creamy Chicken Saltimbocca with Prosciutto |
| 50 | Tandoori, Chicken with Cauliflower Rice | 53 | Tender Spiced Butter Chicken |
| 50 | Tandoori-Style Grilled Chicken | 53 | Chicken Lo Mein with Coleslaw |
| 50 | Chickpea Pasta with Turkey Meatballs in Pomodoro Sauce | 53 | Homemade Juicy Turkey Burgers |

## Easy Lemon Chicken Piccata

**Prep time: 15 minutes | Cook time: 10 minutes | Serves: 4**

1 tablespoon olive oil
1 teaspoon unsalted butter
4 (4-ounce) boneless, skinless chicken breasts
½ teaspoon kosher salt
¼ teaspoon ground black pepper
1½ tablespoons white whole-wheat flour
⅔ cup low-sodium chicken broth
¼ cup dry white wine
3 tablespoons lemon juice
¼ cup chopped fresh parsley
1 tablespoon jarred capers, drained

1. In a skillet, heat oil and butter. 2. Sprinkle tops of chicken evenly with salt, black pepper, and flour. Add chicken, flour side down, to skillet and cook 4 minutes on each side or until cooked through. 3. Place chicken to plate and set aside. Add broth, wine, and lemon juice to skillet, reduce heat, and simmer 2–3 minutes until sauce thickens slightly. 4. Stir in parsley and capers. Place chicken back in skillet approximately 2 minutes to heat through. Serve.
**Per Serving:** Calories 200; Total Fat 8g; Saturated Fat 2g; Sodium 260mg; Carbs 4g; Fiber 1g; Sugar 0g; Protein 26g

## Chicken Cacciatore with Red Wine Sauce

**Prep time: 15 minutes | Cook time: 25 minutes | Serves: 6**

¼ cup white whole-wheat flour
⅛ teaspoon ground black pepper
1½ pounds boneless, skinless thin chicken breasts, cut into 4-ounce pieces
2 teaspoons extra-virgin olive oil
2 green bell peppers, sliced into ¼" strips
12 ounces white mushrooms, sliced
1 (25-ounce) jar low-sodium marinara sauce
½ cup dry red wine

1. Place flour and black pepper in a medium shallow bowl. Dredge chicken on both sides in flour and then discard extra. 2. Heat a large saucepan with lid over medium-high heat and add oil. Add chicken and sauté 3 minutes per side. 3. On top of chicken, add green peppers, mushrooms, marinara sauce, and wine. simmer 20 minutes until vegetables are cooked and sauce is reduced. Serve.
**Per Serving:** Calories 260; Total Fat 6g; Saturated Fat 1g; Sodium 100mg; Carbs 17g; Fiber 2g; Sugar 8g; Protein 30g

## Easy Turkey Bolognese with Mushroom and Cheese

**Prep time: 10 minutes | Cook time: 35 minutes | Serves: 6**

8 ounces white mushrooms, quartered
1⅓ pounds 93% lean ground turkey
1 (25-ounce) jar low-sodium marinara sauce
¼ teaspoon ground black pepper
¼ teaspoon garlic powder
¼ teaspoon dried oregano
½ teaspoon kosher salt
¼ cup grated Parmesan cheese

1. Place mushrooms into a food processor or blender. Pulse until ground. 2. Spray a large pot with nonstick cooking spray over medium-high heat. Add turkey and ground mushrooms side by side. Do not disturb for 5 minutes, then break up turkey and combine with mushrooms, stirring until cooked through, about 3–5 more minutes. 3. Stir in marinara sauce and seasonings, reduce heat to low, and cook an additional 5–10 minutes to reduce. Sprinkle with Parmesan and serve.
**Per Serving:** Calories 220; Total Fat 12g; Saturated Fat 2.5g; Sodium 340mg; Carbs 9g; Fiber 2g; Sugar 5g; Protein 26g

## One-Pot Chicken and Brown Rice

**Prep time: 15 minutes | Cook time: 15 minutes | Serves: 4**

1 tablespoon olive oil
4 (5-ounce) boneless, skinless chicken breasts
⅛ teaspoon kosher salt
⅛ teaspoon ground black pepper
¾ teaspoon garlic powder, divided
¾ teaspoon dried rosemary, divided
1½ cups low-sodium chicken broth
2 cups uncooked instant brown rice

1. In a nonstick skillet heat oil. 2. Sprinkle one side of chicken with salt and black pepper. Add chicken to skillet, salt and pepper side down, and sprinkle with half of garlic powder and half of rosemary. Cover and cook for 4 minutes until cooked through. Remove chicken from skillet and set aside. 3. Add broth to skillet and stir to deglaze pan and bring to a boil. Stir in rice and remaining garlic powder and rosemary. Top with chicken and cover. Lower the heat and cook 5 minutes.
**Per Serving:** Calories 390; Total Fat 9g; Saturated Fat 1.5g; Sodium 125mg; Carbs 40g; Fiber 2g; Sugar 0g; Protein 37g

## Easy Hoisin Chicken Lettuce Wraps

**Prep time: 15 minutes | Cook time: 5 minutes | Serves: 4**

1 tablespoon olive oil
1 pound lean ground chicken
2 large cloves garlic, peeled and minced
1 medium onion, peeled and diced
¼ cup hoisin sauce
2 tablespoons light soy sauce
1 tablespoon unflavored rice wine vinegar
1 (1") piece fresh ginger, grated
½ teaspoon sriracha
1 (8-ounce) can water chestnuts, diced
3 medium scallions, thinly sliced, divided
8 large lettuce leaves (like butter, Bibb, or Boston)

1. In a saucepan, heat oil. 2. Add chicken and cook until browned, 3–5 minutes, crumbling it as it cooks. 3. Stir in garlic, onion, hoisin sauce, soy sauce, vinegar, ginger, and sriracha. Cook 1–2 minutes until onion becomes translucent. 4. Stir in water chestnuts and two-thirds of scallions and cook until tender, 1–2 minutes. 5. Spoon a few tablespoons of chicken mixture into center of each lettuce leaf and sprinkle with remaining scallions to serve.
**Per Serving:** Calories 290; Total Fat 15g; Saturated Fat 0.5g; Sodium 670mg; Carbs 15g; Fiber 2g; Sugar 7g; Protein 22g

## Tasty Manhattan Chicken Salad

Prep time: 15 minutes | Cook time: 0 minutes | Serves: 4

½ teaspoon ground coriander
1½ cups nonfat plain Greek yogurt
½ cup light sour cream
1 tablespoon freshly squeezed orange juice
1 teaspoon orange zest
1 tablespoon honey
¼ teaspoon cayenne pepper
3 cups cooked shredded chicken
½ cup chopped cashews
3 tablespoons dried cranberries
2 tablespoons minced red onion
½ cup chopped fresh parsley

1. In a bowl, combine the coriander, yogurt, sour cream, orange juice, orange zest, honey, and cayenne. Mix well. 2. Add the chicken, cashews, cranberries, red onion, and parsley. Mix well. Taste and adjust the seasoning, if needed.

**Per Serving:** Calories 422; Total Fat 14g; Saturated Fat 2g; Sodium 713mg; Carbs 20g; Fiber 1g; Sugar 12g; Protein 53g

## Homemade Shirataki Noodles with Vegetables and Turkey

Prep time: 15 minutes | Cook time: 20 minutes | Serves: 4

14 ounces angel hair shirataki noodles
4 tablespoons canola oil, divided
14 ounces ground turkey
1 medium onion, thinly sliced
2 red bell peppers, thinly sliced
6 garlic cloves, minced
1 pound mushrooms, stemmed, caps thinly sliced
1 (10-ounce) bag frozen cooked spinach, thawed, excess liquid squeezed out
1⅓ cups water
1½ tablespoons sesame oil
¼ cup reduced-sodium soy sauce
1 tablespoon sesame seeds

1. Rinse the noodles under fresh, running water. In a skillet, heat the noodles for about 5 minutes to remove any excess water. Place noodles in a bowl and set aside. 2. In a skillet, heat oil to shimmer, add the turkey. Cook, stirring for about 5 minutes, or until the meat is no longer pink. Place the turkey with the noodles. 3. Heat the oil to shimmer, add the onion and cook for 3 to 4 minutes, or until translucent. Then add the bell peppers and garlic. Cook until the vegetables are tender. Add the cooked vegetables to the bowl of turkey and noodles. 4. Return the pan to the heat and add the remaining oil. When the oil starts shimmering, add the mushrooms; cook for about 5 minutes, or until tender. Place the mushrooms to the bowl with the cooked turkey and vegetables. Add the spinach to the bowl. 5. In a medium pot, combine the water, sesame oil, and soy sauce. Bring them to a boil over medium-high heat. Add the cooked turkey, noodles, and vegetables to the pot and cook another 2 minutes to reheat. 6. All liquid should be absorbed or evaporated during the cooking process. If it hasn't, turn up the heat and cook until no liquid remains. 7. Transfer to a platter or portion on serving plates. Sprinkle the sesame seeds over the top.

**Per Serving:** Calories 428; Total Fat 29g; Saturated Fat 10g; Sodium 710mg; Carbs 15g; Fiber 5g; Sugar 6g; Protein 29g

## Whole Spatchcock Chicken with Roast Vegetable Medley

Prep time: 10 minutes | Cook time: 45 minutes | Serves:

1 (3½- to 4-pound) whole chicken, butterflied
2½ tablespoons canola oil, divided
3 garlic cloves, minced
4 thyme sprigs, broken apart into large pieces
4 rosemary sprigs, broken apart into large pieces
½ teaspoon kosher salt
½ teaspoon freshly ground black pepper, divided
5 parsnips, cut lengthwise in ½-inch strips
1 rutabaga, cut into ½-inch cubes
1 onion, cut into 1-inch wedges

1. Preheat the oven to 450°F temp setting. 2. Using paper towels, pat dry the chicken. Carefully separate the skin from the chicken, then rub 1 tablespoon of oil between them and on the outside of the skin. Evenly disperse the minced garlic and thyme and rosemary sprigs under the skin. Season the skin on all sides with the salt and ¼ teaspoon of black pepper. Set aside while you prep the vegetables. 3. In a medium bowl, thoroughly combine the remaining 1½ tablespoons of oil and remaining ¼ teaspoon of pepper with the parsnips, rutabaga, and onion. Place the vegetables and place the chicken on top. Position the chicken breasts to be in the center of the baking sheet, skin-side up. The legs should be splayed close to the edges. Roast the chicken and veggies for 40-45 minutes. 4. Transfer the chicken to a clean, sanitized cutting board, cover it with aluminum foil, and allow it to rest for 10 minutes. 5. Meanwhile, place the vegetables on a platter or keep them warm in the oven with the heat turned off. 6. Carve and serve it with the roasted vegetables.

**Per Serving:** Calories 514; Total Fat 25g; Saturated Fat 10g; Sodium 293mg; Carbs 33g; Fiber 8.5g; Sugar 10g; Protein 39g

## Tropical Chicken Salad Sandwiches

Prep time: 15 minutes | Cook time: 10 minutes | Serves: 6

1 pound rotisserie chicken, cut into bite-sized cubes
1 medium ripe mango, peeled, pitted, and diced
1 small red onion, peeled and diced
1 small bell pepper, seeded and diced
1 medium jalapeño pepper, seeded and minced
2 medium cloves garlic, peeled and minced
1 cup canned black beans
2 tablespoons apple cider vinegar
Juice of 1 medium lime
2 tablespoons olive oil
¼ cup chopped fresh cilantro
½ teaspoon ground black pepper
4 cups mixed salad greens
6 high-fiber flatbreads or 8" high-fiber, low-carb flour tortillas

1. In a large bowl, add chicken, mango, onion, bell pepper, jalapeño, garlic, and beans and mix. 2. In a small bowl, add vinegar, lime juice, oil, cilantro, and black pepper and whisk well to combine. Pour over chicken salad and stir well to coat. 3. Divide greens and chicken salad evenly between flatbreads, then roll sandwiches up. Slice each in half using a sharp knife. 4. Serve immediately or cover and refrigerate until ready to serve.

**Per Serving:** Calories 300; Total Fat 10g; Saturated Fat 2.5g; Sodium 650mg; Carbs 37g; Fiber 19g; Sugar 7g; Protein 30g

Chapter 4 Chicken and Poultry Recipes | 49

## Tandoori, Chicken with Cauliflower Rice

**Prep time: 5 minutes | Cook time: 30 minutes | Serves: 4**

**For the Tandoori Chicken**
4 boneless, skinless chicken breasts
4 tablespoons freshly squeezed lemon juice
¼ teaspoon kosher salt
¼ teaspoon ground turmeric
2 garlic cloves, minced
1 tablespoon chopped fresh ginger
½ teaspoon ground cardamom
¾ teaspoon ground cumin
2 teaspoons paprika
½ cup nonfat plain Greek yogurt
½ tablespoon olive oil
**For the Cauliflower Rice**
1 (1½-pound) head cauliflower
½ tablespoon olive oil
¼ teaspoon kosher salt
Freshly ground black pepper

To make the tandoori chicken
1. Prick the chicken with a fork or skewer, then make three diagonal slashes in each breast, ½ inch deep and 1 inch apart. In a bowl, combine the chicken with lemon juice, salt, and turmeric. Cover and let sit while you prepare the rest of the sauce. 2. In a bowl, mix the garlic, ginger, cardamom, cumin, paprika, and yogurt and mix thoroughly. Pour this sauce over the chicken and gently stir to coat evenly. 3. Preheat the oven to 500°F. Manage a baking sheet with parchment paper. 4. Remove the chicken from the marinade, brush it with the olive oil, and place it on the prepared baking sheet. Discard the marinade. 5. Roast it for 20-30 minutes, or until the meat reaches an internal temperature of 165°F. 6. Remove the outer green leaves and core. Roughly chop the florets. 7. In a food processor, pulse the cauliflower to resemble a crumb-like texture, almost like rice, being careful not to overpulse and make it too fine. Put the cauliflower in a bowl and set aside. 8. In a large skillet, heat the oil to shimmer, add the cauliflower and stir to coat it with the hot oil. Season with the salt and pepper. Cook for 5 minutes until the cauliflower browns and becomes tender.
**Per Serving:** Calories 210; Total Fat 7g; Saturated Fat 2g; Sodium 345mg; Carbs 6g; Fiber 1.5g; Sugar 3.5g; Protein 30g

## Tandoori-Style Grilled Chicken

**Prep time: 15 minutes | Cook time: 10 minutes | Serves: 4**

1½ pounds boneless, skinless chicken breast halves, pounded thin
1 tablespoon garam masala
2 cloves garlic, finely chopped
½ cup plain nonfat Greek yogurt

1. Place chicken, garam masala, garlic, and yogurt in a medium shallow dish. Turn to coat chicken fully in marinade. Cover and refrigerate overnight. 2. Preheat broiler. Place chicken on a medium baking sheet lightly coated with nonstick cooking spray. 3. Broil chicken on top rack 4–5 minutes per side until internal temperature reaches 165°F. Serve.
**Per Serving:** Calories 220; Total Fat 4.5g; Saturated Fat 1g; Sodium 125mg; Carbs 2g; Fiber 0g; Sugar 1g; Protein 41g

## Chickpea Pasta with Turkey Meatballs in Pomodoro Sauce

**Prep time: 10 minutes | Cook time: 20 minutes | Serves: 4**

Cooking spray
1 pound ground turkey
1 large egg
1½ teaspoons Italian seasoning
2 teaspoons olive oil
8 ounces chickpea pasta
2 cups Pomodoro Sauce
4 ounces Parmesan cheese (optional)

1. Boil water on high heat. 2. Preheat the broiler. Manage a baking sheet with parchment paper and spray with cooking spray. 3. In a large bowl, combine the turkey, egg, Italian seasoning, and oil. Make the meatballs and place it on the baking tray. 4. Broil until the meatballs reach an internal temperature of 165°F for 10 minutes. 5. Boil pasta, then drain. 6. In a small saucepan, heat the pomodoro sauce over medium-low heat and keep warm until the meatballs have finished cooking. 7. Add the cooked meatballs in the sauce and mix to coat. 8. On each plate, serve about one-quarter of the chickpea noodles. Top with pomodoro sauce, meatballs, and Parmesan.
**Per Serving:** Calories 523; Total Fat 22g; Saturated Fat 10g; Sodium 238mg; Carbs 42g; Fiber 9g; Sugar 5g; Protein 37g

## Flavored Roast Chicken with Collards

**Prep time: 10 minutes | Cook time: 50 minutes | Serves: 2**

4 bone-in, skinless chicken thighs
1½ cups brine from Flash Pickles
½ cup whole-wheat flour
2 teaspoons paprika
1 teaspoon baking powder
3 tablespoons sesame seeds
¼ teaspoon freshly ground black pepper
Cooking spray
1 tablespoon avocado oil
½ bunch collard greens, coarsely shredded
1 garlic clove, minced

1. In a sealable bag, combine the chicken and pickle brine. Seal and marinate in refrigerate for at least 8 hours or overnight. 2. Preheat the oven to 425°F. Place a wire rack to fit over a baking sheet. 3. Using paper towels, pat dry the chicken and set aside. 4. In a bowl, add the flour with paprika, baking powder, sesame seeds, and pepper. Mix well, then toss the chicken thighs in the mixture, making sure each piece is coated. 5. Arrange the chicken pieces ½ inch apart on the wire rack over the baking sheet. Grease the chicken with cooking oil and bake for 40 to 50 minutes. 6. While the chicken rests, prepare the greens. In a skillet, heat the oil to shimmer, add the collards, toss to coat with the hot oil, for 3 minutes, or until the greens begin to wilt. Add the garlic, toss, and cook for 1 to 2 minutes.
**Per Serving:** Calories 562; Total Fat 34g; Saturated Fat 10g; Sodium 375mg; Carbs 23g; Fiber 6g; Sugar 0.5g; Protein 47g

## Turkey Cutlets with Zucchini

**Prep time: 10 minutes | Cook time: 15 minutes | Serves: 4**

¼ cup avocado oil
2 tablespoons molasses
¼ cup chopped scallions, green and white parts
1 tablespoon freshly ground black pepper
¼ teaspoon kosher salt
1 teaspoon dried thyme
½ teaspoon ground cinnamon
⅛ teaspoon ground cloves
½ teaspoon cayenne pepper
2 garlic cloves, minced
1 (1-inch) ginger, minced
¼ cup freshly squeezed lime juice
1 pound turkey breast cutlets
1 small onion, cut into ¼-inch slices
1 medium zucchini, cut into ¼-inch-by-¼-inch-by-3-inch matchsticks

1. In a large bowl, combine the oil, molasses, scallions, black pepper, salt, thyme, cinnamon, cloves, cayenne, garlic, ginger, and lime juice. Whisk until it comes together, then add the turkey cutlets, onion, and zucchini and toss to coat. 2. Preheat a cast-iron skillet or preheat the grill to medium-high. Remove the cutlets from the marinade and cook them in batches for 2 to 3 minutes per side, or until no longer pink. Transfer the cutlets to a platter and allow them to rest for 3 to 5 minutes. 3. Cook the onion and zucchini, stirring continuously, for 2 to 3 minutes, or until tender-crisp. Serve the vegetables with the turkey cutlets.

**Per Serving:** Calories 213; Total Fat 7.5g; Saturated Fat 2g; Sodium 167mg; Carbs 7g; Fiber 1g; Sugar 5.5g; Protein 29g

## Chicken and Shrimp Jambalaya

**Prep time: 30 minutes | Cook time: 2-4 hours | Serves: 6**

3½-4-lb. roasting chicken, trimmed of skin and fat, cut up
3 onions, diced
1 carrot, sliced
3-4 garlic cloves, minced
1 teaspoon dried oregano
1 teaspoon dried basil
½ teaspoon salt
⅛ teaspoon white pepper
14-oz. can crushed tomatoes
1 lb. shelled raw shrimp
2 cups cooked rice

1. Combine all ingredients instead of shrimp and rice in a slow cooker. 2. Cover. Cook on low temp setting for 2-3½ hours, or until chicken is tender. 3. Add shrimp and rice. 4. Cover. Cook on high temp setting for 15-20 minutes, or until shrimp are done.

**Per Serving:** Calories 354; Total Fat 7g; Saturated Fat 1.9g; Sodium 589mg; Carbs 29g; Fiber 4g; Sugar 9g; Protein 41g

## West African–Style Chicken Stew with Potatoes

**Prep time: 10 minutes | Cook time: 30 minutes | Serves: 4**

2 teaspoons avocado oil or olive oil
1 pound chicken breasts, boneless, skinless, cut into 1-inch cubes
1 onion, chopped
2 teaspoons minced garlic
2 teaspoons peeled and grated fresh ginger
1 teaspoon ground cumin
1 (15-ounce) can no-salt-added crushed tomatoes
½ cup Herbed Bone Broth or low-sodium chicken broth
¼ cup peanut butter
Pinch red pepper flakes, optional
2 sweet potatoes, peeled and cut into ½-inch cubes
1 cup chopped baby kale
2 teaspoons chopped fresh cilantro

1. In a skillet, Sauté the chicken until it is just cooked through, about 6 minutes. Set aside. 2. In the same skillet, sauté the onion, garlic, ginger, and cumin until the vegetables are softened, about 4 minutes. Add in the tomatoes, broth, peanut butter, and red pepper flakes, (if using), and bring to a boil. 3. Place back the chicken to the skillet along with the sweet potatoes, reduce the heat to low, manage simmer until the vegetables are tender, about 15 minutes. 4. Turn off the heat, stir in the kale, and let the stew sit for 5 minutes to wilt the greens before serving. Garnish with fresh cilantro.

**Per Serving:** Calories 355; Total Fat 14g; Saturated Fat 3g; Sodium 208mg; Carbs 27g; Fiber 6g; Sugar 4g; Protein 32g

## Sun-Dried Tomato Stuffed Grilled Chicken Breasts

**Prep time: 10 minutes | Cook time: 25 minutes | Serves: 2**

Nonstick cooking spray
2 (5-ounce) boneless, skinless chicken breasts
2 ounces crumbled feta cheese
2 tablespoons chopped oil-packed sun-dried tomatoes
½ teaspoon finely chopped fresh basil
¼ teaspoon minced garlic
Sea salt
Freshly ground black pepper

1. Preheat the oven to 400°F. Spray a 9-inch square baking dish with cooking spray and set aside. 2. Make a slit in the middle of each chicken breast lengthwise to create a pocket. 3. In a small bowl, mix the feta, sun-dried tomatoes, basil, and garlic until well combined. 4. Spoon the filling into the chicken breasts and close the pocket by pressing the edges together and sealing the pockets with wooden toothpicks. Season the breasts with salt and pepper. 5. Place the stuffed breasts into the prepared dish and bake until the chicken is cooked through, about 25 minutes. Remove the toothpicks and serve.

**Per Serving:** Calories 255; Total Fat 10g; Saturated Fat 3g; Sodium 332mg; Carbs 3g; Fiber 1g; Sugar 4g; Protein 36g

## Creamy Mushroom and Kale Sliced Chicken

| Prep time: 10 minutes | Cook time: 20 minutes | Serves: 2 |

1 tablespoon olive oil
½ pound boneless, skinless chicken breasts, cut into thin slices
2 cups quartered mushrooms
½ onion, chopped
2 teaspoons minced garlic
1 cup Herbed Bone Broth or low-sodium chicken broth
¼ cup low-fat plain Greek yogurt
½ cup shredded mozzarella cheese
2 cups chopped baby kale
Sea salt
Freshly ground black pepper
1 tablespoon fresh parsley

1. In a skillet, Sauté the chicken breast slices until they're just cooked through, about 7 minutes; set aside. 2. In the same skillet, sauté the mushrooms, onion, and garlic until the vegetables are softened, about 4 minutes. Add the broth, yogurt, and cheese and bring the sauce to a boil. Manage simmer on low heat, whisking constantly, until it's thickened, about 4 minutes. 3. Add the chicken on the plate back to the skillet, along with the kale, and simmer for 5 minutes longer to wilt the greens. 4. Season with salt and pepper and serve topped with the parsley.
**Per Serving:** Calories 462; Total Fat 21g; Saturated Fat 4g; Sodium 462mg; Carbs 11g; Fiber 1g; Sugar 2g; Protein 33g

## Greek-Inspired Turkey Sauté with vegetables

| Prep time: 10 minutes | Cook time: 20 minutes | Serves: 4 |

1 teaspoon olive oil
1 pound 93 percent lean ground turkey
1 zucchini, halved lengthwise and cut into ½-inch slices
1 red bell pepper, seeded and chopped
½ onion, chopped
2 teaspoons minced garlic
2 teaspoons dried oregano
1 cup cooked lentils
¼ cup halved black olives
1 tablespoon balsamic vinegar
1 cup spinach
Sea salt
Freshly ground black pepper

1. In a skillet, Sauté the turkey, zucchini, bell pepper, onion, garlic, and oregano until the turkey and the veggies are cooked and are tender, about 10 minutes. 2. Add the lentils, olives, and balsamic vinegar and cook until heated through, about 5 minutes. Add in the spinach, and let it sit for 5 minutes until the greens are wilted. 3. Spice lightly with salt and black pepper and serve.
**Per Serving:** Calories 279; Total Fat 12g; Saturated Fat 1g; Sodium 193mg; Carbs 17g; Fiber 6g; Sugar 2g; Protein 27g

## Homemade Chicken Satay with Peach Fennel Salad

| Prep time: 10 minutes | Cook time: 5 minutes | Serves: 4 |

**For the Satay**
⅔ cup ground almonds
5 garlic cloves, minced
1 teaspoon berbere or any hot pepper spice (e.g., cayenne pepper or chili powder)
⅛ teaspoon freshly ground black pepper
¼ teaspoon kosher salt
3 tablespoons canola oil
1 tablespoon maple syrup
1½ pounds chicken breasts, boneless, skinless, cut into ¼-inch-thick strips
½ cup water
**For the Salad**
Zest and juice of 1 lemon
3 tablespoons extra-virgin olive oil
1 large fennel bulb, halved, cored, and very thinly sliced
2 peaches, pitted and thinly cut into wedges
¼ cup fresh parsley leaves

To make the satay
1. In a bowl, add the almonds, garlic, berbere, black pepper, salt, canola oil, and maple syrup. Mix until thoroughly combined. Add the chicken and coat evenly. Marinate for at least 30 minutes. 2. Preheat the grill, or place an oven rack in the topmost position in the oven and preheat the broiler to high. 3. Brush away some of the marinade before threading the chicken onto skewers. Evenly distribute the chicken among the skewers. Grill it for 3 minutes on each side. 4. Scrape the leftover marinade into a saucepan, add the water, and bring it to a boil over high heat. Transfer to a small bowl to serve with the chicken skewers and salad.
To make the salad
1. Put the lemon zest with juice into a medium bowl. Slowly whisk in the olive oil. 2. Add the shaved fennel, peaches, and parsley leaves and toss gently to coat them with the dressing. 3. Allow the salad to rest while you finish preparing the chicken.
**Per Serving:** Calories 539; Total Fat 32g; Saturated Fat 2g; Sodium 236mg; Carbs 23g; Fiber 4.5g; Sugar 13g; Protein 41

## Creamy Chicken Saltimbocca with Prosciutto

Prep time: 10 minutes | Cook time: 15 minutes | Serves: 4

4 (4-ounce) chicken breasts, about ½-inch thick
1 teaspoon salt, divided
½ teaspoon freshly ground black pepper, divided
4 large sage leaves
8 slices of prosciutto
2 tablespoons extra-virgin olive oil
4 tablespoons unsalted butter
¼ cup dry white wine
1 cup chicken stock
½ cup heavy (whipping) cream

1. Spice the chicken with the salt and pepper. Place 1 sage leaf over each breast and wrap each with 2 slices of prosciutto. 2. Heat the olive oil over medium-high heat. Cook chicken in hot oil for 2 to 3 minutes per side, or until the prosciutto is browned and the chicken is almost cooked through. Place to a plate and keep warm. 3. Melt the butter in the skillet. Add the wine along with stock and boil it over high heat. Cook, whisking constantly, until the liquid is reduced by half, 3 to 4 minutes. Reduce the heat to low and whisk in the cream. 4. Place back the chicken to the skillet, cover, and simmer over low heat until the chicken is cooked through, 3 to 4 minutes. Serve the chicken warm, spooning the sauce over each piece.
Per Serving: Calories 447; Total Fat 34g; Saturated Fat 16g; Sodium 1055mg; Carbs 1g; Fiber 0g; Sugar 0g; Protein 32g

## Tender Spiced Butter Chicken

Prep time: 5 minutes | Cook time: 25 minutes | Serves: 4

½ cup coconut oil
1 pound boneless, skinless chicken thighs
2 teaspoons salt
1 teaspoon freshly ground black pepper
4 tablespoons (½ stick) unsalted butter
½ small onion, finely chopped
6 garlic cloves, sliced
2 tablespoons curry powder
1 (13.5-ounce) can full-fat coconut milk
2 tablespoons tomato paste

1. Heat up the coconut oil in a skillet or saucepan over medium-high heat. Season the chicken with salt and pepper. 2. Sear the chicken until browned. 3. To the hot oil, add the butter and onion, reduce the heat to medium, and sauté until the onion is just tender, 3 to 4 minutes. Add the garlic and curry powder and sauté another 1 to 2 minutes. 4. In a bowl, whisk the coconut milk and tomato paste. Add the mixture to the pan and bring to a boil. lower the heat, add the chicken back to the pan, cover, and simmer until cooked through and tender, 15-20 minutes. Serve warm.
Per Serving: Calories 667; Total Fat 63g; Saturated Fat 45g; Sodium 1360mg; Carbs 11g; Fiber 3g; Sugar 0g; Protein 21g

## Chicken Lo Mein with Coleslaw

Prep time: 15 minutes | Cook time: 15 minutes | Serves: 4

2½ tablespoons reduced-sodium soy sauce, divided
1 teaspoon grated fresh ginger
1 tablespoon unflavored rice vinegar
¼ teaspoon ground turmeric
1 pound chicken breast, boneless, skinless, cut into 1" cubes
½ tablespoon canola oil
½ cup sliced scallions
2 teaspoons minced garlic
3 cups shredded coleslaw mix
¼ teaspoon red pepper flakes
2 cups cooked whole-grain spaghetti
1 teaspoon sesame oil
1 teaspoon sesame seeds

1. In a medium bowl, combine 1½ tablespoons soy sauce, ginger, rice vinegar, and turmeric. Mix in cubed chicken and set aside. 2. Heat canola oil in a wok over medium heat and sauté scallions and garlic 1 minute. Add chicken and cook quickly until meat and scallions are slightly browned, about 8–10 minutes. 3. Add coleslaw to skillet and continue to stir-fry another 3–4 minutes. Sprinkle in red pepper flakes. 4. When vegetables are crisp-tender, add cooked pasta, sesame oil, remaining 1 tablespoon soy sauce, and sesame seeds. Toss lightly and serve.
Per Serving: Calories 310; Total Fat 8g; Saturated Fat 1g; Sodium 430mg; Carbs 27g; Fiber 4g; Sugar 2g; Protein 31g

## Homemade Juicy Turkey Burgers

Prep time: 10 minutes | Cook time: 15 minutes | Serves: 4

1 pound 93 percent lean ground turkey
¼ cup almond flour
1 large egg
1 scallion, chopped
1 tablespoon fresh parsley
½ teaspoon minced garlic
Sea salt
Freshly ground black pepper
4 whole-wheat sandwich thins
**Optional Toppings**
Spicy Barbecue Sauce
Onion
Tomato
Lettuce
Avocado
Cheese

1. In a bowl, mix the turkey, almond flour, egg, scallion, parsley, and garlic until they're well combined. Season lightly with salt and pepper. Form the mixture into four patties. 2. Preheat a grill or the oven to broil. Grill the burgers until they're cooked through, turning halfway through, about 12 minutes. Alternatively, broil the burgers on a baking sheet, turning once, about 15 minutes. 3. Serve the burgers on the sandwich thins with the toppings you choose.
Per Serving: Calories 360; Total Fat 21g; Saturated Fat 1.5g; Sodium 375mg; Carbs 18g; Fiber 15g; Sugar 2g; Protein 39g

# Chapter 5 Meat Recipes

| | | | |
|---|---|---|---|
| 55 | Pot-Roasted Spiced Rabbit | 62 | Classic Beef Pot Roast |
| 55 | Slow Cooker Venison Roast | 62 | Baked Lamb Shanks and Vegetable |
| 55 | Simple Pot Roast and Veggies | 63 | Braised Rump Roast and Vegetables |
| 55 | Six-Bean Barbecued Beans with Pork | 63 | Hearty and Nutritious New England Dinner |
| 55 | Main Dish Baked Beans and Beef | 63 | Traditional "Smothered" Steak |
| 55 | Veal and Green Peppers | 63 | Beef and Beans Stew |
| 56 | Venison in Onion Sauce | 63 | Easy Roast |
| 56 | Calico Beans with Beef and Bacon | 64 | Crock Pot Three-Bean Burrito Bake |
| 56 | Herbed Lamb Stew with Peas | 64 | Authentic Beef Stew Bourguignonne |
| 56 | Venison Steak with Tomato Juice | 64 | Easy Homemade Beef Stew |
| 56 | Sausage Beef and Tomato Spaghetti Sauce | 64 | Home-Style Pot Roast with Gravy and Vegetables |
| 57 | Mom's Meatballs with Tomato Sauce | 65 | Three-Pepper Steak Stew |
| 57 | Lamb Stew with Carrot and Potato | 65 | Simple Succulent Steak |
| 57 | Chunky Mushroom and Meat Spaghetti Sauce | 65 | Classic Stroganoff Steak |
| 57 | Nancy's Beef and Mushroom Spaghetti Sauce | 65 | Tasty Garlic Beef Stroganoff |
| 57 | Beef, Onion and Tomato Spaghetti Sauce | 65 | Homemade Machaca Beef |
| 58 | Gourmet Spaghetti Sauce with Red Wine | 66 | Slow Cooker Roast Beef with Apple and Onion |
| 58 | Daily Slow-Cooker Stew | 66 | Healthy Swedish Meatballs |
| 58 | Pheasant a la Elizabeth with Mushroom | 66 | Savory Sweet Crock Pot Roast |
| 58 | Italian-Style Stew | 66 | Slow Cooker Dilled Pot Roast |
| 58 | Easy Pot Roast | 66 | Cowboy Casserole Stew |
| 59 | Tender Venison or Beef Stew | 67 | Beef Braised with Mushroom Barley |
| 59 | Venison Swiss Steak Slow Stew | 67 | Traditional Hungarian Goulash |
| 59 | Homemade Swiss Steak | 67 | Tender Beef Burgundy |
| 59 | Low Calorie Margaret's Swiss Steak | 67 | Authentic Chinese Pot Roast |
| 59 | Juicy Nadine & Hazel's Swiss Steak | 67 | Red Wine Tender Roast |
| 59 | Homemade Sour Beef | 67 | Chuck Wagon Beef Stew |
| 60 | Beef Noodles with Tomatoes | 68 | Classic French Dip Roast |
| 60 | Low Calorie Big Beef Stew | 68 | Crock Pot Dripped Beef |
| 60 | Spanish Delicious Round Steak | 68 | Low calorie Old World Sauerbraten |
| 60 | Slow-Cooked Low Fat Pepper Steak | 68 | Cheesy Chili Rice |
| 60 | Authentic Asian Pepper Steak | 68 | Simple Spanish Rice |
| 60 | Beef Roast with Multiple Vegetables | 68 | Crock Pot Swedish Cabbage Rolls |
| 61 | Slow Cooker Steak San Morco | 69 | Green Chili Stew with Pork |
| 61 | Pat's Meat Slow Stew | 69 | Beef and Lentil Stew |
| 61 | Gone-All-Day Low Calorie Casserole | 69 | Easy Meal-in-One-Casserole |
| 61 | Classic Ernestine's Beef Stew | 69 | Homemade Mary Ellen's Barbecued Meatballs |
| 61 | Slow Cooker Becky's Beef Stew | 70 | Low Fat Cranberry Meatballs |
| 61 | Tasty Santa Fe Stew | 70 | All-Day Pot Roast |
| 62 | Low Carb, Full-Flavored Beef Stew | 70 | Slow Cooker Sweet and Sour Meatballs |
| 62 | Lazy Day Beef Stew | 70 | Beef and Vegetables Stew |
| 62 | Judy's Slow Cooker Beef Stew | | |

## Pot-Roasted Spiced Rabbit

Prep time: 20 minutes | Cook time: 10-12 hours | Serves: 6

2 onions, sliced
4-lb. roasting rabbit, skinned
1 garlic clove, sliced
2 bay leaves
1 whole clove
1 cup hot water
2 tablespoons soy sauce
2 tablespoons flour
½ cup cold water

1. Place onion in base of slow cooker inner pot. 2. Rub rabbit with salt and pepper. Insert garlic in the cavity. Place spiced rabbit in slow cooker. 3. Add bay leaves with clove, hot water, and soy sauce. 4. Cover. Cook on low temp setting for 10-12 hours. 5. Remove rabbit. Thicken the gravy by stirring 2 tablespoons flour blended into ½ cup water into juices in cooker. Stir continuously until gravy thickens. Cut meat into serving-size pieces and enjoy with gravy.
Per Serving: Calories 294; Total Fat 11g; Saturated Fat 3.2g; Sodium 390mg; Carbs 7g; Fiber 1g; Sugar 4g; Protein 40g

## Slow Cooker Venison Roast

Prep time: 15 minutes | Cook time: 10-12 hours | Serves: 10

3-lb. venison roast
¼ cup vinegar
2 garlic cloves, minced
1 teaspoon salt
½ cup chopped onions
15-oz. can no-added-salt tomato sauce
1 tablespoon ground mustard
1 pkg. brown gravy mix
½ teaspoon salt
¼ cup water

1. Place venison in a deep bowl. Add the vinegar, garlic, and salt over venison. Add cold water to cover venison. Marinate it for at least 8 hours. 2. After marination time completes, rinse and dry venison and add in slow cooker pot. 3. Mix remaining ingredients and pour it over venison in slow cooker. 4. Cover. Cook on low temp setting for 10-12 hours.
Per Serving: Calories 186; Total Fat 3g; Saturated Fat 1.4g; Sodium 530mg; Carbs 5g; Fiber 1g; Sugar 4g; Protein 31g

## Simple Pot Roast and Veggies

Prep time: 20 minutes | Cook time: 6-8 hours | Serves: 6

3-4 lb. chuck roast, trimmed of fat
4 medium potatoes, cubed, unpeeled
4 medium carrots, sliced, or 1 lb. baby carrots
2 celery ribs, sliced thin
1 envelope dry onion soup mix
3 cups water

1. Put roast, potatoes, carrots, and celery in slow cooker. 2. Add onion soup mix and water. 3. Cover. Cook on low 6-8 hours.
Per Serving: Calories 325; Total Fat 8g; Saturated Fat 2.9g; Sodium 560mg; Carbs 26g; Fiber 4g; Sugar 6g; Protein 35g

## Six-Bean Barbecued Beans with Pork

Prep time: 25 minutes | Cook time: 4-6 hours | Serves: 24

1-lb. can kidney beans, drained
1-lb. can pinto beans, drained
1-lb. can Great Northern beans, drained
1-lb. can butter beans, drained
1-lb. can navy beans, drained
1-lb. can pork and beans
¼ cup barbecue sauce
⅓ cup prepared mustard
⅓ cup ketchup
2 tablespoons Worcestershire sauce
1 small onion, chopped
1 small bell pepper, chopped
2 tablespoons molasses
½ cup brown sugar
Brown sugar substitute to equal ¼ cup sugar

1. Mix together all ingredients in a slow cooker. 2. Cook on low 4-6 hours.
Per Serving: Calories 122; Total Fat 1g; Saturated Fat 0.1g; Sodium 322mg; Carbs 24g; Fiber 6g; Sugar 7g; Protein 6g

## Main Dish Baked Beans and Beef

Prep time: 20 minutes | Cook time: 4-8 hours | Serves: 8

1 lb. ground beef
28-oz. can baked beans
8-oz. can pineapple tidbits packed in juice, drained
4½-oz. can sliced mushrooms, drained
1 large onion, chopped
1 large green pepper, chopped
½ cup Phyllis' Homemade Barbecue Sauce
2 tablespoons light soy sauce
1 clove garlic, minced
¼ teaspoon pepper

1. Brown ground beef in skillet. Drain. Place in slow cooker. 2. Stir in remaining ingredients. Mix well. 3. Cover. Cook on low 4-8 hours, or until bubbly. Serve in soup bowls.
Per Serving: Calories 238; Total Fat 6g; Saturated Fat 2.4g; Sodium 663mg; Carbs 31g; Fiber 7g; Sugar 13g; Protein 17g

## Veal and Green Peppers

Prep time: 15 minutes | Cook time: 4-7 hours | Serves: 4

1½ lbs. boneless veal, cubed
3 green bell peppers, quartered
2 onions, thinly sliced
½ lb. fresh mushrooms, sliced
1 teaspoon salt
½ teaspoon dried basil
2 cloves garlic, minced
28-oz. can tomatoes

1. Add all ingredients in a slow cooker pot. 2. Cover. Cook on low 7 hours, or on high 4 hours. 3. Serve over rice or noodles.
Per Serving: Calories 194; Total Fat 3g; Saturated Fat 0.9g; Sodium 555mg; Carbs 16g; Fiber 4g; Sugar 9g; Protein 26g

## Venison in Onion Sauce

Prep time: 25 minutes | Cook time: 8-10 hours | Serves: 12

3-4-lb. venison roast
¼ cup vinegar
2 garlic cloves, minced
¼ teaspoon salt
Cold water
2 tablespoons oil
1 large onion, sliced
Half a green bell pepper, sliced
2 ribs celery, sliced
1-2 garlic cloves, minced
1½-2 teaspoons salt
¼ teaspoon pepper
½ teaspoon dried oregano
¼ cup ketchup
1 cup tomato juice

1. Combine vinegar, garlic cloves, and ¼ teaspoon salt. Pour over venison. Add water until meat is covered. Marinate 6-8 hours. 2. Cut meat into pieces. Brown in oil in skillet. Place in slow cooker. 3. Mix remaining ingredients together; then pour into cooker. Stir in meat. 4. Cover. Cook on low 8-10 hours. 5. Pull the meat apart with help of forks and then stir it through the sauce. 6. Serve on sandwich rolls, or over rice or pasta.
**Per Serving:** Calories 176; Total Fat 5g; Saturated Fat 1.4g; Sodium 429mg; Carbs 5g; Fiber 1g; Sugar 3g; Protein 26g

## Calico Beans with Beef and Bacon

Prep time: 25 minutes | Cook time: 3-4 hours | Serves: 12

½ lb. ground beef
¼ lb. bacon, chopped
½ cup chopped onions
½ cup no-added-salt ketchup
⅓ cup brown sugar
Brown sugar substitute to equal 3 Tablespoon sugar
2 tablespoons sugar
1 tablespoon vinegar
1 teaspoon dry mustard
16-oz. can pork and beans, undrained
16-oz. can red kidney beans, undrained
16-oz. can yellow limas, undrained
16-oz. can navy beans, undrained

1. Brown ground beef, bacon, and onions together in skillet. Drain. Spoon meat and onions into slow cooker. 2. Stir ketchup, brown sugar, sugar, vinegar, mustard, and salt. Mix together well. Add to slow cooker. 3. Pour beans into slow cooker and combine all ingredients thoroughly. 4. Cover. Cook on high 3-4 hours.
**Per Serving:** Calories 233; Total Fat 4g; Saturated Fat 1.3g; Sodium 620mg; Carbs 37g; Fiber 7g; Sugar 16g; Protein 12g

## Herbed Lamb Stew with Peas

Prep time: 20-30 minutes | Cook time: 8-10 hours | Serves: 6

1½ lbs. lean lamb, cut into 1-2" cubes
1 tablespoon oil
2 medium onions, chopped
4 cups fat-free, low-sodium beef broth
3 medium potatoes, peeled and thinly sliced
½ teaspoon salt
¼ teaspoon pepper
¼ teaspoon celery seed
¼ teaspoon dried marjoram
¼ teaspoon dried thyme
10-oz. pkg. frozen peas
6 tablespoons flour
½ cup cold water

1. Brown lamb cubes in skillet in oil over medium-high heat. Do in two batches so that cubes brown and don't just steam. 2. Transfer browned meat to slow cooker. 3. Add remaining ingredients except peas, flour, and water. 4. Cover. Cook on low temp setting for 8 to 10 hours, or just until meat is tender. 5. Stir in peas. 6. In a bowl, mix flour in water. When smooth, stir into pot. 7. Cover. Turn cooker to high and cook an additional 15 to 20 minutes, or until broth thickens.
**Per Serving:** Calories 325; Total Fat 9g; Saturated Fat 2.5g; Sodium 590mg; Carbs 32g; Fiber 4g; Sugar 6g; Protein 30g

## Venison Steak with Tomato Juice

Prep time: 15-20 minutes | Cook time: 5 hours | Serves: 4

1 tablespoon olive oil
1 lb. venison tenderloin steak, cubed
1 large onion, chopped
½ teaspoon garlic salt
½ teaspoon garlic powder
1 large bell pepper, diced
1 teaspoon soy sauce
1 tablespoon brown sugar
1 tablespoon chili powder
1 cup V8, or home-canned tomato, juice

1. In a skillet, heat the oil, brown steak and onion with garlic salt and powder. 2. Add chopped pepper, soy sauce, brown sugar, and chili powder to slow cooker. 3. Transfer steak and onion to slow-cooker. 4. Pour juice over top. Cover. Cook 5 hours on low.
**Per Serving:** Calories 225; Total Fat 6g; Saturated Fat 1.5g; Sodium 410mg; Carbs 15g; Fiber 3g; Sugar 10g; Protein 27g

## Sausage Beef and Tomato Spaghetti Sauce

Prep time: 20 minutes | Cook time: 6 ½ hours | Serves: 20

1 lb. ground beef
1 lb. Italian sausage, sliced
2 28-oz. cans crushed tomatoes
¾ can (28-oz. tomato can) water
2 teaspoons garlic powder
1 teaspoon pepper
2 tablespoons parsley
2 tablespoons dried oregano
2 12-oz. cans tomato paste
2 12-oz. cans tomato purée

1. Brown ground beef and sausage in skillet. Drain. Transfer to large slow cooker. 2. Add crushed tomatoes, water, garlic powder, pepper, parsley, and oregano. 3. Cover. Cook on high 30 minutes. Add tomato paste and tomato purée. Cook on low 6 hours.
**Per Serving:** Calories 176; Total Fat 8g; Saturated Fat 2.7g; Sodium 408mg; Carbs 17g; Fiber 4g; Sugar 6g; Protein 10g

## Mom's Meatballs with Tomato Sauce

Prep time: 45 minutes | Cook time: 4-5 hours | Serves: 10

**Sauce:**
2 tablespoons canola oil
¼-½ cup chopped onions
3 garlic cloves, minced
29-oz. can tomato purée
29-oz. can water
12-oz. can tomato paste
12-oz. can water
1 tablespoon sugar
2 teaspoons dried oregano
¼ teaspoon Italian seasoning
½ teaspoon dried basil
⅛ teaspoon pepper
¼ cup diced green peppers
**Meatballs:**
1 lb. 85%-lean ground beef
1 egg
2 tablespoons water
¾ cup Italian bread crumbs
⅛ teaspoon black pepper
⅛ teaspoon salt
1 tablespoon canola oil

1. Sauté onions and garlic in oil in a saucepan. 2. Combine all sauce ingredients in a slow cooker. 3. Cover. Cook on low. 4. Mix together all meatball ingredients except oil. Form into small meatballs, then brown on all sides in oil in saucepan. Drain on paper towels. Add to sauce. 5. Cover. Cook on low 4-5 hours.
**Per Serving:** Calories 221; Total Fat 10g; Saturated Fat 2.4g; Sodium 540mg; Carbs 22g; Fiber 4g; Sugar 7g; Protein 13g

## Lamb Stew with Carrot and Potato

Prep time: 30 minutes | Cook time: 8-10 hours | Serves: 6

2 lbs. lamb, cubed
½ teaspoon sugar
2 tablespoons oil
2 teaspoons salt
¼ teaspoon pepper
¼ cup flour
2 cups water
¾ cup red cooking wine
¼ teaspoon powdered garlic
2 teaspoons Worcestershire sauce
6 medium carrots, sliced
4 small onions, quartered
4 ribs celery, sliced
3 medium potatoes, unpeeled, diced

1. Sprinkle lamb with sugar. Brown in oil in skillet. 2. Remove lamb and place in cooker, reserving drippings. 3. Stir salt, pepper, and flour into drippings until smooth. Stir in water and wine, until smooth, stirring until broth simmers and thickens. 4. Pour into cooker. Add remaining ingredients in it and stir until well combined. 5. Cover. Cook on low 8-10 hours.
**Per Serving:** Calories 388; Total Fat 13g; Saturated Fat 3.2g; Sodium 943mg; Carbs 32g; Fiber 5g; Sugar 9g; Protein 35g

## Chunky Mushroom and Meat Spaghetti Sauce

Prep time: 25 minutes | Cook time: 3-8 hours | Serves: 12

1 lb. ground beef, browned and drained
½ lb. bulk sausage, browned and drained
14½-oz. can no-added-salt Italian tomatoes with basil
15-oz. can Italian tomato sauce
1 medium onion, chopped
1 green pepper, chopped
8-oz. can sliced mushrooms
½ cup dry red wine
2 teaspoons sugar
1 teaspoon minced garlic
1½ teaspoons dried basil

1. Add all ingredients in a slow cooker pot. 2. Cover. Cook on high 3½-4 hours, or low 7-8 hours.
**Per Serving:** Calories 134; Total Fat 7g; Saturated Fat 2.5g; Sodium 397mg; Carbs 8g; Fiber 2g; Sugar 4g; Protein 11g

## Nancy's Beef and Mushroom Spaghetti Sauce

Prep time: 25 minutes | Cook time: 3 hours | Serves: 6

¼ cup minced onion
Garlic powder, to taste
3 cups chopped fresh tomatoes
6-oz. can tomato paste
½ teaspoon salt
Dash of pepper
½ teaspoon dried basil
1 bay leaf
1 chopped green bell pepper
1 lb. ground beef, browned and drained
4-oz. can sliced mushrooms, undrained

1. Add all ingredients in a slow cooker pot. 2. Cover. Cook on low 3 hours.
**Per Serving:** Calories 186; Total Fat 8g; Saturated Fat 3g; Sodium 372mg; Carbs 12g; Fiber 3g; Sugar 4g; Protein 17g

## Beef, Onion and Tomato Spaghetti Sauce

Prep time: 30-35 minutes | Cook time: 4 hours | Serves: 15

1½ lbs. 90%-lean ground beef, cooked and drained
3 onions, coarsely chopped
1 red bell pepper, coarsely chopped
1 green pepper, coarsely chopped
4 cloves garlic, minced
2 28-oz. cans diced tomatoes
14½-oz. can diced tomatoes
2 14½-oz. cans fat-free, low-sodium beef broth
2 tablespoons sugar
2 teaspoons dried basil
2 teaspoons dried oregano
1 teaspoon salt
2 6-oz. cans tomato paste, no salt added

1. Combine all ingredients except tomato paste in slow cooker. 2. Cook for 3½ hours on high. Stir in tomato paste. 3. Cover and cook an additional 30 minutes.
**Per Serving:** Calories 140; Total Fat 4g; Saturated Fat 1.5g; Sodium 475mg; Carbs 15g; Fiber 3g; Sugar 9g; Protein 12g

## Gourmet Spaghetti Sauce with Red Wine

**Prep time: 25 minutes | Cook time: 4-5 hours | Serves: 20**

2 slices bacon
1¼ lbs. ground beef
½ lb. ground pork
1 cup chopped onions
½ cup chopped green bell pepper
3 garlic cloves, minced
2. 3-oz. cans Italian tomatoes
2 6-oz. cans tomato paste
1 cup dry red wine, or water
2½ teaspoons dried oregano
2½ teaspoons dried basil
1 bay leaf, crumbled
¾ cup water
¼ cup chopped fresh parsley
1 teaspoon dried thyme
1 teaspoon salt
¼ teaspoon pepper
¼ cup dry red wine, or water

1. Brown bacon in skillet until crisp. Drain. Remove and crumble. 2. Add ground beef and pork. Crumble and cook until brown. Stir in onions, green peppers, and garlic. Cook 10 minutes. 3. Drain fat and dry with paper towel. 4. Pour tomatoes into slow cooker and crush with back of spoon. 5. Add all other ingredients, except ¼ cup wine, in slow cooker. 6. Cover. Bring to boil on high. Reduce heat to low for 3-4 hours. 7. During last 30 minutes, stir in ¼ cup red wine or water.
**Per Serving:** Calories 115; Total Fat 5g; Saturated Fat 1.8g; Sodium 309mg; Carbs 9g; Fiber 2g; Sugar 4g; Protein 9g

## Daily Slow-Cooker Stew

**Prep time: 35 minutes | Cook time: 8-10 hours | Serves: 8**

2 lbs. boneless beef, cubed, trimmed of fat
4-6 celery ribs, sliced
6-8 medium carrots, sliced
6 medium potatoes, cubed, unpeeled
2 medium onions, sliced
28-oz. can tomatoes
¼ cup minute tapioca
1 teaspoon salt
¼ teaspoon pepper
½ teaspoon dried basil or oregano
1 garlic clove, minced

1. Add all ingredients in a slow cooker. 2. Cover. Cook on low 8-10 hours.
**Per Serving:** Calories 299; Total Fat 5g; Saturated Fat 1.4g; Sodium 549mg; Carbs 42g; Fiber 7g; Sugar 11g; Protein 23g

## Pheasant a la Elizabeth with Mushroom

**Prep time: 30 minutes | Cook time: 6-8 hours | Serves: 8**

6 half boneless, skinless pheasant breasts, 6½ oz. each, cubed
¾ cup teriyaki sauce
⅓ cup flour
1½ teaspoons garlic salt
Pepper to taste
2 tablespoons olive oil
1 large onion, sliced
12-oz. can beer
¾ cup fresh mushrooms, sliced

1. Marinate pheasant in teriyaki sauce for 2-4 hours. Remove breasts from teriyaki sauce and discard sauce. 2. Combine flour, garlic salt, and pepper in a shallow bowl. Dredge pheasant in flour mixture. 3. Brown floured breasts in olive oil in skillet. Add onion and sauté for 3 minutes, stirring frequently. Transfer to slow cooker. 4. Add beer and mushrooms. 5. Cover. Cook on low 6-8 hours.
**Per Serving:** Calories 260; Total Fat 8g; Saturated Fat 0.5g; Sodium 357mg; Carbs 10g; Fiber 1g; Sugar 5g; Protein 34g

## Italian-Style Stew

**Prep time: 30 minutes | Cook time: 8-10 hours | Serves: 6**

1½ lbs. beef cubes
2-3 carrots, cut in 1-inch chunks
3-4 ribs celery, cut in ¾-1-inch pieces
1-1½ cups coarsely chopped onions
14½-oz. can stewed, or diced tomatoes
⅓ cup minute tapioca
1½ teaspoon salt
¼ teaspoon pepper
¼ teaspoon Worcestershire sauce
½ teaspoon Italian seasoning

1. Add all ingredients in a slow cooker. 2. Cover. Cook on low 8-10 hours.
**Per Serving:** Calories 188; Total Fat 5g; Saturated Fat 1.4g; Sodium 508mg; Carbs 18g; Fiber 3g; Sugar 6g; Protein 19g

## Easy Pot Roast

**Prep time: 10 minutes | Cook time: 10-12 hours | Serves: 8**

3 potatoes, thinly sliced
2 large carrots, thinly sliced
1 onion, thinly sliced
1 teaspoon salt
½ teaspoon pepper
3-4 lb. pot roast, trimmed of fat
½ cup water

1. Put vegetables in the slow cooker. Stir in salt and pepper. Add roast. Pour in water. 2. Cover. Cook on low 10-12 hours.
**Per Serving:** Calories 219; Total Fat 6g; Saturated Fat 2.2g; Sodium 361mg; Carbs 14g; Fiber 2g; Sugar 3g; Protein 26g

## Tender Venison or Beef Stew

**Prep time: 35 minutes | Cook time: 8-9 hours | Serves: 6**

1½ lbs. venison or beef cubes
2 tablespoon canola oil
1 medium onion, chopped
4 carrots, cut into 1-inch pieces
1 rib celery, cut into 1-inch pieces
4 medium potatoes, peeled and quartered
12-oz. can whole tomatoes, undrained
10½-oz. can beef broth
1 tablespoon Worcestershire sauce
1 tablespoon parsley flakes
1 bay leaf
¼ teaspoon salt
¼ teaspoon pepper
2 tablespoon quick-cooking tapioca

1. Brown meat cubes in skillet in oil over medium heat. Transfer to slow cooker. 2. Add remaining ingredients. Mix well. 3. Cover. Cook on low 8-9 hours.
Per Serving: Calories 313; Total Fat 8g; Saturated Fat 1.5g; Sodium 552mg; Carbs 29g; Fiber 4g; Sugar 7g; Protein 31g

## Venison Swiss Steak Slow Stew

**Prep time: 25 minutes | Cook time: 7-8 hours | Serves: 6**

2 lbs. round venison steak
¼ cup flour
2 teaspoon salt
½ teaspoon pepper
1 tablespoon canola oil
2 medium onions, sliced
2 ribs celery, diced
1 cup diced carrots
2 cups fresh, or stewed, tomatoes
1 tablespoon Worcestershire sauce

1. Combine flour, salt, and pepper. Dredge steak in flour mixture. Brown in oil in skillet. Place in slow cooker. 2. Add remaining ingredients. 3. Cover. Cook on low 7½-8½ hours.
Per Serving: Calories 277; Total Fat 7g; Saturated Fat 1.7g; Sodium 527mg; Carbs 14g; Fiber 3g; Sugar 6g; Protein 39g

## Homemade Swiss Steak

**Prep time: 25 minutes | Cook time: 3-10 hours | Serves: 6**

1½ lbs. round steak, about ¾" thick, trimmed of fat
2-4 teaspoon flour
½-1 teaspoon salt
¼ teaspoon pepper
1 medium onion, sliced
1 medium carrot, chopped
1 rib celery, chopped
14½-oz. can diced tomatoes, or 15 oz. can tomato sauce

1. Cut steak into serving pieces. 2. Combine flour, salt, and pepper. Dredge meat in seasoned flour. 3. Place onions in bottom of slow cooker. Add meat. Top with carrots and celery and cover with tomatoes. 4. Cover. Cook on low 8-10 hours, or high 3-5 hours. 5. Serve over noodles or rice.
Per Serving: Calories 172; Total Fat 5g; Saturated Fat 1.7g; Sodium 381mg; Carbs 8g; Fiber 2g; Sugar 4g; Protein 22g

## Low Calorie Margaret's Swiss Steak

**Prep time: 25 minutes | Cook time: 9 hour 15 minutes | Serves: 6**

1 cup chopped onions
½ cup chopped celery
2 lb. ½-inch thick round steak, trimmed of fat
¼ cup flour
3 tablespoon oil
1 teaspoon salt
¼ teaspoon pepper
16-oz. can diced tomatoes
¼ cup flour
½ cup water

1. Place onions and celery in the bottom of the slow cooker. 2. Cut steak into serving-size pieces. Dredge in ¼ cup flour. Sear in oil until brown in saucepan. Place in slow cooker pot. 3. Spice with salt and pepper. Pour on tomatoes. 4. Cover. Cook on low temp setting for 9 hours. Remove meat from slow cooker. 5. Turn heat to high temp setting. Blend together ¼ cup flour and water. Stir into sauce in slow cooker. Cover and cook 15 minutes. Serve with steak.
Per Serving: Calories 305; Total Fat 14g; Saturated Fat 2.8g; Sodium 592mg; Carbs 14g; Fiber 2g; Sugar 4g; Protein 30g

## Juicy Nadine & Hazel's Swiss Steak

**Prep time: 30 minutes | Cook time: 6-8 hours | Serves: 8**

3 lb. round steak, trimmed of fat
⅓ cup flour
1 teaspoon salt
½ teaspoon pepper
3 tablespoon canola oil
1 large onion, sliced
1 large pepper, sliced
14½-oz. can stewed tomatoes, or 3-4 fresh tomatoes, chopped
Water

1. Sprinkle meat with flour, salt, and pepper. Pound both sides. Cut into 6 or 8 pieces. Brown meat in canola oil over medium heat on top of stove, about 15 minutes. Transfer to slow cooker. 2. Brown onion and pepper. Add tomatoes and bring to boil. Pour over steak. Add water to completely cover steak. 3. Cover. Cook on low 6-8 hours.
Per Serving: Calories 296; Total Fat 13g; Saturated Fat 2.9g; Sodium 547mg; Carbs 11g; Fiber 1g; Sugar 4g; Protein 33g

## Homemade Sour Beef

**Prep time: 10 minutes | Cook time: 8-10 hours | Serves: 8**

3 lb. pot roast, trimmed of fat
⅓ cup cider vinegar
1 large onion, sliced
3 bay leaves
½ teaspoon salt
¼ teaspoon ground cloves
¼ teaspoon garlic powder

1. Place roast in slow cooker. Add remaining ingredients. 2. Cover. Cook on low 8-10 hours.
Per Serving: Calories 169; Total Fat 6g; Saturated Fat 2.2g; Sodium 194mg; Carbs 3g; Fiber 1g; Sugar 2g; Protein 24g

## Beef Noodles with Tomatoes

**Prep time: 20 minutes | Cook time: 6-8 hours | Serves: 8**

1½ lbs. stewing beef, cubed, trimmed of fat
¼ cup flour
2 cups stewed tomatoes
1 teaspoon salt
¼-½ teaspoon pepper
1 medium onion, chopped
Water
12-oz. bag noodles

1. Combine meat and flour until cubes are coated. Place in slow cooker. 2. Add tomatoes, salt, pepper, and onion. Add water to cover. 3. Cover. Simmer on low 6-8 hours. 4. Serve over cooked noodles.
**Per Serving:** Calories 286; Total Fat 5g; Saturated Fat 1.8g; Sodium 490mg; Carbs 39g; Fiber 2g; Sugar 4g; Protein 20g

## Low Calorie Big Beef Stew

**Prep time: 25 minutes | Cook time: 9 hours | Serves: 8**

3 lb. beef roast, cubed, trimmed of fat
1 large onion, sliced
1 teaspoon dried parsley flakes
1 medium green pepper, sliced
3 ribs celery, sliced
4 medium carrots, sliced
28-oz. can tomatoes with juice, undrained
1 garlic clove, minced
2 cups water

1. Combine all ingredients. 2. Cover. Cook on high 1 hour. Reduce heat to low and cook 8 hours. 3. Serve on rice or noodles.
**Per Serving:** Calories 224; Total Fat 7g; Saturated Fat 2.1g; Sodium 248mg; Carbs 12g; Fiber 3g; Sugar 7g; Protein 28g

## Spanish Delicious Round Steak

**Prep time: 25 minutes | Cook time: 8 hours | Serves: 6**

1 small onion, sliced
1 rib celery, chopped
1 medium green bell pepper, sliced in rings
2 lbs. round steak, trimmed of fat
2 tablespoon chopped fresh parsley
1 tablespoon Worcestershire sauce
1 tablespoon dry mustard
1 tablespoon chili powder
2 cups canned tomatoes
2 teaspoon dry minced garlic
½ teaspoon salt
¼ teaspoon pepper

1. Put half of onion, green pepper, and celery in a slow cooker. 2. Cut steak into serving-size pieces. Place steak pieces in slow cooker. 3. Put remaining onion, green pepper, and celery over steak. 4. Combine remaining ingredients. Pour over meat. 5. Cover. Cook on low 8 hours. 6. Serve over noodles or rice.
**Per Serving:** Calories 222; Total Fat 7g; Saturated Fat 2.3g; Sodium 414mg; Carbs 8g; Fiber 2g; Sugar 5g; Protein 30g

## Slow-Cooked Low Fat Pepper Steak

**Prep time: 25 minutes | Cook time: 6-7 hours | Serves: 8**

1½-2 lbs. beef round steak, cut in 3" × 1" strips, trimmed of fat
2 tablespoon canola oil
¼ cup soy sauce
1 garlic clove, minced
1 cup chopped onion
1 teaspoon sugar
¼ teaspoon pepper
¼ teaspoon ground ginger
2 large green peppers, cut in strips
4 medium tomatoes cut in eighths, or 16 oz. can diced tomatoes
½ cup cold water
1 tablespoon cornstarch

1. Brown beef in oil in saucepan. Transfer to slow cooker. 2. Combine soy sauce, garlic, onions, sugar, salt, pepper, and ginger. Pour over meat. 3. Cover. Cook on low for temp setting for 5-6 hours. 4. Add in tomatoes and peppers. Cook 1 hour longer. 5. Mix water and cornstarch slurry. Stir into slow cooker pot. Cook on high temp setting until thickened, about 10 minutes. 6. Serve over rice or noodles.
**Per Serving:** Calories 174; Total Fat 8g; Saturated Fat 1.5g; Sodium 546mg; Carbs 10g; Fiber 2g; Sugar 6g; Protein 17g

## Authentic Asian Pepper Steak

**Prep time: 20 minutes | Cook time: 6-8 hours | Serves: 6**

1 lb. round steak, sliced thin, trimmed of fat
3 tablespoon light soy sauce
½ teaspoon ground ginger
1 garlic clove, minced
1 medium green pepper, thinly sliced
4-oz. can mushrooms, drained, or 1 cup sliced fresh mushrooms
1 medium onion, thinly sliced
½ teaspoon crushed red pepper

1. Add all ingredients in a slow cooker pot. 2. Cover. Cook on low 6-8 hours. 3. Serve as steak sandwiches topped with provolone cheese, or over rice.
**Per Serving:** Calories 122; Total Fat 4g; Saturated Fat 1.2g; Sodium 368mg; Carbs 6g; Fiber 2g; Sugar 3g; Protein 16g

## Beef Roast with Multiple Vegetables

**Prep time: 20 minutes | Cook time: 8-10 hours | Serves: 6**

3 lb. boneless chuck roast, trimmed of fat
1 garlic clove, minced
1 tablespoon canola oil
2-3 medium onions, sliced
2-3 sweet green and red peppers, sliced
16-oz. jar salsa
2 14½-oz. cans Mexican-style stewed tomatoes

1. Brown roast and garlic in oil in skillet. Place in slow cooker. 2. Add onions and peppers. 3. Mix salsa and tomatoes and pour over in slow cooker. 4. Cover. Cook on low 8-10 hours. 5. Slice meat to serve.
**Per Serving:** Calories 327; Total Fat 11g; Saturated Fat 3.1g; Sodium 565mg; Carbs 19g; Fiber 5g; Sugar 12g; Protein 38g

## Slow Cooker Steak San Morco

**Prep time: 15 minutes | Cook time: 6-10 hours | Serves: 6**

2 lbs. stewing meat, cubed, trimmed of fat
1 envelope sodium-free dry onion soup mix
29-oz. can peeled, or crushed, tomatoes
1 teaspoon dried oregano
garlic powder to taste
2 tablespoon canola oil
2 tablespoon wine vinegar

1. Layer meat evenly in bottom of slow cooker. 2. Combine soup mix, tomatoes, spices, oil, and vinegar in bowl. Blend with spoon. Pour over meat. 3. Cover. Cook on high temp setting for 6 hours, or low 8-10 hours.
**Per Serving:** Calories 237; Total Fat 10g; Saturated Fat 2.1g; Sodium 252mg; Carbs 10g; Fiber 2g; Sugar 5g; Protein 25g

## Pat's Meat Slow Stew

**Prep time: 25 minutes | Cook time: 4-10 hours | Serves: 5**

1-2 lbs. beef roast, cubed, trimmed of fat
1 teaspoon salt
¼ teaspoon pepper
2 cups water
2 small carrots, sliced
2 small onions, sliced
4-6 small potatoes, unpeeled, chunked
¼ cup quick-cooking tapioca
1 bay leaf
10-oz. pkg. frozen peas, or mixed vegetables

1. Brown beef in saucepan. Place in slow cooker. 2. Sprinkle with salt and pepper. Add remaining ingredients except frozen vegetables. Mix well. 3. Cover. Cook on low temp setting for temp setting for8-10 hours, or on high 4-5 hours. Add vegetables during last 1-2 hours of cooking.
**Per Serving:** Calories 257; Total Fat 4g; Saturated Fat 1.1g; Sodium 567mg; Carbs 36g; Fiber 6g; Sugar 7g; Protein 20g

## Gone-All-Day Low Calorie Casserole

**Prep time: 35 minutes | Cook time: 6-8 hours | Serves: 8**

1 cup wild rice, rinsed and drained
1 cup celery, chopped
1 cup carrots, chopped
2 4-oz. cans mushrooms, stems and pieces, drained
1 large onion, chopped
1 clove garlic, minced
½ cup slivered almonds
1 beef bouillon cube
1¼ teaspoon seasoned salt
2 lbs. boneless round steak, cut into 1-inch cubes, trimmed of fat
3 cups water

1. Place ingredients in order listed in slow cooker. 2. Cover. Cook on low temp setting for 6-8 hours or until rice is tender. Stir before serving.
**Per Serving:** Calories 264; Total Fat 9g; Saturated Fat 1.7g; Sodium 615mg; Carbs 23g; Fiber 4g; Sugar 4g; Protein 24g

## Classic Ernestine's Beef Stew

**Prep time: 20 minutes | Cook time: 7-8 hours | Serves: 6**

1½ lbs. stewing meat, cubed, trimmed of fat
2¼ cups no-added-salt tomato juice
10½-oz. can consomme
1 cup chopped celery
2 cups sliced carrots
4 tablespoon quick-cooking tapioca
1 medium onion, chopped
¼ teaspoon salt
¼ teaspoon pepper

1. Add all ingredients in a slow cooker pot. 2. Cover. Cook on low 7-8 hours.
**Per Serving:** Calories 193; Total Fat 4g; Saturated Fat 1.4g; Sodium 519mg; Carbs 17g; Fiber 3g; Sugar 7g; Protein 21g

## Slow Cooker Becky's Beef Stew

**Prep time: 30 minutes | Cook time: 6-8 hours | Serves: 8**

1½ lbs. beef stewing meat, cubed, trimmed of fat
2 10-oz. pkg. frozen vegetables—carrots, corn, peas
4 large potatoes, unpeeled, cubed
1 bay leaf
1 medium onion, chopped
15-oz. can stewed tomatoes of your choice—Italian, Mexican, or regular
8-oz. can tomato sauce
2 tablespoon Worcestershire sauce
1 teaspoon salt
¼ teaspoon pepper

1. Put meat on bottom of slow cooker. Layer frozen vegetables and potatoes over meat. 2. Mix all remaining ingredients and pour over other ingredients. 3. Cover. Cook on low 6-8 hours.
**Per Serving:** Calories 259; Total Fat 3g; Saturated Fat 1g; Sodium 506mg; Carbs 39g; Fiber 6g; Sugar 9g; Protein 19g

## Tasty Santa Fe Stew

**Prep time: 25 minutes | Cook time: 4-6 hours | Serves: 6**

2 lbs. sirloin, or stewing meat, cubed, trimmed of fat
2 tablespoon canola oil
1 large onion, diced
2 garlic cloves, minced
1½ cups water
1 tablespoon dried parsley flakes
1 beef bouillon cube
1 teaspoon ground cumin
¼ teaspoon salt
3 medium carrots, sliced
1 lb. frozen green beans
1 lb. frozen corn
4-oz. can diced green chilies

1. Sear meat, onion, and garlic in oil in a pan until meat is brown no longer pink. 2.Place all ingredients in slow cooker pot. 3. Cover. Cook on high temp setting for 30 minutes. Lower the heat and cook 4-6 hours.
**Per Serving:** Calories 322; Total Fat 11g; Saturated Fat 2.2g; Sodium 554mg; Carbs 30g; Fiber 7g; Sugar 10g; Protein 28g

## Low Carb, Full-Flavored Beef Stew

**Prep time: 30 minutes | Cook time: 8 hours | Serves: 6**

2 lb. beef roast, cubed, trimmed of fat
2 cups sliced carrots
2 cups diced potatoes, unpeeled
1 medium onion, sliced
1½ cups frozen or fresh peas
2 teaspoon quick-cooking tapioca
½ teaspoon salt
½ teaspoon pepper
8-oz. can tomato sauce
1 cup water
1 tablespoon brown sugar

1. Combine beef and vegetables in the slow cooker. Sprinkle with tapioca, salt, and pepper. 2. Combine tomato sauce and water. Pour over ingredients in slow cooker. Sprinkle with brown sugar. 3. Cover. Cook on low 8 hours.
**Per Serving:** Calories 271; Total Fat 6g; Saturated Fat 1.9g; Sodium 539mg; Carbs 26g; Fiber 5g; Sugar 11g; Protein 28g

## Lazy Day Beef Stew

**Prep time: 30 minutes | Cook time: 8 hours | Serves: 8**

2 lbs. stewing beef, cubed, trimmed of fat
2 cups diced carrots
2 cups diced potatoes, unpeeled
2 medium onions, chopped
1 cup chopped celery
10-oz. pkg. lima beans
2 teaspoon quick-cooking tapioca
1 teaspoon salt
½ teaspoon pepper
8-oz. can tomato sauce
1 cup water
1 Tablespoon brown sugar

1. Place beef in bottom of slow cooker. Add vegetables. 2. Sprinkle tapioca, salt, and pepper over ingredients. 3. Mix together tomato sauce and water. Pour over top. 4. Sprinkle brown sugar over all. 5. Cover. Cook on low 8 hours.
**Per Serving:** Calories 229; Total Fat 5g; Saturated Fat 1.4g; Sodium 558mg; Carbs 25g; Fiber 5g; Sugar 8g; Protein 22g

## Judy's Slow Cooker Beef Stew

**Prep time: 35 minutes | Cook time: 5-12 hours | Serves: 6**

2 lbs. stewing meat, cubed, trimmed of fat
5 medium carrots, sliced
1 medium onion, diced
3 ribs celery, diced
5 medium potatoes, cubed
28 oz. can tomatoes
⅓-½ cup quick-cooking tapioca
½ teaspoon salt
½ teaspoon pepper

1. Add all ingredients in a slow cooker. 2. Cover. Cook on low temp setting for 10-12 hours, or high 5-6 hours.
**Per Serving:** Calories 357; Total Fat 6g; Saturated Fat 1.8g; Sodium 518mg; Carbs 47g; Fiber 7g; Sugar 10g; Protein 29g

## Classic Beef Pot Roast

**Prep time: 30 minutes | Cook time: 10-12 hours | Serves: 10**

2 medium potatoes, cubed, or 2 medium sweet potatoes, cubed
8 small carrots, cut in small chunks
2 small onions, cut in wedges
2 ribs celery, chopped
2½-3 lb. beef chuck, or pot roast, trimmed of fat
2 tablespoon canola oil
¾ cup water, dry wine, or tomato juice
1 tablespoon Worcestershire sauce
1 teaspoon instant beef bouillon granules
1 teaspoon dried basil

1. Place vegetables in bottom of slow cooker. 2. Brown roast in oil in skillet. Place on top of vegetables. 3. Combine water, Worcestershire sauce, bouillon, and basil. Pour over meat and vegetables. 4. Cover. Cook on low 10-12 hours.
**Per Serving:** Calories 233; Total Fat 9g; Saturated Fat 2.1g; Sodium 231mg; Carbs 16g; Fiber 3g; Sugar 5g; Protein 22g

## Baked Lamb Shanks and Vegetable

**Prep time: 20 minutes | Cook time: 4-10 hours | Serves: 6**

1 medium onion, thinly sliced
2 small carrots, cut in thin strips
1 rib celery, chopped
3 (1 lb. each) lamb shanks, cracked, trimmed of fat
1-2 cloves garlic, split
⅛ teaspoon salt
¼ teaspoon pepper
1 teaspoon dried oregano
1 teaspoon dried thyme
2 bay leaves, crumbled
½ cup dry white wine
8-oz. can tomato sauce

1. Place onions with carrots, and celery in a slow cooker pot. 2. Rub lamb with garlic and season with salt and pepper. Add to slow cooker. 3. Mix remaining ingredients together in separate bowl and add to meat and vegetables. 4. Cover. Cook on low 8-10 hours, or high 4-6 hours.
**Per Serving:** Calories 182; Total Fat 5g; Saturated Fat 1.7g; Sodium 386mg; Carbs 7g; Fiber 2g; Sugar 4g; Protein 26g

## Braised Rump Roast and Vegetables

**Prep time: 20 minutes | Cook time: 5-12 hours | Serves: 8**

1½ lbs. small potatoes (about 10), or medium potatoes (about 4), halved, unpeeled
2 medium carrots, cubed
1 small onion, sliced
10-oz. pkg. frozen lima beans
1 bay leaf
2 tablespoon quick-cooking tapioca
2-2½ lb. boneless beef round rump, round tip, or pot roast, trimmed of fat
2 tablespoon canola oil
10¾-oz. can of condensed vegetable beef soup
¼ cup water
¼ teaspoon pepper

1. Place potatoes, carrots, and onions in slow cooker. Add frozen beans and bay leaf. Sprinkle with tapioca. 2. Sear roast until brown in oil in skillet. Place over vegetables in slow cooker. 3. Combine soup, water, and pepper. Pour over roast. 4. Cover. Cook on low temp setting for 10-12 hours, or high 5-6 hours. 5. Discard bay leaf before serving.

Per Serving: Calories 288; Total Fat 8g; Saturated Fat 1.9g; Sodium 34mg; Carbs 32g; Fiber 6g; Sugar 5g; Protein 22g

## Hearty and Nutritious New England Dinner

**Prep time: 40 minutes | Cook time: 8-10 hours | Serves: 8**

2 medium carrots, sliced
1 medium onion, sliced
2 cups water
1 tablespoon vinegar
1 celery rib, sliced
3 lb. boneless chuck roast, trimmed of fat
¼ teaspoon pepper
1 dry onion soup mix
1 bay leaf
Half head of cabbage, cut in wedges
2 tablespoon melted margarine, or butter
2 tablespoon flour
1 tablespoon dried minced onion
2 tablespoon prepared horseradish
½ teaspoon salt

1. Place carrots, onion, and celery in slow cooker. Place roast on top. Sprinkle with pepper. Add soup mix with water, vinegar, and bay leaf. 2. Cover. Cook on low temp setting for 7-9 hours. 3. Discard bay leaf. Add cabbage to juice in slow cooker. 4. Cover. Cook on high temp setting for 1 hour, or until cabbage is tender. 5. Melt margarine in saucepan. Stir in flour and onion. 6. Add 1½ cups liquid from slow cooker. Stir in horseradish and ½ teaspoon salt. Bring to boil. 7. Cook over low setting until thicken and smooth, about 2 minutes. Return to cooker and blend with remaining sauce in cooker. 8. When blended, serve over or alongside meat and vegetables.

Per Serving: Calories 234; Total Fat 9g; Saturated Fat 2.7g; Sodium 607mg; Carbs 11g; Fiber 3g; Sugar 6g; Protein 26g

## Traditional "Smothered" Steak

**Prep time: 20 minutes | Cook time: 8 hours | Serves: 6**

1½-lb. chuck, or round, steak, cut into strips, trimmed of fat
⅓ cup flour
¼ teaspoon pepper
1 large onion, sliced
1 green pepper, sliced
14½-oz. can of stewed tomatoes
4-oz. can of mushrooms, drained
2 Tablespoon soy sauce
10-oz. pkg. frozen French-style green beans

1. Layer steak in bottom of slow cooker. Sprinkle with flour, salt, and pepper. Stir well to coat steak. 2. Add remaining ingredients. Mix together gently. 3. Cover. Cook on low 8 hours. 4. Serve over rice.

Per Serving: Calories 222; Total Fat 6g; Saturated Fat 1.7g; Sodium 613mg; Carbs 19g; Fiber 4g; Sugar 7g; Protein 25g

## Beef and Beans Stew

**Prep time: 20 minutes | Cook time: 6-9 hours | Serves: 8**

1 tablespoon prepared mustard
1 tablespoon chili powder
½ teaspoon salt
¼ teaspoon pepper
1½-lb. boneless round steak, cut into thin slices, trimmed of fat
2 14½-oz. cans diced tomatoes, undrained
1 medium onion, chopped
1 beef bouillon cube, crushed
16-oz. can kidney beans, rinsed and drained

1. Combine mustard, chili powder, salt, and pepper. Add beef slices and toss to coat. Place meat in slow cooker. 2. Add tomatoes, onion, and bouillon. 3. Cover. Cook on low 6-8 hours. 4. Stir in beans. Cook 30 minutes longer. 5. Serve over rice.

Per Serving: Calories 182; Total Fat 4g; Saturated Fat 1.3g; Sodium 582mg; Carbs 16g; Fiber 4g; Sugar 6g; Protein 21g

## Easy Roast

**Prep time: 15 minutes | Cook time: 5-12 hours | Serves: 6**

2 lb. shoulder roast, trimmed of fat
1 teaspoon pepper
1 teaspoon garlic salt
1 small onion, sliced in rings
1 cup boiling water
1 beef bouillon cube

1. Place roast in slow cooker. Sprinkle with pepper, and garlic salt. Place onion rings on top. 2. Dissolve bouillon cube in water. Pour over roast. 3. Cover. Cook on low temp setting for 10-12 hours, or on high 5-6 hours.

Per Serving: Calories 148; Total Fat 5g; Saturated Fat 1.9g; Sodium 407mg; Carbs 2g; Fiber 0g; Sugar 1g; Protein 22g

## Crock Pot Three-Bean Burrito Bake

| Prep time: 20 minutes | Cook time: 8-10 hours | Serves: 8 |

1 tablespoon canola oil
1 onion, chopped
1 green bell pepper, chopped
2 garlic cloves, minced
16-oz. can pinto beans, drained
16-oz. can kidney beans, drained
15-oz. can black beans, drained
4-oz. can sliced black olives, drained
4-oz. can green chilies
2 15-oz. cans no-added-salt diced tomatoes
1 teaspoon chili powder
1 teaspoon ground cumin
6 flour tortillas
1 cup shredded Co-Jack cheese
Sour cream

1. Sauté onions, peppers, and garlic in skillet in oil. 2. Add beans and olives, chilies, tomatoes, chili powder, and cumin. 3. In greased slow cooker pot, layer ¾ cup vegetables, a tortilla, ⅓ cheese. Repeat layers ending with sauce. 4. Cover. Cook on low 8-10 hours. 5. Serve with sour cream.
**Per Serving:** Calories 346; Total Fat 11g; Saturated Fat 3.3g; Sodium 573mg; Carbs 48g; Fiber 12g; Sugar 8g; Protein 16g

## Authentic Beef Stew Bourguignonne

| Prep time: 25 minutes | Cook time: 10-12 hours | Serves: 6 |

2 lbs. stewing beef, cut in 1-inch cubes, trimmed of fat
2 tablespoon canola oil
10¾-oz. can of condensed golden cream of mushroom soup
1 teaspoon Worcestershire sauce
⅓ cup dry red wine
½ teaspoon dried oregano
¼ teaspoon salt
½ teaspoon pepper
½ cup chopped onions
½ cup chopped carrots
4-oz. can mushroom pieces, drained
½ cup cold water
¼ cup flour

1. Brown meat in oil in saucepan. Transfer to slow cooker. 2. Mix together soup, Worcestershire sauce, wine, oregano, salt and pepper, onions, carrots, and mushrooms. Pour over meat. 3. Cover. Cook on low 10-12 hours. 4. Combine water and flour. Stir into beef mixture. Turn cooker to high. 5. Cook until thickened and bubbly. 6. Serve over noodles.
**Per Serving:** Calories 266; Total Fat 12g; Saturated Fat 2.5g; Sodium 585mg; Carbs 12g; Fiber 2g; Sugar 2g; Protein 26g

## Easy Homemade Beef Stew

| Prep time: 35 minutes | Cook time: 6-8 hours | Serves: 6 |

1 lb. stewing beef
1 cup cubed turnip
2 medium potatoes, cubed, unpeeled
1 large onion, sliced
1 garlic clove, minced
2 large carrots, sliced
½ cup green beans, cut up
½ cup peas
1 bay leaf
½ teaspoon dried thyme
1 teaspoon chopped parsley
2 tablespoon tomato paste
2 tablespoon celery leaves
¼ teaspoon salt
¼ teaspoon pepper
1 qt., or 2 14½-oz. cans, lower-sodium beef broth

1. Place meat, vegetables, and seasonings in the slow cooker. Pour broth over all. 2. Cover. Cook on low 6-8 hours.
**Per Serving:** Calories 175; Total Fat 3g; Saturated Fat 0.9g; Sodium 466mg; Carbs 21g; Fiber 5g; Sugar 6g; Protein 16g

## Home-Style Pot Roast with Gravy and Vegetables

| Prep time: 30 minutes | Cook time: 4-10 hours | Serves: 6 |

3-4 lb. bottom round, rump, or arm roast, trimmed of fat
¼ teaspoon salt
2-3 teaspoon pepper
2 tablespoon flour
¼ cup cold water
1 teaspoon Kitchen Bouquet, or gravy browning seasoning sauce
1 garlic clove, minced
2 medium onions, cut in wedges
4 medium potatoes, cubed, unpeeled
2 carrots, quartered
1 green bell pepper, sliced

1. Place roast in slow cooker. Sprinkle with salt and pepper. 2. Make paste of flour and cold water. Stir in Kitchen Bouquet and spread over roast. 3. Add garlic, onions, potatoes, carrots, and green pepper. 4. Cover. Cook on low temp setting for 8-10 hours, or high 4-5 hours. 5. Taste and adjust seasonings before serving.
**Per Serving:** Calories 336; Total Fat 8g; Saturated Fat 2.9g; Sodium 577mg; Carbs 28g; Fiber 4g; Sugar 7g; Protein 36g

## Three-Pepper Steak Stew

Prep time: 15 minutes | Cook time: 5-8 hours | Serves: 10

3 bell peppers—one red, one orange, and one yellow pepper, cut into ¼"-thick slices
2 garlic cloves, sliced
1 large onion, sliced
1 teaspoon ground cumin
½ teaspoon dried oregano
1 bay leaf
3-lb. beef flank steak, cut in ¼-½"-thick slices across the grain
Salt to taste
14½-oz. can of diced tomatoes in juice
Jalapeño chilies, sliced, optional

1. Place sliced peppers, garlic, onion, cumin, oregano, and bay leaf in the slow cooker. Stir gently to mix. 2. Put steak slices on top of vegetable mixture. Season with salt. 3. Spoon tomatoes with juice over top. Sprinkle with jalapeño pepper slices if you wish. Do not stir. 4. Cover. Cook on low temp setting for 5-8 hours, depending on your slow cooker. Check after 5 hours to see if meat is tender. If not, continue cooking until tender but not dry.
Per Serving: Calories 220; Total Fat 8g; Saturated Fat 3g; Sodium 135mg; Carbs 7g; Fiber 1g; Sugar 3g; Protein 30g

## Simple Succulent Steak

Prep time: 20 minutes | Cook time: 9-10 hours | Serves: 4

1½-lb. round steak, cut ½-¾-inch thick, trimmed of fat
¼ cup flour
½ teaspoon salt
¼ teaspoon pepper
¼ teaspoon paprika
2 medium onions, sliced
4-oz. can of sliced mushrooms, drained
½ cup beef broth
2 teaspoon Worcestershire sauce
2 tablespoon flour
3 tablespoon water

1. Mix together ¼ cup flour, salt, pepper, and paprika. 2. Cut steak into 5-6 pieces. Dredge steak in seasoned flour until lightly coated. 3. Layer half of onions, half of the steak, and half of mushrooms into cooker. Repeat. 4. Combine beef broth and Worcestershire sauce. Pour over mixture in slow cooker. 5. Cover. Cook on low 8-10 hours. 6. Place steak to serving platter and keep warm. Mix together 2 Tablespoon flour with water. Stir into drippings and cook on high temp setting until thickened, about 10 minutes. Pour over steak and serve.
Per Serving: Calories 295; Total Fat 8g; Saturated Fat 2.6g; Sodium 601mg; Carbs 18g; Fiber 3g; Sugar 6g; Protein 36g

## Classic Stroganoff Steak

Prep time: 15 minutes | Cook time: 3-7 hours | Serves: 6

2 tablespoon flour
½ teaspoon garlic powder
½ teaspoon pepper
¼ teaspoon paprika
1¾-lb. boneless beef round steak, trimmed of fat
10¾-oz. can reduced-sodium, 98% fat-free cream of mushroom soup
½ cup water
1 envelope sodium-free dried onion soup mix
9-oz. jar sliced mushrooms, drained
½ cup fat-free sour cream
1 tablespoon minced fresh parsley

1. Add flour, garlic powder, pepper, and paprika in a slow cooker. 2. Cut meat into 1½ × ½-inch strips. Stir in flour mix and toss until meat is well coated. 3. Add mushroom soup, water, and soup mix. Stir until well blended. 4. Cover. Cook on high 3-3½ hours, or low 6-7 hours. 5. Stir in mushrooms, sour cream, and parsley. Cover and cook on high temp setting for 10-15 minutes, or until heated through.
Per Serving: Calories 256; Total Fat 7g; Saturated Fat 2.4g; Sodium 390mg; Carbs 17g; Fiber 2g; Sugar 5g; Protein 29g

## Tasty Garlic Beef Stroganoff

Prep time: 20 minutes | Cook time: 7-8 hours | Serves: 6

2 teaspoons sodium-free beef bouillon powder
2 4½-oz. jars sliced mushrooms, drained with juice reserved
1 cup mushroom juice, with boiling water added to make a full cup
10¾-oz. can 98% fat-free, lower-sodium cream of mushroom soup
1 large onion, chopped
3 garlic cloves, minced
1 tablespoon Worcestershire sauce
1½ lbs. boneless round steak, cut into thin strips, trimmed of fat
2 tablespoon canola oil
6-oz. fat-free cream cheese, cubed and softened

1. Dissolve bouillon in mushroom juice and water in slow cooker. 2. Add soup, mushrooms, onion, garlic, and Worcestershire sauce. 3. Sauté beef in oil in skillet. Transfer to slow cooker and stir into sauce. 4. Cover. Cook on low 7-8 hours. Turn off heat. 5. Stir in cream cheese until smooth. 6. Serve over noodles.
Per Serving: Calories 202; Total Fat 8g; Saturated Fat 1.8g; Sodium 474mg; Carbs 10g; Fiber 2g; Sugar 4g; Protein 21g

## Homemade Machaca Beef

Prep time: 15 minutes | Cook time: 10-12 hours | Serves: 12

1½-lb. beef roast
1 large onion, sliced
4-oz. can chopped green chilies
2 beef bouillon cubes
1½ teaspoon dry mustard
½ teaspoon garlic powder
1 teaspoon seasoning salt
½ teaspoon pepper
1 cup salsa

1. Combine all ingredients instead of salsa in slow cooker. Add just enough water to cover. 2. Cover cooker and cook on low for 10-12 hours, or until beef is tender. Drain and reserve liquid. 3. Shred beef with help of forks. 4. Combine beef with salsa, and reserved liquid to make desired consistency. 5. Use this filling for burritos, chalupas, quesadillas, or tacos.
Per Serving: Calories 69; Total Fat 2g; Saturated Fat 0.7g; Sodium 392mg; Carbs 3g; Fiber 1g; Sugar 2g; Protein 9g

## Slow Cooker Roast Beef with Apple and Onion

**Prep time: 25 minutes | Cook time: 5-6 hours | Serves: 8**

3-lb. boneless beef roast, cut in half, trimmed of fat
2 Tablespoon canola oil
1 cup water
1 teaspoon seasoning salt
½ teaspoon soy sauce
½ teaspoon Worcestershire sauce
¼ teaspoon garlic powder
1 large tart apple, quartered
1 large onion, sliced
2 tablespoon cornstarch
2 tablespoon water

1. Sea roast on all sides in oil in skillet. Transfer to slow cooker. 2. Add water to skillet to loosen browned bits. Pour over roast. 3. Sprinkle with seasoning salt, soy sauce, Worcestershire sauce, and garlic powder. 4. Top with apple and onion. 5. Cover. Cook on low 5-6 hours. 6. Remove roast and onion. Discard apple. Let stand 15 minutes. 7. To make gravy, pour juices from roast into saucepan and simmer until reduced to 2 cups. 8. Mix cornstarch and water into slurry. Stir into beef broth. 9. Bring to boil. stir for 2 minutes until thicken. 10. Slice pot roast and serve with gravy.
**Per Serving:** Calories 208; Total Fat 9g; Saturated Fat 2.4g; Sodium 265mg; Carbs 5g; Fiber 1g; Sugar 2g; Protein 24g

## Healthy Swedish Meatballs

**Prep time: 40 minutes | Cook time: 4-5 hours | Serves: 12**

¾ lb. ground beef
½ lb. ground pork
½ cup minced onions
¾ cup fine dry bread crumbs
1 tablespoon minced parsley
1 teaspoon salt
⅛ teaspoon pepper
½ teaspoon garlic powder
1 tablespoon Worcestershire sauce
1 egg
½ cup fat-free milk
2 tablespoon canola oil
**Gravy:**
¼ cup flour
¼ teaspoon salt
¼ teaspoon garlic powder
⅛ teaspoon pepper
1 teaspoon paprika
2 cups boiling water
¾ cup fat-free sour cream

1. Combine meats, onions, bread crumbs, parsley, salt, pepper, garlic powder, Worcestershire sauce, egg, and milk. 2. Shape into balls. Brown in oil in skillet. Reserve drippings, and place meatballs in slow cooker. 3. Cover. Cook on high 10-15 minutes. 4. Stir flour, salt, garlic powder, pepper, and paprika into hot drippings in skillet. Stir in water and sour cream. Pour over meatballs. 5. Cover. Reduce heat to low. Cook 4-5 hours. 6. Serve over rice or noodles.
**Per Serving:** Calories 168; Total Fat 9g; Saturated Fat 2.5g; Sodium 368mg; Carbs 11g; Fiber 0g; Sugar 2g; Protein 11g

## Savory Sweet Crock Pot Roast

**Prep time: 20 minutes | Cook time: 12-16 hours | Serves: 8**

3-lb. blade, or chuck, roast, trimmed of fat
2 tablespoon canola oil
1 onion, chopped
10¾-oz. can reduced-sodium, 99% fat-free cream of mushroom soup
½ cup water
¼ cup sugar
¼ cup vinegar
¾ teaspoon salt
1 teaspoon prepared mustard
1 teaspoon Worcestershire sauce

1. Sear meat until brown on both side in hot oil in a saucepan. Put in slow cooker. 2. Blend together remaining ingredients. Pour over meat. 3. Cover. Cook on low 12-16 hours.
**Per Serving:** Calories 241; Total Fat 10g; Saturated Fat 2.7g; Sodium 424mg; Carbs 11g; Fiber 0g; Sugar 8g; Protein 25g

## Slow Cooker Dilled Pot Roast

**Prep time: 15 minutes | Cook time: 7-9 hours | Serves: 6**

3-lb. beef pot roast, trimmed of fat
¾ teaspoon salt
¼ teaspoon pepper
2 teaspoon dried dillweed, divided
¾ cup water, divided
1 tablespoon vinegar
3 tablespoon flour
1 cup fat-free sour cream

1. Sprinkle both sides of meat with salt, pepper, and 1 teaspoon dill. Place in slow cooker. Add ¼ cup water and vinegar. 2. Cover. Cook on low temp setting for 7-9 hours, or until tender. Remove meat from pot. Turn to high. 3. Dissolve flour in ½ cup water. Stir into meat drippings. Stir in additional 1 teaspoon dill. Cook on high 5 minutes. Stir in sour cream. Cook on high another 5 minutes. 4. Slice meat and serve with sour cream sauce over top.
**Per Serving:** Calories 260; Total Fat 8g; Saturated Fat 2.9g; Sodium 403mg; Carbs 10g; Fiber 0g; Sugar 3g; Protein 34g

## Cowboy Casserole Stew

**Prep time: 25 minutes | Cook time: 5-6 hours | Serves: 6**

1 medium onion, chopped
1¼ lbs. 90%-lean ground beef, browned, drained, and patted dry
6 medium potatoes, sliced, unpeeled
1 clove garlic, minced
16-oz. can kidney beans
15-oz. can diced tomatoes mixed with 2 Tablespoon flour, or 10¾-oz. can tomato soup
¼ teaspoon salt
¼ teaspoon pepper

1. Layer onions, ground beef, potatoes, garlic, and beans in a slow cooker. 2. Spread tomatoes or soup over all. Sprinkle with salt and pepper. 3. Cover. Cook on low temp setting for 5-6 hours, or until potatoes are tender.
**Per Serving:** Calories 373; Total Fat 8g; Saturated Fat 3.2g; Sodium 567mg; Carbs 48g; Fiber 7g; Sugar 8g; Protein 27g

## Beef Braised with Mushroom Barley

**Prep time: 10 minutes | Cook time: 6-8 hours | Serves: 6**

1 cup pearl barley
½ cup onion, diced
6½-oz. can mushroom, undrained
1 teaspoon minced garlic
1 teaspoon Italian seasoning
¼ teaspoon black pepper
2-lb. beef chuck roast, visible fat removed
1¾ cups beef broth

1. Put barley, onion, mushrooms with liquid, and garlic in slow cooker. 2. Sprinkle seasoning and pepper over top. 3. Add roast. Pour broth over all. 4. Cover. Cook 6-8 hours on low, or until meat is fork-tender and barley is also tender.
Per Serving: Calories 275; Total Fat 5g; Saturated Fat 2g; Sodium 395mg; Carbs 29g; Fiber 6g; Sugar 1g; Protein 26g

## Traditional Hungarian Goulash

**Prep time: 20 minutes | Cook time: 8 hours | Serves: 6**

2 lbs. beef chuck, cubed, trimmed of fat
1 medium onion, sliced
½ teaspoon garlic powder
½ cup ketchup
2 tablespoon Worcestershire sauce
1 tablespoon brown sugar
¼ teaspoon salt
2 teaspoons paprika
½ teaspoon dry mustard
1 cup cold water
¼ cup flour
½ cup water

1. Place meat in slow cooker. Add onion. 2. Add garlic powder along with ketchup, Worcestershire sauce, brown sugar, salt, paprika, mustard, and 1 cup water. Pour over meat. 3. Cover. Cook on low 8 hours. 4. Dissolve flour in ½ cup water. Add into meat mix. Cook on high temp setting until thickened, about 10 minutes. 5. Serve over noodles.
Per Serving: Calories 207; Total Fat 6g; Saturated Fat 2g; Sodium 444mg; Carbs 15g; Fiber 1g; Sugar 7g; Protein 23g

## Tender Beef Burgundy

**Prep time: 20 minutes | Cook time: 8-10 hours | Serves: 6**

5 medium onions, thinly sliced
2 lbs. stewing meat, cubed, trimmed of fat
1½ Tablespoon flour
½ lb. fresh mushrooms, sliced
1 teaspoon salt
¼ teaspoon dried marjoram
¼ teaspoon dried thyme
⅛ teaspoon pepper
¾ cup beef broth
1½ cups burgundy wine

1. Place onions in slow cooker. 2. Dredge meat in flour. Put in slow cooker. 3. Add mushrooms, salt, marjoram, thyme, and pepper. 4. Pour in broth and wine. 5. Cover. Cook 8-10 hours on low. 6. Serve over cooked noodles.
Per Serving: Calories 219; Total Fat 6g; Saturated Fat 1.9g; Sodium 576mg; Carbs 14g; Fiber 2g; Sugar 5g; Protein 26g

## Authentic Chinese Pot Roast

**Prep time: 20 minutes | Cook time: 8-10 hours | Serves: 6**

3-lb. boneless beef pot roast, trimmed of fat
2 tablespoon flour
1 tablespoon canola oil
2 large onions, chopped
¼ cup light soy sauce
¼ cup water
½ teaspoon ground ginger

1. Dredge roast in flour and sear on both sides in oil until brown in saucepan. Place in slow cooker. 2. Top with onions. 3. Combine soy sauce, water, and ginger. Pour over meat. 4. Cover. Cook on high 10 minutes. Lower the heat to low and cook 8-10 hours. 5. Slice and serve with rice.
Per Serving: Calories 272; Total Fat 10g; Saturated Fat 3.1g; Sodium 446mg; Carbs 9g; Fiber 1g; Sugar 4g; Protein 34g

## Red Wine Tender Roast

**Prep time: 15 minutes | Cook time: 8-10 hours | Serves: 10**

2½-lb. chuck roast
1 cup thinly sliced onion
½ cup chopped apple, peeled or unpeeled
3 cloves garlic, chopped
1 cup red wine
Salt and pepper

1. Put roast in slow cooker. Layer onions, apples, and garlic on top of roast. 2. Carefully pour wine over roast without disturbing its toppings. 3. Sprinkle with salt and pepper. 4. Cover. Cook on low temp setting for 8-10 hours.
Per Serving: Calories 160; Total Fat 5g; Saturated Fat 2g; Sodium 85mg; Carbs 2g; Fiber 0g; Sugar 1g; Protein 25g

## Chuck Wagon Beef Stew

**Prep time: 20 minutes | Cook time: 8-10 hours | Serves: 10**

4-lb. boneless chuck roast, trimmed of fat
1 teaspoon garlic salt
¼ teaspoon black pepper
2 tablespoon canola oil
6 garlic cloves, minced
1 large onion, sliced
1 cup water
1 bouillon cube
2 teaspoons instant coffee
1 bay leaf, or 1 Tablespoon mixed Italian herbs
3 tablespoon cold water
2 tablespoon cornstarch

1. Sprinkle roast with garlic salt and pepper. Brown on all sides in oil in saucepan. Place in slow cooker. 2. Sauté garlic and onion in meat drippings in saucepan. 3. Add water, bouillon cube, and coffee. Cook for several minutes, stirring until drippings loosen. Pour over meat in cooker. 4. Add bay leaf or herbs. 5. Cover. Cook on low 8-10 hours, or until very tender. Remove bay leaf and discard. Remove meat to serving platter and keep warm. 6. Mix water and cornstarch together until paste forms. Stir into hot liquid and onions in cooker. 7. Cover. Cook 10 minutes on high or until thickened. 8. Slice meat and serve with gravy over top or on the side.
Per Serving: Calories 211; Total Fat 9g; Saturated Fat 2.5g; Sodium 271mg; Carbs 4g; Fiber 1g; Sugar 2g; Protein 26g

## Classic French Dip Roast

**Prep time: 15 minutes | Cook time: 5-12 hours | Serves: 8**

1 large onion, sliced
3-lb. beef bottom roast, trimmed of fat
½ cup dry white wine, or water
½ of 1-oz. pkg. dry au jus gravy mix
2 cups lower sodium 100% fat-free beef broth

1. Place onion in slow cooker. Add roast. 2. Combine wine and gravy mix. Pour over roast. 3. Add enough broth to cover roast. 4. Cover. Cook on high temp setting for 5-6 hours, or low 10-12 hours. 5. Slicing thinly across the grain when serving.
**Per Serving:** Calories 177; Total Fat 6g; Saturated Fat 2.2g; Sodium 376mg; Carbs 3g; Fiber 1g; Sugar 2g; Protein 25g

## Crock Pot Dripped Beef

**Prep time: 10 minutes | Cook time: 6-7 hours | Serves: 8**

3 lb. chuck roast, trimmed of fat
½ teaspoon salt
1 teaspoon seasoned salt
1 teaspoon white pepper
1 tablespoon rosemary
1 tablespoon dried oregano
1 tablespoon garlic powder
1 cup water

1. Add all ingredients in a slow cooker pot. 2. Cover. Cook on low 6-7 hours. 3. Shred meat using two forks. Strain liquid and return liquid and meat to slow cooker. Serve meat and au jus over mashed potatoes, noodles, or rice.
**Per Serving:** Calories 165; Total Fat 6g; Saturated Fat 2.2g; Sodium 384mg; Carbs 2g; Fiber 1g; Sugar 0g; Protein 24g

## Low calorie Old World Sauerbraten

**Prep time: 15 minutes | Cook time: 6-8 hours | Serves: 8**

3½-lb. beef rump roast, trimmed of fat
1 cup water
1 cup vinegar
1 lemon, sliced
10 whole cloves
1 large onion, sliced
4 bay leaves
6 whole peppercorns
1 tablespoon salt
2 tablespoon sugar
12 gingersnaps, crumbled

1. Place meat in a deep ceramic or glass bowl. 2. Combine water, vinegar, lemon, cloves, onion, bay leaves, peppercorns, salt, and sugar. Pour over meat. Cover and refrigerate 24-36 hours. Turn meat several times during marinating. 3. Place beef in slow cooker. Pour 1 cup marinade over meat.4. Cover. Cook on low 6-8 hours. Remove meat. 5. Strain meat juices and return to pot. Turn to high. Stir in gingersnaps. Cover and cook on high 10-14 minutes. Slice meat. Pour finished sauce over meat.
**Per Serving:** Calories 235; Total Fat 8g; Saturated Fat 2.6g; Sodium 416mg; Carbs 10g; Fiber 0g; Sugar 4g; Protein 29g

## Cheesy Chili Rice

**Prep time: 15 minutes | Cook time: 4 hours | Serves: 6**

1 lb. extra-lean ground beef
1 medium onion, diced
1 teaspoon dried basil
1 teaspoon dried oregano
16-oz. can light red kidney beans
15½-oz. can chili beans
1½ cups stewed tomatoes, drained
2 cups cooked rice
6 tablespoon fat-free grated cheddar cheese

1. Sear beef and onion in skillet until brown and juices are released. Drain. Season with basil and oregano. 2. Combine all ingredients except rice and cheese in slow cooker. 3. Cover. Cook on low 4 hours. 4. Serve over cooked rice. Top with cheese.
**Per Serving:** Calories 371; Total Fat 9g; Saturated Fat 3.2g; Sodium 745mg; Carbs 46g; Fiber 9g; Sugar 7g; Protein 26g

## Simple Spanish Rice

**Prep time: 20 minutes | Cook time: 6-10 hours | Serves: 8**

1¾ lbs. 90%-lean ground beef, browned
2 medium onions, chopped
2 medium green peppers, chopped
28-oz. can tomatoes
8-oz. can tomato sauce
1½ cups water
2½ teaspoon chili powder
½ teaspoon salt
2 teaspoon Worcestershire sauce
1½ cups rice, uncooked

1. Add all ingredients in a slow cooker pot. 2. Cover. Cook on low 8-10 hours, or high 6 hours.
**Per Serving:** Calories 335; Total Fat 9g; Saturated Fat 3.3g; Sodium 550mg; Carbs 40g; Fiber 3g; Sugar 8g; Protein 24g

## Crock Pot Swedish Cabbage Rolls

**Prep time: 35 minutes | Cook time: 7-9 hours | Serves: 6**

12 large cabbage leaves
1 egg, beaten
¼ cup fat-free milk
¼ cup finely chopped onions
¾ teaspoon salt
¼ teaspoon pepper
1 lb. ground beef, browned and drained
1 cup cooked rice
8-oz. can tomato sauce
1 tablespoon brown sugar
1 tablespoon lemon Juice
1 teaspoon Worcestershire sauce

1. Immerse cabbage leaves in boiling water for about 3 minutes or until limp. Drain. 2. Combine egg, milk, onions, salt, pepper, beef, and rice. Place about ¼ cup meat mixture in center of each leaf. Fold in sides and roll ends over meat. Place in slow cooker. 3. Combine tomato sauce, brown sugar, lemon juice, and Worcestershire sauce. Pour over cabbage rolls. 4. Cover. Cook on low 7-9 hours.
**Per Serving:** Calories 219; Total Fat 9g; Saturated Fat 3.4g; Sodium 603mg; Carbs 18g; Fiber 2g; Sugar 7g; Protein 17g

## Green Chili Stew with Pork

| Prep time: 25 minutes | Cook time: 4-6 hours | Serves: 8 |

2 Tablespoon oil
2 garlic cloves, minced
1 large onion, diced
1 lb. extra-lean ground sirloin
⅓ lb. ground pork
3 cups reduced-sodium chicken broth
2 cups water
2 4-oz. cans diced green chilies
4 large potatoes, diced
10-oz. pkg. frozen corn
1 teaspoon black pepper
1 teaspoon crushed dried oregano
½ teaspoon ground cumin
½ teaspoon salt

1. Brown onion, garlic, sirloin, and pork in oil in skillet. Cook until meat is no longer pink. Drain. 2. Add all ingredients in a slow cooker pot. 3. Cover. Cook on low 4-6 hours, or until potatoes are soft.
Per Serving: Calories 309; Total Fat 11g; Saturated Fat 3.1g; Sodium 529mg; Carbs 33g; Fiber 5g; Sugar 5g; Protein 20g

## Beef and Lentil Stew

| Prep time: 30 minutes | Cook time: 6-8 hours | Serves: 12 |

1 medium onion
3 whole cloves
5 cups water
1 lb. dry lentils
1 teaspoon salt
1 bay leaf
1 lb. ground beef
½ cup ketchup
¼ cup molasses
2 tablespoon brown sugar
1 teaspoon dry mustard
¼ teaspoon Worcestershire sauce
1 medium onion, finely chopped

1. Stick cloves into whole onion. Set aside. 2. In a pan, combine water, lentils, salt, bay leaf, and whole onion with cloves. Simmer 30 minutes. 3. Meanwhile, Add all remaining ingredients in slow cooker pot. Add in simmered ingredients also from pan. Add additional water if mixture seems dry. 4. Cover. Cook on low 6 hours and check to see if the lentils are tender. If not, cook an additional hour and check again. Repeat if needed.
Per Serving: Calories 230; Total Fat 4g; Saturated Fat 1.5g; Sodium 342mg; Carbs 32g; Fiber 9g; Sugar 11g; Protein 17g

## Easy Meal-in-One-Casserole

| Prep time: 20 minutes | Cook time: 3 hours | Serves: 8 |

1 lb. ground beef
1 medium onion, chopped
1 medium green pepper, chopped
15¼-oz. can whole kernel corn, drained
4-oz. can mushroom, drained
¼ teaspoon pepper
11-oz. jar salsa
5 cups uncooked medium egg noodles
28-oz. can no-added-salt diced tomatoes, undrained
1 cup shredded fat-free cheddar cheese

1. Cook beef and onion in saucepan over medium heat until meat is no longer pink. Drain. Transfer to slow cooker. 2. Top with green pepper, corn, and mushrooms. Sprinkle with pepper. Pour salsa over mushrooms. 3. Cover and cook on low 3 hours. 4. Cook noodles according to package in separate pan. 5. Drain and add to slow cooker after mixture in cooker has cooked for 3 hours. Top with tomatoes. Sprinkle with cheese.
Per Serving: Calories 282; Total Fat 7g; Saturated Fat 2.7g; Sodium 393mg; Carbs 34g; Fiber 4g; Sugar 8g; Protein 21g

## Homemade Mary Ellen's Barbecued Meatballs

| Prep time: 40 minutes | Cook time: 5 hours | Serves: 10 |

**Meatballs:**
¾ lb. ground beef
¾ cup bread crumbs
1½ tablespoon minced onion
½ teaspoon horseradish
3 drops Tabasco sauce
2 eggs, beaten
¼ teaspoon salt
½ teaspoon pepper
1 Tablespoon canola oil
**Sauce:**
¾ cup ketchup
½ cup water
¼ cup cider vinegar
2 tablespoon brown sugar
1 tablespoon minced onion
2 teaspoon horseradish
1 teaspoon dry mustard
3 drops Tabasco
Dash pepper

1. Combine all meatball ingredients except canola oil. Shape into ¾-inch balls. Brown in oil in skillet. Place in slow cooker. 2. Combine all sauce ingredients. Pour over meatballs. 3. Cover. Cook on low 5 hours.
Per Serving: Calories 148; Total Fat 6g; Saturated Fat 1.8g; Sodium 378mg; Carbs 14g; Fiber 1g; Sugar 6g; Protein 9g

## Low Fat Cranberry Meatballs

**Prep time: 30 minutes | Cook time: 2 hours | Serves: 30**

**Meatballs**
2 lbs. 90%-lean ground beef
⅓ cup parsley flakes
2 tablespoon soy sauce
½ teaspoon garlic powder
2 tablespoon minced onion
1 cup cornflake crumbs
2 eggs
½ cup ketchup

**Sauce**
14-oz. can jellied cranberry sauce
12-oz. bottle chili sauce
2 tablespoon brown sugar
1 tablespoon lemon juice

1. In a large mixing bowl, combine meatball ingredients until well mixed. 2. Form into 50-60 meatballs and put in lightly greased 9 × 13 baking pan. 3. Bake at 350° temp setting for about 30 minutes, or until meatballs are cooked through. (Cut one open to test.) 4. While meatballs are baking, combine sauce ingredients in a saucepan. Heat over low heat until cranberry sauce and brown sugar melt. Stir frequently. 5. Place baked meatballs in the slow cooker. Pour sauce over meatballs, making sure that all are covered in sauce if you've layered them into the cooker. 6. Cover. Cook on low temp setting for 2 hours, or until sauce is bubbly. 7. Turn slow cooker to warm and serve with toothpicks.
**Per Serving:** Calories 105; Total Fat 3g; Saturated Fat 1g; Sodium 310mg; Carbs 12g; Fiber 1g; Sugar 7g; Protein 7g

## All-Day Pot Roast

**Prep time: 20 minutes | Cook time: 7-9 hours | Serves: 10**

3 carrots, cut in 1" chunks
4 medium potatoes, cut in 1" chunks
1 lb. frozen or fresh green beans
1 large onion, cut in wedges
1½ cups water
3-lb. beef roast, visible fat removed
2 cloves garlic, minced
Salt to taste
Pepper to taste
10¾-oz. can cream of mushroom soup
2 tablespoon Worcestershire sauce
1 recipe Onion Soup Mix, Salt-Free

1. Place vegetables and water into slow cooker. 2. Place beef roast on top of vegetables. 3. Sprinkle garlic salt and pepper to taste over the meat.3. Add cream of mushroom soup over spiced meat. 4. Gently pour Worcestershire sauce over soup. 5. Sprinkle with dry onion soup mix. 6. Cover. Cook on high 5-6 hours.7. Reset temperature to low setting. Continue cooking 2-3 more hours, until vegetables and meat are tender.
**Per Serving:** Calories 290; Total Fat 8g; Saturated Fat 3g; Sodium 340mg; Carbs 26g; Fiber 4g; Sugar 5g; Protein 29g

## Slow Cooker Sweet and Sour Meatballs

**Prep time: 45 minutes | Cook time: 6 hours | Serves: 8**

**Meatballs:**
2 lbs. ground beef
1¼ cups bread crumbs
¼ teaspoon salt
1 teaspoon pepper
2-3 Tablespoon Worcestershire sauce
1 egg
½ teaspoon garlic salt
¼ cup finely chopped onions

**Sauce:**
20-oz. can pineapple chunks, juice reserved
½ cup chopped green peppers
3 tablespoon cornstarch
¼ cup cold water
1 cups ketchup
2 tablespoon Worcestershire sauce
¼ teaspoon salt
¼ teaspoon pepper
¼ teaspoon garlic salt

1. Combine all meatball ingredients. Shape into 60 meatballs. Brown in skillet, rolling so all sides are browned. Place meatballs in slow cooker. 2. Pour juice from pineapples into skillet. Stir into drippings. 3. Combine cornstarch and cold water. Add to skillet and stir until thickened. 4. Stir in ketchup and Worcestershire sauce. Season with salt, pepper, and garlic salt. Add green peppers and pineapples. Pour over meatballs. 5. Cover. Cook on low 6 hours.
**Per Serving:** Calories 150; Total Fat 5g; Saturated Fat 1.9g; Sodium 430mg; Carbs 16g; Fiber 1g; Sugar 7g; Protein 10g

## Beef and Vegetables Stew

**Prep time: 25 minutes | Cook time: 6-8 hours | Serves: 6**

3 cups grated raw carrots
2½ cups onions, sliced thin
6 cups grated raw potatoes
1 lb. 90%-lean ground beef, browned and drained
Salt to taste
Pepper to taste
1 tablespoon Worcestershire sauce
10¾-oz. can cream of mushroom soup

1. Grate and slice vegetables either in the amounts above, or to suit tastes of those you're serving and size of your slow cooker. 2. Place layer of grated carrots in bottom. 3. Lay onion slices on top of carrots. Season with salt and pepper. 4. Place potatoes on top of onions. 5. Put ground beef on top of vegetables. 6. Combine soup and Worcestershire sauce in a small bowl. 7. Spoon soup mixture over all. 8. Cover. Cook 6-8 hours on low, or until vegetables are as tender as you like them.
**Per Serving:** Calories 300; Total Fat 9g; Saturated Fat 3.5g; Sodium 535mg; Carbs 34g; Fiber 5g; Sugar 7g; Protein 19g

# Chapter 6 Stew, Soups, Salads, and Sandwiches Recipes

| | | | |
|---|---|---|---|
| 72 | Bacon and Fruit Baked Bean Casserole | 78 | Burger with Jicama Chips |
| 72 | Slow Cooker Apple Bean Bake | 79 | Quinoa and Cucumber Feta Salad |
| 72 | Sweet and Sour Beans with Bacon Drippings | 79 | Apple and Bulgur Salad |
| 72 | Spiced Lamb Chops | 79 | Nutritional Sweet Beet Grain Bowl |
| 72 | Authentic Mexican Tortilla Soup | 79 | Grilled Romaine with White Beans Salad |
| 73 | Pizza Beans with Tomato and Sausage | 79 | Easy Chickpea Fattoush Salad |
| 73 | New Orleans Red Beans with Sausage | 80 | Oven Roasted Carrot and Quinoa with Goat Cheese |
| 73 | Low-Fat Cajun Sausage and Beans | 80 | Roasted Tomato Tartine with Ricotta Cheese |
| 73 | Slow Cooker Four-Bean Medley | 80 | Simple Cauli-Lettuce Wraps |
| 73 | Easy Low Cooker Beans with Sausage | 80 | Miso Baked Tempeh and Carrot Wraps |
| 73 | Slow Cooker Kidney Beans with Apple | 81 | Chicken Salad with Apricots and Almonds |
| 74 | Creole Black Beans with Celery and Green Pepper | 81 | Green Tofu Soup |
| 74 | Tuna Noodle Casserole with Almonds Topping | 81 | Shortcut Wonton Soup |
| 74 | Cowboy Beans with Sliced Bacon | 81 | Lentil Sloppy Joes with Roasted Asparagus |
| 74 | New Mexico - Style Pinto Beans | 81 | Homemade Turkey Pastrami and Pimento Cheese Sandwich |
| 74 | Spicy Asian-Style Tofu Salad | 82 | Easy Turkey Taco Soup |
| 74 | Simple Broccoli Slaw Crab Salad | 82 | Super Easy Minted Sweet Pea Soup |
| 75 | Fresh Chickpea and Salmon Salad Dijon | 82 | Homemade Egg Drop Soup |
| 75 | Chicken and Mushroom Soup | 82 | Manhattan-Style Seafood Chowder |
| 75 | Tasty Herbed Chicken Stew with Noodles | 82 | Shaved Asparagus Salad with Chile-Lime Dressing |
| 75 | Healthy Cream of Carrot Soup | 83 | Roasted Tomato-Basil Soup with Grilled Cheese Croutons |
| 75 | Traditional English Beef Stew | 83 | West African Peanut Soup |
| 75 | Fresh Fish Chowder Soup | 83 | Chickpea and Spinach Soup |
| 76 | Hearty Italian Minestrone Soup | 84 | Traditional Golden Chicken Soup |
| 76 | Daily Lentil Soup | 84 | Easy Smoked Turkey Chili |
| 76 | Low Fat Manhattan Clam Chowder | 84 | Quick Moroccan Style Chicken Stew |
| 76 | Classic Pasta e Fagioli | 84 | Roasted Butternut Squash and Pear Soup |
| 76 | Quick Chicken and Shrimp Gumbo | 85 | Cauliflower and Mushroom Soup |
| 76 | Fresh Herbed Tomato Salad | 85 | Classic Tuscan Pasta Fagioli |
| 77 | Easy Spanish Black Bean Soup | 85 | Chicken Noodle Soup |
| 77 | Healthy Citrus Avocado Salad | 85 | Jalapeño Lime Chicken Soup |
| 77 | Shaved Brussels Sprouts and Kale Salad with Poppy Seed Dressing | 85 | Garden Fresh Tomato Soup |
| 77 | Baby Spinach Salad with Strawberries and Toasted Almonds | 86 | Creamy White Bean and Collard Green Soup |
| 77 | Spicy Slow Cooker Turkey Chili | 86 | Spicy Vegetable and Bean Chili Soup |
| 77 | Quick and Easy Minestrone Soup | 86 | Winter White Turkey Chili Soup |
| 78 | Creamy White Bean Soup | 86 | Creamy Smoked Salmon on Toast |
| 78 | Vegan Kale Caesar Salad | 86 | Healthy Low-Cal Garden Soup |
| 78 | Simple Pomegranate "Tabbouleh" with Cauliflower | | |

## Bacon and Fruit Baked Bean Casserole

**Prep time: 25 minutes | Cook time: 2-3 hours | Serves: 8**

½ lb. bacon
3 medium onions, chopped
cooking spray
16-oz. can lima beans, drained
16-oz. can kidney beans, drained
16-oz. can baked beans
14.8-oz. can no-added-salt baked beans
15½-oz. can pineapple chunks, canned in juice
2 tablespoons brown sugar
brown sugar substitute to equal 2 tablespoons sugar
¼ cup cider vinegar
2 tablespoons molasses
½ cup ketchup
2 tablespoons prepared mustard
½ teaspoon garlic powder
1 medium green pepper, chopped

1. Cook bacon in skillet. Crumble. Place bacon in slow cooker. Rinse skillet. 2. Sauté onions in non-stick skillet with cooking spray until soft. Drain. Add to bacon in slow cooker. 3. Add beans and pineapple to cooker. Mix well. 4. Combine brown sugar, vinegar, molasses, ketchup, mustard, garlic powder and green pepper. Mix well. Stir into mixture in slow cooker. 5. Cover. Cook on high 2-3 hours.
**Per Serving:** Calories 350; Total Fat 5g; Saturated Fat 1.5g; Sodium 577mg; Carbs 65g; Fiber 13g; Sugar 32g; Protein 15g

## Slow Cooker Apple Bean Bake

**Prep time: 25 minutes | Cook time: 2-4 hours | Serves: 12**

4 tablespoons margarine
2 large Granny Smith apples, unpeeled, cubed
¼ cup brown sugar
Brown sugar substitute to equal 2 tablespoons sugar
2 tablespoons sugar
white sugar substitute to equal 1 tablespoon sugar
½ cup no-added-salt ketchup
1 teaspoon cinnamon
1 tablespoon molasses
24-oz. can Great Northern beans, undrained
24-oz. can pinto beans, undrained

1. Melt butter in skillet. Add apples and cook until tender. 2. Stir in brown sugar and sugar. Cook until they melt. Stir in ketchup, cinnamon, and molasses. 3. Add beans and ham chunks. Mix well. Pour into slow cooker. 4. Cover. Cook on high 2-4 hours.
**Per Serving:** Calories 195; Total Fat 5g; Saturated Fat 0.8g; Sodium 399mg; Carbs 32g; Fiber 6g; Sugar 17g; Protein 6g

## Sweet and Sour Beans with Bacon Drippings

**Prep time: 20 minutes | Cook time: 3 hours | Serves: 8**

5 slices bacon
4 medium onions, cut in rings
¼ cup brown sugar
Brown sugar substitute to equal 2 tablespoons sugar
1 teaspoon dry mustard
½ teaspoon salt
¼ cup cider vinegar
1-lb. can green beans, drained
2 1-lb. cans butter beans, drained
2 14.8-oz. cans baked beans, no-added-salt

1. Brown bacon in skillet and crumble. Drain all but 3 teaspoons bacon drippings. Stir in onions, brown sugar, mustard, salt, and vinegar. Simmer 20 minutes. 2. Add all ingredients in a slow cooker pot. 3. Cover. Cook on low 3 hours.
**Per Serving:** Calories 289; Total Fat 4g; Saturated Fat 1.5g; Sodium 519mg; Carbs 51g; Fiber 13g; Sugar 22g; Protein 13g

## Spiced Lamb Chops

**Prep time: 15 minutes | Cook time: 4-6 hours | Serves: 8**

1 medium onion, sliced
1 teaspoon dried oregano
½ teaspoon dried thyme
½ teaspoon garlic powder
¼ teaspoon salt
⅛ teaspoon pepper
8 loin lamb chops (1¾-2 lbs.), bone-in, trimmed of visible fat
2 garlic cloves, minced
¼ cup water

1. Place onion in slow cooker. 2. Combine oregano with thyme, garlic powder, salt, and pepper. Rub the spice mix over lamb chops. Place in slow cooker. Top with garlic. 3. Pour water down along the side of the crock, so as not to disturb the rub on the chops. 4. Cover. Cook on low 4-6 hours.
**Per Serving:** Calories 117; Total Fat 5g; Saturated Fat 1.7g; Sodium 116mg; Carbs 2g; Fiber 0g; Sugar 1g; Protein 15g

## Authentic Mexican Tortilla Soup

**Prep time: 10 minutes | Cook time: 40 minutes | Serves: 8**

2 tablespoons extra-virgin olive oil
1 onion, chopped
2 cloves garlic, minced
¼ cup freshly chopped cilantro
1 tablespoon cumin
1 teaspoon cayenne pepper
1 quart low-sodium chicken broth
One 15-ounce can low-sodium whole tomatoes, drained and coarsely chopped
1 medium zucchini, sliced
1 medium yellow squash, sliced
1 cup yellow corn
Six 6-inch corn tortillas
½ cup reduced-fat shredded cheddar cheese

1. Preheat the oven to 350 degrees. 2. In a saucepan, sauté the onion and garlic in hot oil for 5 minutes. 3. Add the cilantro, cumin, and cayenne pepper; sauté for 3 more minutes. Add all the remaining ingredients instead of the tortillas and cheese. Bring to a boil; cover and let simmer for 30 minutes. 4. Cut each tortilla into about 10 strips. Place it on a sheet and bake for 5–6 minutes at 350 degrees until slightly browned and toasted. Remove from the oven. 5. To serve the soup, place strips of tortilla into each bowl. Ladle the soup on top of the tortilla strips. Top with cheese.
**Per Serving:** Calories 150; Total Fat 6g; Saturated Fat 1.5g; Sodium 125mg; Carbs 18g; Fiber 3g; Sugar 4g; Protein 8g

## Pizza Beans with Tomato and Sausage

**Prep time: 20 minutes | Cook time: 7-9 hours | Serves: 6**

16-oz. can pinto beans, drained
16-oz. can kidney beans, drained
2.25-oz. can ripe olives sliced, drained
28-oz. can no-added-salt stewed or whole tomatoes
¾ lb. bulk lean Italian turkey sausage
1 tablespoon oil
1 green pepper, chopped
1 medium onion, chopped
1 garlic clove, minced
1 teaspoon dried oregano
1 teaspoon dried basil

1. Combine beans, olives, and tomatoes in a slow cooker. 2. Brown sausage in ½ tablespoon oil in skillet. Drain. Transfer sausage to slow cooker. 3. Sauté green pepper in ½ tablespoon oil for 1 minute, stirring constantly. Cook onions until become translucent. Add garlic and cook 1 more minute. Transfer to slow cooker. 4. Stir in seasonings. 5. Cover. Cook on low 7-9 hours. 6. To serve, sprinkle with Parmesan cheese.
Per Serving: Calories 335; Total Fat 12g; Saturated Fat 2.2g; Sodium 632mg; Carbs 39g; Fiber 10g; Sugar 8g; Protein 23g

## New Orleans Red Beans with Sausage

**Prep time: 15 minutes | Cook time: 9-11 hours | Serves: 6**

2 cups dried kidney beans
5 cups water
8 oz. low-fat smoked sausage, diced
2 medium onions, chopped
2 cloves garlic, minced
¼ teaspoon salt

1. Wash and sort beans. In a saucepan, combine beans and water. Boil 2 minutes. Remove from heat. Soak 1 hour. 2. Brown sausage slowly in a skillet. If needed, use non-fat cooking spray. Add onions and garlic and sauté until tender. 3. Combine all ingredients, including the bean water, in slow cooker. 4. Cover. Cook on low 8-10 hours. In the last 15-20 minutes of cooking time, stir frequently and mash lightly with a spoon.
Per Serving: Calories 260; Total Fat 3g; Saturated Fat 0.8g; Sodium 422mg; Carbs 42g; Fiber 10g; Sugar 8g; Protein 18g

## Low-Fat Cajun Sausage and Beans

**Prep time: 15 minutes | Cook time: 8 hours | Serves: 6**

1 lb. low-fat smoked sausage, sliced into ¼-inch pieces
16-oz. can no-salt-added red kidney beans
16-oz. can crushed tomatoes with green chilies
1 cup chopped celery
Half an onion, chopped
2 tablespoons Italian seasoning
Tabasco sauce to taste

1. Add all ingredients in a slow cooker pot. 2. Cover. Cook on low 8 hours. 3. Serve over rice or as a thick zesty soup.
Per Serving: Calories 158; Total Fat 2g; Saturated Fat 0.8g; Sodium 588mg; Carbs 23g; Fiber 7g; Sugar 7g; Protein 11g

## Slow Cooker Four-Bean Medley

**Prep time: 20 minutes | Cook time: 6-8 hours | Serves: 8**

8 bacon slices, diced and browned until crisp
2 medium onions, chopped
6 tablespoons brown sugar
Brown sugar substitute to equal 3 tablespoons sugar
½ cup vinegar
1 teaspoon dry mustard
½ teaspoon garlic powder
16-oz. can baked beans, undrained
16-oz. can kidney beans, drained
15½-oz. can butter beans, drained
14½-oz. can green beans, drained
2 tablespoons ketchup

1. Mix together all ingredients. Pour into slow cooker. 2. Cover. Cook on low 6-8 hours.
Per Serving: Calories 242; Total Fat 4g; Saturated Fat 1.1g; Sodium 619mg; Carbs 44g; Fiber 09g; Sugar 19g; Protein 11g

## Easy Low Cooker Beans with Sausage

**Prep time: 30 minutes | Cook time: 4-10 hours | Serves: 8**

15-oz. can Great Northern beans, drained
15½-oz. can black beans, rinsed and drained
16-oz. can red kidney beans, drained
15-oz. can butter beans, drained
1½ cups no-salt-added ketchup
½ cup chopped onions
1 green pepper, chopped
1 lb. low-fat smoked sausage, cooked and cut into ½-inch slices
2 tablespoons brown sugar
Brown sugar substitute to equal 1 tablespoon sugar
2 garlic cloves, minced
1 teaspoon Worcestershire sauce
½ teaspoon dry mustard
½ teaspoon Tabasco sauce

1. Add all ingredients in a slow cooker pot. 2. Cover. Cook on low for 9-10 hours, or high 4-5 hours.
Per Serving: Calories 328; Total Fat 3g; Saturated Fat 1.2g; Sodium 764mg; Carbs 56g; Fiber 11g; Sugar 22g; Protein 19g

## Slow Cooker Kidney Beans with Apple

**Prep time: 20 minutes | Cook time: 6-7 hours | Serves: 12**

2 30-oz. cans kidney beans, rinsed and drained
28-oz. can no-salt-added diced tomatoes, drained
2 medium red bell peppers, chopped
1 cup ketchup
¼ cup brown sugar
brown sugar substitute to equal 2 tablespoons sugar
2 tablespoons honey
2 tablespoons molasses
1 tablespoon Worcestershire sauce
1 teaspoon dry mustard
2 medium red apples, cored and chopped

1. Add all ingredients, instead of apples, in a slow cooker. 2. Cover. Cook on low 4-5 hours. 3. Stir in apples. 4. Cover. Cook 2 more hours.
Per Serving: Calories 216; Total Fat 1g; Saturated Fat 0g; Sodium 445mg; Carbs 46g; Fiber 9g; Sugar 20g; Protein 10g

## Creole Black Beans with Celery and Green Pepper

**Prep time: 25 minutes | Cook time: 4-8 hours | Serves: 8**

14 oz. low-fat smoked sausage, sliced in ½" pieces, browned
3 15-oz. cans black beans, drained
1½ cups chopped onions
1½ cups chopped green peppers
1½ cups chopped celery
4 garlic cloves, minced
2 teaspoons dried thyme
1½ teaspoons dried oregano
1½ teaspoons pepper
1 teaspoon salt-free chicken bouillon powder
3 bay leaves
8-oz. can no-added-salt tomato sauce
1 cup water

1. Add all ingredients in a slow cooker pot. 2. Cover. Cook on low 8 hours or on high 4 hours. 3. Remove bay leaves.
**Per Serving:** Calories 223; Total Fat 3g; Saturated Fat 1.0g; Sodium 566mg; Carbs 34g; Fiber 10g; Sugar 9g; Protein 15g

## Tuna Noodle Casserole with Almonds Topping

**Prep time: 20 minutes | Cook time: 3-9 hour | Serves: 6**

2 6½-oz. cans water-packed tuna, drained
2 10½-oz. cans 98% fat-free, lower sodium cream of mushroom soup
1 cup milk
2 tablespoons dried parsley
10-oz. pkg. frozen mixed vegetables, thawed
8-oz. pkg. noodles, cooked and drained
½ cup toasted sliced almonds

1. Combine tuna, soup, milk, parsley, and vegetables. Fold in noodles. Pour into greased slow cooker. Top with almonds. 2. Cover. Cook on low temp setting for 7-9 hours, or high 3-4 hours.
**Per Serving:** Calories 395; Total Fat 11g; Saturated Fat 1.9g; Sodium 637mg; Carbs 46g; Fiber 5g; Sugar 8g; Protein 27g

## Cowboy Beans with Sliced Bacon

**Prep time: 25 minutes | Cook time: 3-7 hours | Serves: 12**

6 slices bacon, cut in pieces
½ cup onions, chopped
1 garlic clove, minced
16-oz. can baked beans
16-oz. can kidney beans, drained
15-oz. can butter beans or pinto beans, drained
2 tablespoons dill pickle relish or chopped dill pickles
⅓ cup chili sauce or ketchup
2 teaspoons Worcestershire sauce
¼ cup brown sugar
Brown sugar substitute to equal 2 tablespoons sugar
⅛ teaspoon hot pepper sauce, optional

1. Lightly brown bacon, onions, and garlic in skillet. Drain. 2. Combine all ingredients in slow cooker. Mix well. 3. Cover. Cook on low 5-7 hours or high 3-4 hours.
**Per Serving:** Calories 138; Total Fat 2g; Saturated Fat 0.6g; Sodium 441mg; Carbs 25g; Fiber 5g; Sugar 9g; Protein 7g

## New Mexico - Style Pinto Beans

**Prep time: 10 minutes | Cook time: 6-10 hours | Serves: 10**

2½ cups dried pinto beans
3 qts. water
½ cup ham, or salt pork, diced
2 garlic cloves, crushed
1 teaspoon crushed red chili peppers, optional

1. Sort beans. Discard pebbles, shriveled beans, and floaters. Wash beans under running water. Place in saucepan, cover with 3 quarts water, and soak overnight. 2. Drain beans and discard soaking water. Pour beans into slow cooker. Cover with fresh water. 3. Add meat, garlic, chili, salt, and pepper. Cook on low temp setting for 6-10 hours, or until beans are soft.
**Per Serving:** Calories 145; Total Fat 1g; Saturated Fat 0.2g; Sodium 95mg; Carbs 25g; Fiber 8g; Sugar 2g; Protein 10g

## Spicy Asian-Style Tofu Salad

**Prep time: 20 minutes | Cook time: 15 minutes | Serves: 4**

1 (14-ounce) package firm tofu, drained
2 tablespoons canola oil
2 tablespoons rice vinegar
2 teaspoons reduced-sodium soy sauce
1 teaspoon toasted sesame oil
1 teaspoon ground ginger
1 large carrot, peeled and shredded
1 (8-ounce) can water chestnuts, chopped
1 (8-ounce) package frozen snow peas, thawed
4 cups mixed Asian-style salad greens, including bok choy, Chinese cabbage, and red leaf lettuce
4 tablespoons sesame seeds, divided

1. Pat the tofu dry with paper towels and cut into 1-inch cubes. 2. In a large bowl, whisk together the canola oil, vinegar, soy sauce, sesame oil, and ginger. 3. Add the tofu chunks and toss to coat thoroughly with the sauce. Marinate the tofu in the refrigerator for at least 15 minutes. 4. Toss the carrot, water chestnuts, and snow peas with the tofu to coat. 5. Divide the salad greens into 4 bowls and top with the tofu mixture. Sprinkle 1 tablespoon of sesame seeds on top of each serving.
**Per Serving:** Calories 340; Total Fat 17g; Saturated Fat 3g; Sodium 160mg; Carbs 34g; Fiber 4g; Sugar 4g; Protein 15g

## Simple Broccoli Slaw Crab Salad

**Prep time: 15 minutes | Cook time: 0 minutes | Serves: 4**

⅔ cup mayonnaise
1 tablespoon freshly squeezed lime juice
1 teaspoon minced garlic
½ teaspoon freshly ground black pepper
1 (16-ounce) package broccoli slaw
2 (6-ounce) cans crabmeat, drained and flaked
1 small onion, diced
2 large celery stalks, chopped
1 red bell pepper, chopped
Chopped fresh parsley, for garnish

1. In a bowl, whisk the mayonnaise, lime juice, garlic, and pepper until smooth. 2. Add the broccoli slaw, crab meat, onion, celery, and bell pepper and mix until all the ingredients are coated. 3. Garnish with parsley.
**Per Serving:** Calories 411; Total Fat 32g; Saturated Fat 5g; Sodium 867mg; Carbs 15g; Fiber 4g; Sugar 5g; Protein 15g

## Fresh Chickpea and Salmon Salad Dijon

Prep time: 10 minutes | Cook time: 0 minutes | Serves: 4

½ cup bottled Dijon mustard dressing
2 (5-ounce) cans salmon, drained and flaked
1 (15-ounce) can chickpeas, rinsed and drained
1 large cucumber, peeled and sliced
½ cup chopped walnuts
1 (10- to 12-ounce) package mixed salad greens, divided

1. Pour the dressing into a large mixing bowl and stir until creamy. Add the salmon, chickpeas, cucumber, and walnuts and stir until all the ingredients are coated with dressing. 2. Divide ¼ of the package of salad greens into 4 bowls and top with the salmon mixture.
Per Serving: Calories 377; Total Fat 18g; Saturated Fat 2g; Sodium 311mg; Carbs 34g; Fiber 6g; Sugar 15g; Protein 22g

## Chicken and Mushroom Soup

Prep time: 5 minutes | Cook time: 20 minutes | Serves: 6

1 quart low-sodium chicken broth
1 tablespoon light soy sauce
1 cup sliced mushrooms, stems removed
1 tablespoon finely chopped scallions
1 tablespoon dry sherry
½ pound boneless, skinless chicken breast, cubed

1. In a stockpot, simmer all ingredients except the chicken for 10 minutes. 2. Add the chicken cubes, and simmer for 6–8 minutes more. Serve with additional soy sauce if desired.
Per Serving: Calories 70; Total Fat 1g; Saturated Fat 0.2g; Sodium 200mg; Carbs 1g; Fiber 0g; Sugar 0g; Protein 13g

## Tasty Herbed Chicken Stew with Noodles

Prep time: 10 minutes | Cook time: 40 minutes | Serves: 8

1 tablespoon extra-virgin olive oil
1 onion, chopped
2 garlic cloves, minced
1 pound boneless, skinless chicken breast, cubed
2 tablespoons flour
3 cups low-sodium chicken broth
1 cup dry white wine
1 tablespoon fresh thyme
4 cups cooked egg noodles, hot (from 1/2 pound dry egg noodles)
½ cup minced parsley

1. In a pan, sauté the onion and garlic in hot oil for about 5 minutes. Add the chicken cubes, and sauté until the chicken is cooked (about 10 minutes). 2. Sprinkle the flour over the chicken. Add the chicken broth, wine, and thyme. Boil, and then lower the heat and manage simmer for 30 minutes. 3. Toss the noodles and the parsley in a large bowl. Serve stew with noodles and enjoy.
Per Serving: Calories 220; Total Fat 5g; Saturated Fat 1g; Sodium 85mg; Carbs 24g; Fiber 2g; Sugar 1g; Protein 18g

## Healthy Cream of Carrot Soup

Prep time: 5 minutes | Cook time: 15 minutes | Serves: 4

1 cup plus 2 tablespoons chicken broth, divided
3 tablespoons chopped shallots
2 tablespoons flour
2 cups fat-free milk, scalded and hot
1 teaspoon cinnamon
1 cup cooked, pureed carrots
Freshly ground black pepper

1. In a stockpot, heat the broth. Cook the shallots until limp. Sprinkle the flour on shallots and cook 2–3 minutes. 2. Add in the hot milk and cook until thickens. Add the all remaining ingredients. Boil it, stirring often, and cook for 5 minutes. Add pepper to taste.
Per Serving: Calories 90; Total Fat 0g; Saturated Fat 0.1g; Sodium 110mg; Carbs 14g; Fiber 2g; Sugar 9g; Protein 7g

## Traditional English Beef Stew

Prep time: 10 minutes | Cook time: 2 ½ hours | Serves: 8

2 pounds lean beef, cut into large chunks
1½ tablespoons flour
2 tablespoons canola oil
2 garlic cloves, chopped
2 cups boiling water
1 tablespoon Worcestershire sauce
1 teaspoon
1 yellow onion, quartered
4 carrots, peeled and quartered
3 potatoes, cut into 1-inch cubes
1 cup canned stewed tomatoes

1. Roll the beef in the flour. In a saucepan heat the canola oil. Cook the beef. When the beef browned, add the garlic and stir. Pour in the boiling water. 2. Add the Worcestershire sauce with salt, and pepper. reduce the heat, cover, and manage to simmer for 1½–2 hours until the meat is tender. 3 Add the onion along with carrots, potatoes, and tomatoes. Let veggies simmer about 30 minutes until tender. Transfer to a serving bowl and serve.
Per Serving: Calories 260; Total Fat 8g; Saturated Fat 2.2g; Sodium 120mg; Carbs 21g; Fiber 3g; Sugar 5g; Protein 24g

## Fresh Fish Chowder Soup

Prep time: 10 minutes | Cook time: 50 minutes | Serves: 6

2 tablespoons extra-virgin olive oil
1 large garlic clove, minced
1 small onion, chopped
1 large green bell pepper, chopped
One 14.5-ounce can no-salt-added crushed tomatoes
1 tablespoon tomato paste
½ teaspoon dried basil
½ teaspoon dried oregano
¼ cup dry red wine
1 teaspoon
½ cup uncooked brown rice
½ pound fresh halibut, cubed
2 tablespoons freshly chopped parsley

1. In a saucepan, cook the garlic, onion, and green pepper in hot oil; sauté for 10 minutes over low heat until the vegetables are just tender. 2. Add the tomatoes, tomato paste, basil, oregano, wine, salt, and pepper. Let simmer for 15 minutes. Add the rice and continue to cook for 15 minutes. 3. Add the halibut, and cook for about 5–7 minutes, until the fish is cooked through.
Per Serving: Calories 180; Total Fat 6g; Saturated Fat 0.9g; Sodium 75mg; Carbs 21g; Fiber 3g; Sugar 4g; Protein 11g

## Hearty Italian Minestrone Soup

**Prep time: 10 minutes | Cook time: 50 minutes | Serves: 8**

½ cup sliced onion
1 tablespoon extra-virgin olive oil
4 cups low-sodium chicken broth
¾ cup diced carrot
½ cup diced potato (with skin)
2 cups sliced cabbage or coarsely chopped spinach
1 cup diced zucchini
½ cup cooked garbanzo beans
½ cup cooked navy beans
One 14.5-ounce can low-sodium tomatoes, with liquid
½ cup diced celery
2 tablespoons fresh basil, finely chopped
½ cup uncooked whole-wheat rotini or other shaped pasta
2 tablespoons fresh parsley, for garnish

1. In a stockpot, sauté the onion in oil until the onion is slightly browned. Add the chicken broth, carrot, and potato. Cover and cook for 30 minutes over medium heat. 2. Add the remaining ingredients and cook for 15–20 minutes, until the pasta is cooked through. Garnish with parsley and serve hot.

**Per Serving:** Calories 110; Total Fat 2.5g; Saturated Fat 0.3g; Sodium 90mg; Carbs 16g; Fiber 4g; Sugar 4g; Protein 7g

## Daily Lentil Soup

**Prep time: 10 minutes | Cook time: 55 minutes | Serves: 8**

1 large onion, diced
1 large carrot, peeled and diced
2 stalks celery, diced
2 tablespoons extra-virgin olive oil
1 pound lentils
1½ quarts low-sodium chicken or beef broth
2 medium russet or white potatoes, peeled and diced
1 tablespoon finely chopped fresh oregano
1 teaspoon finely chopped fresh thyme

1. In a stockpot or Dutch oven, sauté the onion, carrot, and celery in the olive oil for 10 minutes. Add the lentils, broth, and potatoes. 2. Continue to cook for 30–45 minutes, adding the oregano and thyme 15 minutes before serving.

**Per Serving:** Calories 270; Total Fat 4g; Saturated Fat 0.6g; Sodium 120mg; Carbs 41g; Fiber 14g; Sugar 5g; Protein 20g

## Low Fat Manhattan Clam Chowder

**Prep time: 10 minutes | Cook time: 1½ hours | Serves: 8**

3 carrots, coarsely chopped
3 potatoes, coarsely chopped
4 celery stalks, coarsely chopped
2½ cups minced clams, drained
2 cups canned tomatoes, slightly crushed
½ teaspoon dried thyme
Ground black pepper

1. Add all ingredients to a stockpot. Cover and let simmer for 1½ hours. Serve hot.

**Per Serving:** Calories 150; Total Fat 1g; Saturated Fat 0.1g; Sodium 180mg; Carbs 21g; Fiber 3g; Sugar 4g; Protein 15g

## Classic Pasta e Fagioli

**Prep time: 10 minutes | Cook time: 25 minutes | Serves: 12**

1 tablespoon extra-virgin olive oil
1 large onion, chopped
3 cloves garlic, crushed
2 medium carrots, sliced
2 medium zucchini, sliced
2 tablespoons finely chopped fresh basil
2 teaspoons finely chopped fresh oregano
Two 14.5-ounce cans unsalted tomatoes with liquid
Two 15-ounce cans low-sodium white cannellini or navy beans, drained and rinsed
¾ pound whole-wheat uncooked rigatoni or shell pasta

1. In a saucepan, sauté the onion and garlic in hot oil for 5 minutes. 2. Add the carrots, zucchini, basil, oregano, tomatoes with their liquid, and beans. Cook until veggies are tender, about 15–17 minutes. 3. In a separate saucepan, cook the pasta according to package directions (without adding salt). Add the pasta to the soup, and mix thoroughly. Serve warm with crusty bread.

**Per Serving:** Calories 210; Total Fat 2g; Saturated Fat 0.3g; Sodium 25mg; Carbs 40g; Fiber 8g; Sugar 6g; Protein 9g

## Quick Chicken and Shrimp Gumbo

**Prep time: 10 minutes | Cook time: 40 minutes | Serves: 4**

2 cups low-sodium canned tomatoes, undrained
¼ cup chopped green bell pepper
1 medium onion, chopped
1 cup cooked brown rice
½ cup low-sodium chicken broth
1 medium garlic clove, minced
Dash hot pepper sauce
Freshly ground black pepper
12 ounces precooked fresh jumbo shrimp

1. Place all the ingredients instead of the shrimp in a large stockpot and bring to a boil. Manage simmer on low heat for 25–30 minutes. 2. Add the shrimp, cover, and simmer for 5–10 minutes or until the shrimp is thoroughly heated. Serve hot.

**Per Serving:** Calories 190; Total Fat 1g; Saturated Fat 0.2g; Sodium 125mg; Carbs 22g; Fiber 3g; Sugar 5g; Protein 24g

## Fresh Herbed Tomato Salad

**Prep time: 7 minutes | Cook time: 0 minutes | Serves: 2 to 4**

1 pint cherry tomatoes, halved
1 bunch fresh parsley, leaves only
1 cup cilantro, leaves only (stems discarded)
¼ cup fresh dill
1 teaspoon sumac (optional)
2 tablespoons extra-virgin olive oil
Kosher salt
Freshly ground black pepper

1. In a medium bowl, carefully toss together the tomatoes, parsley, cilantro, dill, sumac (if using), olive oil, and salt, pepper to taste.

**Per Serving:** Calories 161; Total Fat 14g; Saturated Fat 3g; Sodium 322mg; Carbs 8g; Fiber 3g; Sugar 5g; Protein 3g

## Easy Spanish Black Bean Soup

Prep time: 5 minutes | Cook time: 1 hour 10 minutes | Serves: 6

1½ cups plus 2 teaspoons low-sodium chicken broth, divided
1 teaspoon extra-virgin olive oil
3 garlic cloves, minced
1 yellow onion, minced
1 teaspoon minced fresh oregano
1 teaspoon cumin
1 teaspoon chili powder or ½ teaspoon cayenne pepper
1 red bell pepper, chopped
1 carrot, coarsely chopped
3 cups cooked black beans
½ cup dry red wine

1. In a large pot, heat 2 teaspoons of the chicken broth and the olive oil. Sauté the garlic, onion, for 3 minutes. Add the oregano with cumin seeds, and chili powder; stir for another minute. Add the red pepper and carrot. 2. Puree 1½ cups of the black beans in a blender or food processor. Add the pureed beans, the remaining 1½ cups of whole black beans, the remaining 1½ cups of chicken broth, and the red wine to the stockpot. Simmer 1 hour. 3. Taste before serving; add additional spices if you like.
Per Serving: Calories 160; Total Fat 1.5g; Saturated Fat 0.3g; Sodium 55mg; Carbs 26g; Fiber 9g; Sugar 5g; Protein 10g

## Healthy Citrus Avocado Salad

Prep time: 10 minutes | Cook time: 0 minutes | Serves: 2

4 cups salad greens
1 grapefruit, peeled and segmented
1 orange, peeled and segmented
2 tablespoons minced red onion
¼ cup fresh mint leaves, torn
3 tablespoons Lemon Vinaigrette Dressing or store-bought
1 avocado, thinly sliced
¼ cup Stovetop Granola (optional)

1. In a bowl, toss the salad greens, grapefruit, orange, red onion, mint, and dressing. 2. Place the salad on a plate with the slices of avocado and a sprinkling of granola.
Per Serving: Calories 364; Total Fat 26g; Saturated Fat 2g; Sodium 125mg; Carbs 32g; Fiber 9g; Sugar 5g; Protein 6g

## Shaved Brussels Sprouts and Kale Salad with Poppy Seed Dressing

Prep time: 20 minutes | Cook time: 0 minutes | Serves: 4-6

1 pound Brussels sprouts, shaved
1 bunch kale, thinly shredded
4 scallions, thinly sliced
4 ounces shredded Romano cheese
Poppy Seed Dressing or store-bought
Kosher salt
Freshly ground black pepper

1. In a bowl, toss the Brussels sprouts, kale, scallions, and Romano cheese. 2. Add the dressing to the greens and toss to combine. Season with salt and pepper to taste.
Per Serving: Calories 251; Total Fat 12g; Saturated Fat 1g; Sodium 122mg; Carbs 23g; Fiber 6g; Sugar 3g; Protein 14g

## Baby Spinach Salad with Strawberries and Toasted Almonds

Prep time: 7 minutes | Cook time: 0 minutes | Serves: 2 to 4

8 cups packed fresh baby spinach
16 strawberries, quartered
4 ounces goat cheese, crumbled
¼ cup chopped toasted almonds
2 tablespoons Lemon Vinaigrette Dressing or store-bought
Kosher salt
Freshly ground black pepper

1. In a bowl, gently toss together the spinach, strawberries, goat cheese, and almonds. Drizzle the salad with the vinaigrette and season with salt and pepper to taste. 2. Store any leftovers in an airtight container in the refrigerator for up to 3 days, but the salad is best consumed on the day it is dressed.
Per Serving: Calories 516; Total Fat 39g; Saturated Fat 0.6g; Sodium 455mg; Carbs 21g; Fiber 8g; Sugar 2g; Protein 25g

## Spicy Slow Cooker Turkey Chili

Prep time: 10 minutes | Cook time: 50 minutes | Serves: 6

2 onions, chopped
2 garlic cloves, minced
½ cup green bell pepper
1 tablespoon olive oil
1 pound lean ground turkey meat
2 cups cooked kidney beans
2 cups tomatoes with liquid
1 cup low-sodium chicken broth
2 tablespoon chili powder
2 teaspoons cumin
Freshly ground black pepper

1. In a saucepan, sauté the onion, garlic, green pepper in the hot oil for 10 minutes. Add the turkey meat in it, and sauté until the turkey is cooked, about 5–10 minutes. 2 Add all the remaining ingredients, boil it, manage simmer on low heat uncovered for 30 minutes.
Per Serving: Calories 240; Total Fat 5g; Saturated Fat 0.9g; Sodium 200mg; Carbs 24g; Fiber 7g; Sugar 5g; Protein 27g

## Quick and Easy Minestrone Soup

Prep time: 10 minutes | Cook time: 15 minutes | Serves: 8

2 cups diced zucchini
½ cup dry whole-wheat elbow pasta
⅛ teaspoon ground black pepper
2 medium cloves garlic, peeled and minced
4 cups low-sodium chicken broth
1 (14.5-ounce) can Italian style diced tomatoes, undrained
1 (16-ounce) can low-sodium red kidney beans, drained and rinsed
1 (10-ounce) bag frozen peas and carrots, defrosted
½ cup grated Parmesan cheese

1. In a large pot over high heat, combine all ingredients except Parmesan. Bring to a boil. 2. Once boiling, cover and reduce heat to medium-low; simmer 10 minutes, stirring occasionally until pasta is done. 3. Transfer to medium bowls and serve with 1 tablespoon Parmesan sprinkled over each serving.
Per Serving: Calories 140; Total Fat 3g; Saturated Fat 1.5g; Sodium 320mg; Carbs 20g; Fiber 4g; Sugar 5g; Protein 9g

## Creamy White Bean Soup

**Prep time: 5 minutes | Cook time: 2 ½ hours | Serves: 6**

¼ cup chopped onion
1 garlic clove, minced
2 tablespoons extra-virgin olive oil
½ pound dried great northern, white navy, or cannellini beans, soaked in boiling water for 1 hour and drained
2 quarts water
2 bay leaves
1 teaspoon dried basil
teaspoon salt
teaspoon freshly ground black pepper
2 medium scallions, chopped
2 tablespoons minced fresh parsley

1. In a saucepan, sauté the onion and garlic in the oil for 5 minutes. Add the beans, water, bay leaves, and basil; stir well. Boil the mix, lower the heat, cover, and let simmer. 2. Continue to cook the soup for 1–1½ hours or until the beans are tender. Add water (if necessary), salt, and pepper; mix well. 3. Remove and discard the bay leaves. In a food processor, puree the mixture. Return the soup to the saucepan and serve hot. Garnish with scallions and parsley.
**Per Serving:** Calories 150; Total Fat 5g; Saturated Fat 0.8g; Sodium 25mg; Carbs 20g; Fiber 7g; Sugar 2g; Protein 8g

## Vegan Kale Caesar Salad

**Prep time: 8 minutes | Cook time: 15 minutes | Serves: 2 to 4**

**For the Oat Croutons**
½ cup rolled oats
1 tablespoon sunflower seeds
1 tablespoon chopped almonds
1 tablespoon canola oil
1 tablespoon honey
Pinch kosher salt
**For the Salad**
1 bunch kale, cleaned, ribs removed, and chopped
1 bunch fresh parsley, leaves only
¼ cup Parmesan cheese
¼ to ½ cup Caesar Dressing or store-bought
1 lemon, cut into wedges (optional)

To make the oat croutons
1. Preheat the oven to 350°F temp setting. 2. In a small bowl, combine the oats, sunflower seeds, almonds, oil, honey, and a pinch of salt. Toss to coat evenly, then spread the mixture on a nonstick baking sheet. Bake for 12 to 15 minutes, then remove from the oven to cool on the baking sheet for 15 minutes.
To make the salad
3. In a bowl, toss the kale, parsley, and Parmesan cheese with the Caesar Dressing until all the leaves are coated. Place salad on plates. 4. Spread the croutons and serve. 5. If the dressing and oats are kept separately from the greens, then the salad and dressing will keep separately for 5 days in airtight containers in the refrigerator. The croutons will keep in an airtight container in the refrigerator for up to 1 month.
**Per Serving:** Calories 340; Total Fat 20g; Saturated Fat 5g; Sodium 302mg; Carbs 31g; Fiber 6g; Sugar 6g; Protein 12g

## Simple Pomegranate "Tabbouleh" with Cauliflower

**Prep time: 20 minutes | Cook time: 5 minutes | Serves: 4-6**

⅓ cup extra-virgin olive oil, divided
4 cups grated cauliflower
Juice of 1 lemon
¼ red onion, minced
4 large tomatoes, diced
3 large bunches flat-leaf parsley, chopped
1 large bunch mint, chopped
½ cup pomegranate arils
Kosher salt
Freshly ground black pepper

1. In a skillet, heat extra-virgin olive oil. When it's hot, add the cauliflower and sauté for 3 to 5 minutes or until it starts to crisp. Allow the cauliflower to cool while you prep the remaining ingredients. 2. In a large bowl, combine the remaining extra-virgin olive oil with the lemon juice and red onion. Mix well, then mix in the tomatoes, parsley, mint, and pomegranate arils. 3. After the cauliflower cools, 5 to 7 minutes, add it to the bowl with the other ingredients. Spice with salt and pepper and serve.
**Per Serving:** Calories 270; Total Fat 19g; Saturated Fat 3g; Sodium 388mg; Carbs 22g; Fiber 8g; Sugar 6g; Protein 7g

## Burger with Jicama Chips

**Prep time: 5 minutes | Cook time: 22minutes | Serves: 2**

¼ pound ground bison
¼ pound ground beef
½ teaspoon garlic powder
½ teaspoon onion powder
½ teaspoon extra-virgin olive oil
1 small jicama, peeled
Juice of 1 lime
Chili powder (optional)
Bun (optional)
1 tomato, thinly sliced
4 lettuce leaves
Optional Toppings
Other burger toppings (cheese, onions, mushrooms, etc.)

1. Preheat a grill to medium-high heat. 2. In a bowl, combine the bison with beef, garlic powder, and onion powder until mixed well. Do not over handle, squeeze, or compress the meat. 3. Divide the meat into two equal pieces and form each into a patty. 4. Lightly oil both sides of the burger to prevent sticking and grill on the first side for 5 to 6 minutes, or until juices start to come through. until the internal temperature is 160°F. If you want to add cheese, layer on a slice during the last minute. 5. If you do not have a grill, heat a grill pan or cast-iron skillet with 1 tablespoon of oil over medium-high heat and cook the burgers, turning once, until they reach the correct internal temperature, about 14 minutes in total. 6. Let the burgers rest 5 to 10 minutes, so the juices settle, then add the desired toppings. 7. Meanwhile, slice the jicama into ¼-inch-thick slices, then into quarters. Put the jicama in a medium bowl and add the lime juice and chili powder (if using) to taste. 8. Serve the burgers on a bun, or wrapped in lettuce if you're watching carbs, with your favorite toppings and a side of jicama.
**Per Serving:** Calories 348; Total Fat 15g; Saturated Fat 0.1g; Sodium 308mg; Carbs 23g; Fiber 11g; Sugar 33g; Protein 32g

## Quinoa and Cucumber Feta Salad

**Prep time:** 10 minutes | **Cook time:** 15 minutes | **Serves:** 2

1 cup quinoa, rinsed
2 cups water
Kosher salt
Freshly ground black pepper
1 bunch fresh parsley, minced
1 medium cucumber, cut into ¼-inch dice
¼ cup minced red onion
2 tablespoons toasted sesame seeds
¼ to ½ cup Tahini Dressing or store-bought
4 ounces crumbled feta

1. In a saucepan, mix the quinoa with the water and a pinch each of salt and pepper. Boil it over medium-high heat, then decrease to a gentle simmer and allow to cook for 10-15 minutes, until the quinoa absorbed all water. Remove the pot from the heat, cover, and allow to rest. 2. In a bowl, mix the parsley, cucumber, red onion, sesame seeds, and dressing. 3. Add the cooked quinoa to the bowl with the other ingredients. Toss well to coat evenly and spice with salt and pepper. 4. Top the salad with feta and serve. 5. Store any leftovers in an airtight container in the refrigerator for 3 to 5 days.
**Per Serving:** Calories 653; Total Fat 27g; Saturated Fat 6g; Sodium 633mg; Carbs 78g; Fiber 13g; Sugar 14g; Protein 25g

## Apple and Bulgur Salad

**Prep time:** 10 minutes | **Cook time:** 15 minutes | **Serves:** 2

2 cups water
1 cup bulgur
1 teaspoon dried thyme
2 tablespoons extra-virgin olive oil
2 teaspoons cider vinegar
Kosher salt
Freshly ground black pepper
6 kale leaves, shredded
1 small apple, cored and diced
3 tablespoons sliced, toasted almonds

1. In a saucepan, boil water over high heat and remove it from the heat. Add the bulgur and thyme, cover, and allow the grain to rest for 7 to 15 minutes or until cooked through. 2. In a bowl, whisk the extra-virgin olive oil and cider vinegar with a pinch of salt and pepper. Add the cooked bulgur, kale, apple, and almonds to the dressing and toss to combine. Adjust the seasonings as desired.
**Per Serving:** Calories 550; Total Fat 20g; Saturated Fat 3g; Sodium 321mg; Carbs 82g; Fiber 21g; Sugar 13g; Protein 15g

## Nutritional Sweet Beet Grain Bowl

**Prep time:** 1 minutes | **Cook time:** 20 minutes | **Serves:** 2

3 cups water
1 cup farro, rinsed
2 tablespoons extra-virgin olive oil
1 tablespoon honey
3 tablespoons cider vinegar
Pinch freshly ground black pepper
4 small cooked beets, sliced
1 pear, cored and diced
6 cups mixed greens
⅓ cup pumpkin seeds, roasted
¼ cup ricotta cheese

1. In a saucepan, stir the water and farro over high heat and bring to a boil. Reduce the heat and manage simmer until the farro is tender, 15 to 20 minutes. Drain and rinse the farro under cold running water until cool. Set aside. 2. In a bowl, Mix the oil with honey, and vinegar. Season with black pepper. 3. Evenly divide the farro between two bowls. Top each with the beets, pear, greens, pumpkin seeds, and ricotta. Drizzle the bowls with the dressing before serving and adjust the seasonings as desired.
**Per Serving:** Calories 779; Total Fat 29g; Saturated Fat 0.1g; Sodium 322mg; Carbs 108g; Fiber 15g; Sugar 20g; Protein 26g

## Grilled Romaine with White Beans Salad

**Prep time:** 5 minutes | **Cook time:** 8 minutes | **Serves:** 4-6

3 tablespoons extra-virgin olive oil, divided
2 large heads romaine lettuce, halved lengthwise
2 tablespoons white miso
1 tablespoon water, plus more as needed
1 (15-ounce) can white beans
½ cup chopped fresh parsley

1. Preheat the grill. 2. Drizzle 2 tablespoons of extra-virgin olive oil over the cut sides of the romaine lettuce. 3. In a medium bowl, whisk the remaining 1 tablespoon of extra-virgin olive oil with the white miso and about 1 tablespoon of water. Add the white beans and parsley to the bowl, stir, adjust the seasonings as desired, and set aside. 4. When the grill is hot, put the romaine on the grill and cook for 1 to 2 minutes on each side or until lightly charred with grill marks. Remove the lettuce from the grill and repeat with remaining lettuce halves. Set the lettuce aside on a platter or individual plates and top with the beans. 5. Serve.
**Per Serving:** Calories 291; Total Fat 12g; Saturated Fat 0.3g; Sodium 258mg; Carbs 38g; Fiber 14g; Sugar 15g; Protein 14g

## Easy Chickpea Fattoush Salad

**Prep time:** 15 minutes | **Cook time:** 5 minutes | **Serves:** 4

2 tablespoons extra-virgin olive oil
2 pitas, torn into bite-size pieces
1 (15-ounce) can chickpeas, rinsed and drained
1 head romaine lettuce, cut into bite-size pieces
1 cucumber, diced
½ pint cherry tomatoes, halved
8 radishes, thinly sliced
1 bunch fresh parsley, chopped
1 cup mint, chopped
½ teaspoon sumac (optional)
½ cup Lemon Vinaigrette Dressing or store-bought

1. Heat the extra-virgin olive oil and sauté the pita bread until toasted and crisp, about 3 minutes. Remove the skillet from the heat and transfer the pita bread to a medium bowl. 2. Add the chickpeas, romaine, cucumber, tomatoes, radishes, parsley, mint, and sumac (if using) to the medium bowl. Add the dressing and toss to combine. Serve. 3. Store any leftovers in an airtight container in the refrigerator for up to 3 days.
**Per Serving:** Calories 466; Total Fat 30g; Saturated Fat 0.5g; Sodium 369mg; Carbs 42g; Fiber 10g; Sugar 11g; Protein 11g

## Oven Roasted Carrot and Quinoa with Goat Cheese

**Prep time: 10 minutes | Cook time: 20 minutes | Serves: 4**

4 large carrots, cut into ⅛-inch-thick rounds
4 tablespoons oil (olive, safflower, or grapeseed), divided
2 teaspoons paprika
1 teaspoon turmeric
2 teaspoons ground cumin
2 cups water
1 cup quinoa, rinsed
½ cup shelled pistachios, toasted
4 ounces goat cheese
12 ounces salad greens

1. Preheat the oven to 400°F temp setting. Manage a baking sheet with parchment paper. 2. In a large bowl, toss together the carrots, 2 tablespoons of oil, the paprika, turmeric, and cumin until the carrots are well coated. Spread them evenly on the prepared baking sheet and roast until tender, 15 to 17 minutes. 3. In a saucepan, mix the water and quinoa over high heat. Boil it, lower the heat and simmer until tender, about 15 minutes. 4. Transfer the roasted carrots to a large bowl and add the cooked quinoa, remaining 2 tablespoons of oil, the pistachios, and goat cheese and toss to combine. 5. Evenly divide the greens among four plates and top with the carrot mixture. Serve. 6. Store any leftovers in an airtight container in the refrigerator for up to 2 days.

**Per Serving:** Calories 527; Total Fat 31g; Saturated Fat 10g; Sodium 257mg; Carbs 48g; Fiber 10g; Sugar 11g; Protein 17g

## Roasted Tomato Tartine with Ricotta Cheese

**Prep time: 5 minutes | Cook time: 15 minutes | Serves: 2**

3 tomatoes, cut into eighths
2 tablespoons extra-virgin olive oil, divided
1 tablespoon balsamic vinegar
2 garlic cloves, minced
Pinch kosher salt
Pinch freshly ground black pepper
½ cup ricotta cheese
2 slices whole-grain bread
2 tablespoons chopped fresh basil
4 cups arugula

1. Preheat the oven to 450°F. Manage a baking sheet with parchment paper. 2. In a medium-sized bowl, toss the tomatoes with 1 tablespoon of extra-virgin olive oil, the vinegar, garlic, salt, and pepper. 3. Spread the tomatoes on the baking sheet and bake for 15 minutes. 4. Meanwhile, place the ricotta in the bowl of a food processor and, while it is running, add the remaining 1 tablespoon of extra-virgin olive oil in a thin stream. Taste and adjust the seasonings as needed. Whisk the ricotta and extra-virgin olive oil in a medium bowl. 5. Toast the bread and divide the ricotta between the slices, spreading it out evenly. Top the ricotta with the tomatoes and garnish with chopped basil. 6. Serve with the greens on the side.

**Per Serving:** Calories 375; Total Fat 22g; Saturated Fat 10g; Sodium 231mg; Carbs 34g; Fiber 6g; Sugar 7g; Protein 13g

## Simple Cauli-Lettuce Wraps

**Prep time: 10 minutes | Cook time: 20 minutes | Serves: 2-4**

1½ tablespoons sesame oil
½ yellow onion, chopped
8 ounces mushrooms, thinly sliced
4 garlic cloves, minced
1½ tablespoons low-sodium soy sauce or tamari
4 teaspoons rice wine vinegar
5 ounces water chestnuts, drained and liquid reserved
2½ cups Cauliflower Rice
½ cup coarsely chopped cashews
4 large green leaf lettuce leaves
2 scallions, thinly sliced (optional)
1 cup chopped cilantro (optional)

1. Heat the sesame oil and sauté the onion until translucent, about 3 minutes. Add the mushrooms, garlic, tamari, vinegar, and water chestnuts to the skillet. Cover and cook until the mushrooms are softened, about 5 minutes. 2. Add the cauliflower and cashews and mix well. Cover and cook for 2 minutes. 3. Adjust the seasonings as desired and evenly divide the cauliflower mixture among the lettuce leaves. 4. Serve garnished with scallions (if using) and cilantro (if using).

**Per Serving:** Calories 413; Total Fat 25g; Saturated Fat 8g; Sodium 452mg; Carbs 38g; Fiber 9g; Sugar 9g; Protein 17g

## Miso Baked Tempeh and Carrot Wraps

**Prep time: 10 minutes | Cook time: 10 minutes | Serves: 1**

2 collard green leaves, washed
½ cup shredded carrots
1 teaspoon grated ginger (optional)
½ tablespoon white or yellow miso
½ tablespoon rice vinegar
½ tablespoon sesame oil
Nonstick cooking oil spray
4 ounces smoky tempeh, sliced
1 cup bean sprouts
4 radishes, thinly sliced

1. Fill a saucepan of water and bring it to a boil over high heat. Blanch the collard greens for 3 minutes, remove them from the water, and cool immediately under cold running water. Allow to dry and blot with a towel to remove excess water. 2. In a bowl, mix the carrots, ginger (if using), miso, vinegar, and sesame oil until well mixed. 3. Lightly grease a skillet and heat it over medium heat. Panfry the tempeh slices until crispy on each side, about 2 minutes per side. 4. Place the collard greens on a clean work surface and evenly divide the carrot mixture, tempeh, bean sprouts, and radishes between them. Fold over the end of each leaf, tuck one side under, and roll like a burrito. Serve. 5. Store any leftovers in an airtight container in the refrigerator for up to 2 days.

**Per Serving:** Calories 396; Total Fat 22g; Saturated Fat 12g; Sodium 536mg; Carbs 19g; Fiber 6g; Sugar 3g; Protein 31g

## Chicken Salad with Apricots and Almonds

**Prep time: 10 minutes | Cook time: 0 minutes | Serves: 4**

1 cup plain Greek yogurt
2 tablespoons minced shallots
1 teaspoon ground coriander
1 teaspoon Dijon mustard (optional)
1 tablespoon freshly squeezed lemon juice
¼ teaspoon cayenne pepper
12 ounces cooked rotisserie chicken, shredded
2 cups chopped celery with the leaves
¼ cup slivered almonds, toasted
¼ cup thinly sliced dried apricots
1 bunch fresh parsley, chopped

1. In a bowl, add the yogurt along with shallots, coriander, mustard (if using), lemon juice, and cayenne until well combined. 2. Add the chicken, celery, almonds, apricots, and parsley. 3. Serve on your food of choice.
Per Serving: Calories 288; Total Fat 16g; Saturated Fat 3g; Sodium 333mg; Carbs 12g; Fiber 3g; Sugar 4g; Protein 25g

## Green Tofu Soup

**Prep time: 10 minutes | Cook time: 25 minutes | Serves: 8**

8 cups low-sodium vegetable broth
3 medium carrots, peeled and diced
4 ounces mushrooms, sliced
6 medium scallions, sliced, divided
8 medium cloves garlic, peeled and minced
1 (1") piece fresh ginger, minced
¼ teaspoon ground white pepper
1 pound tofu, cut into cubes

1. In a stockpot, add broth, carrots, mushrooms, 4 scallions, garlic, ginger, and white pepper. Bring to a boil. 2. Once boiling, add tofu. Reduce heat to low, cover, and simmer 5 minutes. 3. Remove from heat, ladle soup into medium bowls, and garnish with remaining 2 scallions. Serve immediately.
Per Serving: Calories 90; Total Fat 2.5g; Saturated Fat 0g; Sodium 170mg; Carbs 9g; Fiber 2g; Sugar 3g; Protein 7g

## Shortcut Wonton Soup

**Prep time: 10 minutes | Cook time: 25 minutes | Serves: 8**

8 ounces lean ground pork
1 tablespoon minced fresh ginger
4 medium cloves garlic, peeled and minced
8 cups low-sodium chicken broth
2 cups sliced mushrooms
6 ounces dry whole-grain egg noodles
¼ teaspoon ground white pepper
4 medium scallions, chopped

1. Place a stockpot. Add pork, ginger, and garlic and sauté 5 minutes. Drain any excess fat and return to stovetop over medium heat. 2. Add broth and bring to a boil. Once boiling, stir in mushrooms, noodles, and white pepper. Cover and simmer 10 minutes. 3. Remove stockpot from heat. Stir in scallions and serve immediately.
Per Serving: Calories 160; Total Fat 5g; Saturated Fat 1.5g; Sodium 100mg; Carbs 19g; Fiber 2g; Sugar 1g; Protein 11g

## Lentil Sloppy Joes with Roasted Asparagus

**Prep time: 8 minutes | Cook time: 20 minutes | Serves: 2**

1 bunch asparagus, woody ends removed
1 tablespoon extra-virgin olive oil, divided
½ cup chopped onion
2 teaspoons chopped serrano pepper (optional)
2 garlic cloves, minced
1½ cups water
½ cup red lentils, rinsed
2 tablespoons ketchup
1 teaspoon paprika
1 sandwich thin or other bread option

1. Preheat the oven to 450°F. Manage a baking sheet with parchment paper. 2. In a small bowl, toss the asparagus with 1½ teaspoons of extra-virgin olive oil until well coated, and spread the vegetables on the prepared baking sheet. Bake for 12 to 15 minutes. 3. Meanwhile, heat the remaining 1½ teaspoons of extra-virgin olive oil in a medium saucepan over medium heat and sauté the onion and pepper (if using) until soft and translucent, 2 to 3 minutes. Cook the garlic for 1 minute. 4. Add the water and lentils and bring to a boil. Lower the heat to low and manage simmer, until the lentils are tender but not falling apart, about 10 minutes. 5. Add the ketchup and paprika. Adjust seasonings as desired and allow the mixture to thicken over the heat for a couple of minutes. 6. Serve on a sandwich thin or slice of bread with a side of roasted asparagus. 7. Store any leftover filling in an airtight container in the refrigerator for up to 5 days.
Per Serving: Calories 370; Total Fat 9g; Saturated Fat 0.1g; Sodium 308mg; Carbs 61g; Fiber 14g; Sugar 33g; Protein 20g

## Homemade Turkey Pastrami and Pimento Cheese Sandwich

**Prep time: 5 minutes | Cook time: 0 minutes | Serves: 2**

**For the Pimento Cheese** (enough for 4 sandwiches)
6 ounces sharp cheddar cheese, shredded
3 tablespoons cream cheese, softened
1 tablespoon plain Greek yogurt
2 teaspoons diced pimentos
**For the Turkey Pastrami Sandwich**
4 ounces Pimento Cheese
4 slices marble rye bread
6 ounces low-sodium turkey pastrami or peppered turkey
4 lettuce leaves
1 red bell pepper, cut into strips

To make the pimento cheese
1. In a bowl, cream the cheddar, cream cheese, and yogurt using a spoon. 2. Add the pimentos and stir to combine. If it's too thick, add a bit of water or pimento juice.
To make the turkey pastrami sandwich
1. Spread the pimento cheese on each slice of marble rye bread. Layer the turkey pastrami and lettuce on the cheese spread on two of the bread slices. Place the other two slices of bread, cheese-side down, on the fillings, creating the sandwich. 2. Serve the sandwiches accompanied by sliced red bell pepper.
Per Serving: Calories 510; Total Fat 25g; Saturated Fat 0.1g; Sodium 308mg; Carbs 37g; Fiber 4g; Sugar 33g; Protein 31g

## Easy Turkey Taco Soup

**Prep time: 15 minutes | Cook time: 20 minutes | Serves: 12**

1 tablespoon olive oil
1 ⅓ pounds package lean ground turkey
2 (28-ounce) cans crushed tomatoes, undrained
1 (14-ounce) can low-sodium black beans, drained and rinsed.
1 (14-ounce) can low-sodium pinto beans, drained and rinsed.
1 (14-ounce) can low-sodium kidney beans, drained and rinsed
1 (14-ounce) can corn kernels, drained and rinsed
2 tablespoons taco seasoning, less sodium

1. In a large Dutch oven or stockpot over medium-high heat, heat oil for 30 seconds. Cook turkey for 8 minutes or until no longer pink. 2. Add tomatoes, beans, corn, and taco seasoning and stir to combine. Cook 20 minutes, stirring occasionally. Serve.
**Per Serving:** Calories 230; Total Fat 6g; Saturated Fat 1g; Sodium 440mg; Carbs 32g; Fiber 8g; Sugar 9g; Protein 18g

## Super Easy Minted Sweet Pea Soup

**Prep time: 10 minutes | Cook time: 10 minutes | Serves: 2-4**

2 tablespoons extra-virgin olive oil
1 small yellow onion, minced
Pinch kosher salt
Pinch freshly ground black pepper
2 garlic cloves, minced
1 zucchini, diced
4 cups low-sodium vegetable broth
3 cups frozen peas
Juice of 1 lemon
½ cup plain Greek yogurt (optional)
½ cup thinly sliced fresh mint
2 tablespoons chopped pistachios (optional)

1. Heat the extra-virgin olive oil in a stockpot over medium heat. Add the onion, salt, and pepper and sauté until translucent. 2. Add the garlic and zucchini and sauté until tender, about 3 minutes. 3. Transfer the vegetables to a blender and puree them with the vegetable broth, peas, and lemon juice. 4. Adjust the seasonings and serve the soup warmed in a saucepan over medium heat or cooled in the refrigerator. To cool it in an ice bath, transfer the soup to a medium bowl and nestle in a large bowl filled with ice water. 5. Serve with a dollop of optional Greek yogurt (if using) and topped with mint and pistachios (if using). 6. Store the cooled soup in an airtight container in the refrigerator for up to 5 days, with garnishes kept separately.
**Per Serving:** Calories 345; Total Fat 15g; Saturated Fat 0.1g; Sodium 308mg; Carbs 34g; Fiber 13g; Sugar 33g; Protein 12g

## Homemade Egg Drop Soup

**Prep time: 10 minutes | Cook time: 15 minutes | Serves: 4**

3½ cups low-sodium vegetable broth, divided
1 teaspoon grated fresh ginger (optional)
2 garlic cloves, minced
3 teaspoons low-sodium soy sauce or tamari
1 tablespoon cornstarch
2 large eggs, lightly beaten
2 scallions, both white and green parts, thinly sliced

1. In a large saucepan, bring 3 cups plus 6 tablespoons of vegetable broth and the ginger (if using), garlic, and tamari to a boil over medium-high heat. 2. In a small bowl, make a slurry by combining the cornstarch and the remaining 2 tablespoons of broth. Stir until dissolved. Slowly add the cornstarch mixture to the rest of the heated soup, stirring until thickened, 2 to 3 minutes. 3. Reduce the heat to low and simmer. While stirring the soup, pour the eggs in slowly. Turn off the heat, add the scallions, and serve. 4. Store the cooled soup in an airtight container in the refrigerator for up to 3 days.
**Per Serving:** Calories 66; Total Fat 3g; Saturated Fat 0.1g; Sodium 308mg; Carbs 6g; Fiber 1g; Sugar 33g; Protein 4g

## Manhattan-Style Seafood Chowder

**Prep time: 10 minutes | Cook time: 25 minutes | Serves: 4**

1½ teaspoons olive oil
1 large onion, peeled and diced
4 medium cloves garlic, peeled and minced
2 (15-ounce) cans diced tomatoes, undrained
2 cups low-sodium chicken broth
2 medium carrots, peeled and thinly sliced
8 ounces white-fleshed fish such as tilapia, cut into 1" chunks
1 medium jalapeño pepper, seeded and minced
1 large bay leaf
8 ounces small shrimp, shelled
⅓ cup chopped fresh parsley
½ teaspoon orange zest
½ teaspoon ground black pepper
¼ cup grated Parmesan cheese

1. In a stockpot over medium heat, heat oil. Add onion and garlic and cook, stirring for 3 minutes. 2. Add tomatoes with juice, broth, carrots, fish, jalapeños, and bay leaf and stir to combine. 3. Cover stockpot and cook, stirring occasionally, 15 minutes. 4. Add shrimp, parsley, orange zest, and black pepper and stir well. Manage to Simmer until shrimp are pink, about 5 minutes, then remove from heat. 5. Carefully remove bay leaf and serve immediately. Top each serving with 1 tablespoon Parmesan.
**Per Serving:** Calories 240; Total Fat 5g; Saturated Fat 2g; Sodium 590mg; Carbs 16g; Fiber 4g; Sugar 9g; Protein 30g

## Shaved Asparagus Salad with Chile-Lime Dressing

**Prep time: 15 minutes | Cook time: 0 minutes | Serves: 2 to 4**

1 bunch asparagus, woody ends trimmed and stalks peeled into ribbons
12 ounces leftover rotisserie chicken (optional)
2 cups shredded cabbage
1 cup arugula
1 bunch (about 8) radishes, thinly sliced
½ cup mint, stemmed and finely sliced
3 scallions, finely sliced
¼ to ½ cup Chile-Lime Dressing or store-bought
⅓ cup chopped, roasted (unsalted) peanuts
Pickled Red Onions (optional)

1. Combine the asparagus ribbons, chicken (if using), cabbage, arugula, radishes, mint, and scallions in a large bowl. Pour dressing and toss to combine with your hands or tongs. 2. Place the salad on a large serving plate and garnish it with the chopped peanuts, pickled red onions, and more chopped mint if you like.
**Per Serving:** Calories 391; Total Fat 30g; Saturated Fat 5g; Sodium 312mg; Carbs 25g; Fiber 10g; Sugar 6g; Protein 13g

## Roasted Tomato-Basil Soup with Grilled Cheese Croutons

**Prep time: 10 minutes | Cook time: 20 minutes | Serves: 4-6**

**For the Tomato Soup**
2 tablespoons extra-virgin olive oil
1 onion, chopped
1 tablespoon minced garlic
3 pounds fresh tomatoes, cored and chopped, or canned diced tomatoes
8 cups low-sodium vegetable broth
4 tablespoons tomato paste
½ cup coconut milk
½ teaspoon garlic powder
Pinch kosher salt
Pinch freshly ground black pepper
⅓ cup fresh basil, chopped

**For the Grilled Cheese Croutons**
1 tablespoon butter or cooking spray
4 slices whole-wheat bread
4 ounces cheese (cheddar or Gruyère), shredded
Freshly ground black pepper (optional)

To make the tomato soup
1. Heat the olive oil and Sauté the onion and minced garlic until translucent, about 3 minutes. 2. Add the tomatoes and vegetable broth, increase the heat to medium-high, cover, and simmer until the tomato skin wrinkles and pulls back from the tomato flesh, 8 to 10 minutes. 3. Add the tomato paste, coconut milk, garlic powder, salt, and pepper and simmer for 3 to 5 minutes. 4. Blend soup until smooth, in batches if necessary. Leave the center piece out of the lid and cover the lid with a clean kitchen towel while blending to allow the steam to escape. 5. Pour the soup back into the stockpot. 6. Serve the soup topped with basil and the grilled cheese croutons (if using). 7. Store the cooled soup in an airtight container in the refrigerator for 3 to 5 days. Keep the garnishes separate.

To make the grilled cheese croutons
1. Meanwhile, apply the butter on one side of each slice of bread. 2. Put a small nonstick skillet over medium heat, and place 1 slice of bread in the skillet, buttered-side down. Top with half of the cheese and season with pepper (if using). Then top with the second slice of bread, buttered-side up. When the underside is golden brown, 3 to 4 minutes, turn the sandwich. Cook until the second side of the bread is golden and crispy. 3. Repeat with the remaining ingredients. 4. Cut each sandwich into 1-inch squares and use them to garnish the soup.

**Per Serving:** Calories 230; Total Fat 13g; Saturated Fat 2g; Sodium 222mg; Carbs 27g; Fiber 7g; Sugar 5g; Protein 4g

## West African Peanut Soup

**Prep time: 10 minutes | Cook time: 20 minutes | Serves: 4-6**

6 garlic cloves, minced
1½-inch piece ginger, grated
1 jalapeño pepper, stemmed, halved, and minced, divided
Kosher salt
2 (14-ounce) cans coconut milk, divided
2 tablespoons vegetable oil, divided
1 teaspoon turmeric
½ cup unsweetened peanut butter
8 cups vegetable broth
2 sweet potatoes, cut into ½-inch cubes
1 bunch collard greens, chopped
Juice of 1 lime
Freshly ground black pepper
½ cup chopped cilantro

1. Place the garlic, ginger, half the jalapeño, and a pinch of salt in a mound on a cutting board. 2. Scoop 3 tablespoons of the solid white coconut fat off the top of one can of coconut milk and place it in a large Dutch oven or stockpot. Add vegetable oil to the coconut fat and heat over medium-high heat, stirring frequently, until the coconut fat separates and the solids start to sizzle, about 2 minutes. Continue cooking, stirring constantly, until the solids turn pale golden brown, about 1 minute longer. Add the garlic paste, turmeric, and peanut butter. Cook, stirring, until aromatic, about 30 seconds. 3. Add the remaining coconut milk from both cans, the broth, and sweet potatoes. Bring to a boil, lower the heat to low, and simmer until the sweet potatoes are tender, about 15 minutes. 4. When the potatoes are cooked through, use a large spoon to smash about half of the sweet potatoes against the side of the stockpot to help thicken the stew. Add the collard greens and lime juice. 5. Spice the soup with salt and pepper and serve topped with cilantro and the remaining minced jalapeños. 6. Store the cooled soup in an airtight container in the refrigerator for 3 to 5 days.

**Per Serving:** Calories 706; Total Fat 58g; Saturated Fat 20g; Sodium 621mg; Carbs 42g; Fiber 8g; Sugar 7g; Protein 13g

## Chickpea and Spinach Soup

**Prep time: 5 minutes | Cook time: 25 minutes | Serves: 4**

4 medium carrots, cut into ¼-inch pieces
3 tablespoons extra-virgin olive oil, divided
1 teaspoon ground cumin
1 teaspoon paprika
½ teaspoon ground coriander
½ teaspoon ground cinnamon
2 (15-ounce) cans chickpeas, drained and rinsed
1 onion, thinly sliced
2 tablespoons minced fresh ginger
5 cups low-sodium vegetable broth
1 pound fresh baby spinach
1 cup Greek yogurt (optional)

1. Preheat the oven to 425°F. Manage a baking sheet with parchment paper. 2. In a medium bowl, toss the carrots with 2 tablespoons of extra-virgin olive oil, the cumin, paprika, coriander, and cinnamon. Spread the carrots evenly on the baking sheet and roast for 8 to 10 minutes. Add half the chickpeas to the carrots, place the baking sheet back in the oven, and roast until the carrots are tender, about 10 minutes more. Set aside. 3. Meanwhile, heat the remaining 1 tablespoon of extra-virgin olive oil in a large stockpot over medium-high heat. Sauté the onion in the oil until translucent, about 3 minutes, then add the ginger, remaining chickpeas, broth, and spinach. Bring the soup to a boil, reduce the heat to low, and simmer until the greens begin to wilt, 2 to 3 minutes. 4. Blend soup until smooth. Leave the center piece out of the lid and cover the lid with a clean dish towel to allow the steam to escape. Adjust the seasonings as desired and thin the soup with water or additional broth if you prefer a thinner soup. 5. Serve topped with yogurt (if using) and the carrot and chickpea topping. 6. Store the cooled soup in an airtight container in the refrigerator for 3 to 5 days.

**Per Serving:** Calories 344; Total Fat 14g; Saturated Fat 2g; Sodium 302mg; Carbs 45g; Fiber 13g; Sugar 6g; Protein 12g

## Traditional Golden Chicken Soup

**Prep time: 10 minutes | Cook time: 20 minutes | Serves: 4-6**

1 tablespoon extra-virgin olive oil
1 yellow onion, chopped
2 teaspoons garlic powder
1 tablespoon ginger powder
2 teaspoons turmeric
½ teaspoon freshly ground black pepper
6 cups low-sodium chicken broth
3 (5- to 6-ounce) boneless, skinless chicken breasts
4 celery stalks, cut into ¼-inch-thick slices
1 fennel bulb, thinly sliced

1. Heat the olive oil in a stockpot and Sauté the onion until translucent, about 3 minutes. Add the garlic powder, ginger powder, turmeric, black pepper, and chicken broth. 2. Bring to a boil, then carefully add the chicken, celery, and fennel. Lower the heat to medium-low, cover, and simmer until the internal temperature of the chicken is 160°F, 5 to 10 minutes. 3. Allow them to cool for 5 minutes while the soup keeps simmering. 4. Shred the chicken using two forks and return it to the stockpot. Heat the soup for about 1 minute and adjust the seasonings as desired. 5. Store the cooled soup in an airtight container in the refrigerator for 3 to 5 days.

**Per Serving:** Calories 218; Total Fat 7g; Saturated Fat 0.6g; Sodium 322mg; Carbs 13g; Fiber 4g; Sugar 3g; Protein 29g

## Easy Smoked Turkey Chili

**Prep time: 10 minutes | Cook time: 20 minutes | Serves: 4**

1 tablespoon extra-virgin olive oil
1 yellow onion, diced
2 bell peppers, diced
½ pound ground turkey
1½ teaspoons ground cumin
1 teaspoon ground coriander
1 tablespoon cocoa powder (optional)
3 tablespoons adobo sauce
1 cup low-sodium chicken or vegetable broth
1 (28-ounce) can crushed fire-roasted tomatoes
2 (15-ounce) cans cooked beans (kidney beans, black beans, or navy beans), rinsed and drained

1. Heat the olive oil. Add the onion and bell peppers and sauté until softened, about 5 minutes. 2. Add the ground turkey and sauté until cooked through, 3 to 5 minutes. Add the cumin, coriander, cocoa powder (if using), and adobo sauce. Stir well and add the broth, tomatoes, and beans. 3. Boil it, lower the heat to low, and simmer for at least 15 minutes. The longer you have, the better the flavors will be enhanced. Serve. 4. Store the cooled chili in an airtight container in the refrigerator for 3 to 5 days.

**Per Serving:** Calories 329; Total Fat 12g; Saturated Fat 0.7g; Sodium 203mg; Carbs 37g; Fiber 13g; Sugar 8g; Protein 19g

## Quick Moroccan Style Chicken Stew

**Prep time: 5 minutes | Cook time: 15 minutes | Serves: 4-6**

2 teaspoons ground cumin
1 teaspoon ground cinnamon
½ teaspoon turmeric
½ teaspoon paprika
1½ pounds boneless, skinless chicken, cut into strips
2 tablespoons extra-virgin olive oil
5 garlic cloves, smashed and coarsely chopped
2 onions, thinly sliced
1 tablespoon fresh lemon zest
½ cup coarsely chopped olives
2 cups low-sodium chicken broth
Cilantro, for garnish (optional)

1. In a bowl, mix the cumin, cinnamon, turmeric, and paprika until well blended. Add the chicken, tossing to coat, and set aside. 2. Heat the oil in a skillet or medium Dutch oven over medium-high heat. Add the chicken and garlic in one layer and cook, browning on all sides, about 2 minutes. 3. Add the onions, lemon zest, olives, and broth and bring the soup to a boil. Lower the heat, cover, and simmer for 8 minutes. 4. Uncover the soup and let it simmer for another 2 to 3 minutes for the sauce to thicken slightly. Adjust the seasonings as desired and serve garnished with cilantro (if using).

**Per Serving:** Calories 315; Total Fat 14g; Saturated Fat 3g; Sodium 412mg; Carbs 9g; Fiber 2g; Sugar 3g; Protein 40g

## Roasted Butternut Squash and Pear Soup

**Prep time: 10 minutes | Cook time: 30 minutes | Serves: 6**

3 cups frozen cubed butternut squash
2 tablespoons extra-virgin olive oil, divided
½ teaspoon kosher salt
1 small onion, peeled and sliced (approximately 1 cup)
1 medium pear, cored and cut into cubes
2¼ cups low-sodium chicken or vegetable broth
⅛ teaspoon ground black pepper
⅛ teaspoon ground cumin
⅛ teaspoon ground cayenne pepper
½ cup unsweetened vanilla almond milk
2 tablespoons roasted shelled pumpkin seeds

1. Preheat oven to 400°F. In a medium microwave-safe bowl, microwave butternut squash according to package directions, approximately 7–9 minutes. Add 1 tablespoon oil and salt and toss squash together to mix; set aside. 2. Meanwhile, heat remaining 1 tablespoon oil in a large stockpot over medium heat. Add onion and pear and sauté 3 minutes. Add broth, black pepper, cumin, and cayenne and heat for 2 minutes. 3. Add squash and heat through 2–3 minutes. Turn off heat. 4. Use an immersion blender or add mixture to a kitchen blender and purée until smooth. Once desired consistency is reached, blend in milk. 5. Pour into six medium bowls and garnish each serving with 1 teaspoon pumpkin seeds. Serve.

**Per Serving:** Calories 120; Total Fat 6g; Saturated Fat 1g; Sodium 135mg; Carbs 15g; Fiber 4g; Sugar 5g; Protein 3g

## Cauliflower and Mushroom Soup

**Prep time: 10 minutes | Cook time: 30 minutes | Serves: 6**

1 tablespoon olive oil
1 medium yellow onion, peeled and chopped
4 cups riced cauliflower
8 ounces white mushrooms, thinly sliced
4 cups low-sodium chicken or vegetable broth
½ teaspoon kosher salt
¼ teaspoon ground black pepper
¼ teaspoon ground smoked paprika
½ cup unsweetened almond milk

1. In a pot over heat oil. Add onion and sauté until translucent, about 5 minutes. 2. Add cauliflower and cook 3 minutes. Add mushrooms and sauté an additional 7–8 minutes. 3. Add broth, salt, black pepper, and smoked paprika and bring to a boil; cook 5 more minutes. 4. Turn off heat, stir in almond milk, and blend in pot with an immersion blender until desired consistency is achieved. Serve.

**Per Serving:** Calories 70; Total Fat 2.5g; Saturated Fat 0g; Sodium 180mg; Carbs 7g; Fiber 2g; Sugar 3g; Protein 4g

## Classic Tuscan Pasta Fagioli

**Prep time: 10 minutes | Cook time: 20 minutes | Serves: 8**

2 tablespoons olive oil
⅓ cup chopped onion
3 medium cloves garlic, peeled and minced
1 (8-ounce) can diced tomatoes, undrained
5 cups low-sodium vegetable broth
¼ teaspoon ground black pepper
1 teaspoon kosher salt
½ teaspoon dried oregano
¼ teaspoon red pepper flakes
2 teaspoons lemon juice
¼ cup chopped fresh parsley
2 (15-ounce) cans cannellini beans, divided
2 ½ cups dry whole-grain pasta shells
3 tablespoons grated Parmesan cheese

1. In a large pot over medium heat, heat oil. Add onion and garlic and cook until soft but not browned, about 5 minutes. Add tomatoes with juice, broth, black pepper, salt, oregano, red pepper flakes, lemon juice, and parsley. 2. In a food processor, blend 1½ cups cannellini beans, adding small amounts of hot broth or water to make a smooth purée. Add puréed beans to broth mixture and stir. Cover and simmer 20 minutes. 3. While broth is simmering, cook pasta until al dente and drain. 4. Add remaining beans and pasta to pot and heat through 2–3 minutes. Pour into bowls and sprinkle with Parmesan before serving.

**Per Serving:** Calories 230; Total Fat 5g; Saturated Fat 1.5g; Sodium 430mg; Carbs 37g; Fiber 7g; Sugar 3g; Protein 10g

## Chicken Noodle Soup

**Prep time: 10 minutes | Cook time: 25 minutes | Serves: 4**

2 cups shredded cooked chicken
2 medium carrots, peeled and sliced
1 medium stalk celery, sliced
1 small onion, peeled and diced
3 medium cloves garlic, peeled and minced
4 cups low-sodium chicken broth
1 teaspoon all-purpose seasoning
½ teaspoon ground sage
¼ teaspoon ground rosemary
⅛ teaspoon ground black pepper
1½ cups dry whole-grain egg noodles

1. In a stockpot, combine all ingredients except noodles. Bring to a boil. 2. Once boiling, add noodles, reduce heat to medium-low, and simmer 10 minutes. 3 Remove from heat. Ladle soup into four medium bowls and serve immediately.

**Per Serving:** Calories 210; Total Fat 3g; Saturated Fat 0.5g; Sodium 570mg; Carbs 19g; Fiber 4g; Sugar 3g; Protein 26g

## Jalapeño Lime Chicken Soup

**Prep time: 10 minutes | Cook time: 25 minutes | Serves: 8**

2 cups shredded cooked chicken
1 medium red onion, peeled and diced
3 medium cloves garlic, peeled and minced
2 medium carrots, peeled and sliced
1 medium stalk celery, sliced
1 red bell pepper, diced
2 tablespoons minced jalapeño pepper
1 (15-ounce) can diced tomatoes, undrained
Juice of 2 medium limes (about ¼ cup)
8 cups low-sodium chicken broth
1 teaspoon ground cumin
½ teaspoon ground coriander
¼ teaspoon dried oregano
⅛ teaspoon ground black pepper
2 tablespoons chopped fresh cilantro
1 medium lime, cut into wedges

1. In a stockpot, add all ingredients except cilantro and lime wedges. Bring to a boil. 2. Once boiling, reduce heat to low, cover, and simmer 15 minutes. 3. Remove from heat, ladle into medium bowls, and garnish with cilantro and lime wedges. Serve immediately.

**Per Serving:** Calories 110; Total Fat 1.5g; Saturated Fat 0g; Sodium 310mg; Carbs 8g; Fiber 2g; Sugar 3g; Protein 14g

## Garden Fresh Tomato Soup

**Prep time: 10 minutes | Cook time: 20 minutes | Serves: 4**

1 tablespoon olive oil
3 cups peeled, chopped, and seeded tomatoes
1 cup chopped onion
1 cup chopped red bell pepper
1 tablespoon minced garlic
4 cups low-sodium vegetable broth
2 tablespoons tomato paste
1 tablespoon chopped fresh basil
1 teaspoon chopped fresh oregano
½ teaspoon chopped fresh thyme
⅛ teaspoon ground black pepper

1. In a stockpot, heat oil. Add tomatoes, onion, bell pepper, and garlic and cook, stirring, 10 minutes. 2. Add remaining ingredients and stir to combine. Turn heat to high and bring to a boil. 3. Once boiling, reduce heat to low, cover, and simmer 10 minutes. 4. Remove from heat. Transfer mix to a blender and purée until smooth. Serve immediately.

**Per Serving:** Calories 110; Total Fat 4.5g; Saturated Fat 0.5g; Sodium 135mg; Carbs 15g; Fiber 4g; Sugar 9g; Protein 2g

## Creamy White Bean and Collard Green Soup

**Prep time: 10 minutes | Cook time: 25 minutes | Serves: 4**

1 tablespoon olive oil
1 cup finely chopped yellow onion
4 medium cloves garlic, peeled and minced
½ cup dry white wine
¼ teaspoon ground black pepper
¼ teaspoon kosher salt
4 cups thinly shredded collard greens
¾ teaspoon dried thyme
4 cups low-sodium chicken broth
1 (15-ounce) can low-sodium cannellini or great northern beans, drained and rinsed
1 teaspoon red wine vinegar

1. In a pot, heat oil. Add onion and garlic and sauté 5 minutes or until onion is tender. 2. Add wine, black pepper, and salt and reduce heat to a simmer for 5 minutes or until wine mostly evaporates. 3. Add greens, thyme, and broth. Cover and cook 8 minutes or until greens are tender. 4. Add beans and vinegar and heat through, about 5 minutes. Serve.
**Per Serving:** Calories 180; Total Fat 4g; Saturated Fat 1g; Sodium 270mg; Carbs 22g; Fiber 6g; Sugar 3g; Protein 9g

## Spicy Vegetable and Bean Chili Soup

**Prep time: 15 minutes | Cook time: 35 minutes | Serves: 8**

4 teaspoons olive oil
2 cups chopped onions
½ cup chopped green bell pepper
3 medium cloves garlic, peeled and chopped
1 small jalapeño pepper, seeded and finely chopped
1 tablespoon chili powder
1 teaspoon ground cumin
2 (28-ounce) cans low-sodium chopped tomatoes, undrained
1 medium zucchini, diced
2 (15-ounce) cans low-sodium red kidney beans, drained and rinsed
1 tablespoon chopped semisweet chocolate
3 tablespoons chopped fresh cilantro

1. Heat a pot. Add oil, onions, bell pepper, garlic, and jalapeño and sauté until vegetables are softened, about 5 minutes. Add chili powder and cumin and sauté 1 minute, stirring frequently to mix well. 2. Add tomatoes with juice and zucchini and boil. Reduce heat and manage to simmer, partially covered, 10 minutes, stirring occasionally. 3. Stir in beans and chocolate and simmer, stirring occasionally, an additional 10 minutes or until beans are heated through and chocolate is melted. 4. Stir in cilantro and serve.
**Per Serving:** Calories 170; Total Fat 3.5g; Saturated Fat 1g; Sodium 150mg; Carbs 29g; Fiber 8g; Sugar 10g; Protein 8g

## Winter White Turkey Chili Soup

**Prep time: 10 minutes | Cook time: 20 minutes | Serves: 6**

2 teaspoons olive oil
1 ⅓ pounds 93% lean ground turkey
1 cup chopped onion
1 (4-ounce) can diced green chilies, drained
¾ teaspoon dried oregano
¾ teaspoon ground cumin
¼ teaspoon ground cayenne pepper
2 (15-ounce) cans low-sodium great northern beans, drained and rinsed
3 cups low-sodium chicken broth
1½ tablespoons apple cider vinegar

1. In a pot over medium-high heat, heat oil. Place turkey on one side of the pot and onions on the other. Cook turkey undisturbed for 4 minutes while stirring onions a few times. Break up turkey to combine with onions and cook until turkey is no longer pink, about 3 minutes. 2. Add chilies, oregano, cumin, and cayenne and stir occasionally for 2 minutes. 3. Add beans and broth and bring to a simmer. Cook an additional 15 minutes to reduce liquid, stirring occasionally. 4. Add vinegar and cook an additional 3 minutes. Serve.
**Per Serving:** Calories 270; Total Fat 9g; Saturated Fat 1.5g; Sodium 330mg; Carbs 24g; Fiber 5g; Sugar 3g; Protein 28g

## Creamy Smoked Salmon on Toast

**Prep time: 10 minutes | Cook time: 0 minutes | Serves: 4**

**For the Cream Cheese Spread**
4 ounces cream cheese
Juice of 1 lemon
1 teaspoon stone-ground mustard
**For the Sandwich**
4 slices whole-grain bread
8 ounces smoked salmon
4 radishes, thinly sliced
1 teaspoon capers, rinsed and dried (optional)
¼ cup chopped fresh dill
1 medium cucumber, sliced

To make the cream cheese spread
1. In a bowl, add the cream cheese, 1 teaspoon of lemon juice, and mustard. Cream together evenly and add more lemon juice if it's too thick. You should be able to spread it on a slice of bread easily.
To make the sandwich
2. Spread the cream cheese mixture on each slice of bread and top with the salmon, radish slices, capers (if using), and fresh dill. 3. Serve with cucumber slices on the side.
**Per Serving:** Calories 287; Total Fat 14g; Saturated Fat 0.1g; Sodium 308mg; Carbs 23g; Fiber 3g; Sugar 33g; Protein 18g

## Healthy Low-Cal Garden Soup

**Prep time: 10 minutes | Cook time: 30 minutes | Serves: 8**

1 teaspoon olive oil
¾ cup chopped white onion
1½ cups chopped celery
1½ cups chopped carrots
1½ cups chopped zucchini
1½ cups cut green beans
½ teaspoon garlic powder
1 teaspoon dried oregano
4 cups low-sodium chicken broth
1 (14-ounce) can stewed tomatoes, undrained
¼ cup chopped fresh basil

1. In a pot, heat oil for 30 seconds. Add onion, celery, and carrots and sauté until crisp-tender, about 10 minutes. 2. Add zucchini, green beans, garlic powder, oregano, broth, and tomatoes with juice and bring to a light boil. 3. Reduce heat to low and simmer until vegetables are tender, about 10 minutes. Garnish with basil before serving.
**Per Serving:** Calories 50; Total Fat 1g; Saturated Fat 0g; Sodium 150mg; Carbs 9g; Fiber 2g; Sugar 5g; Protein 2g

# Chapter 7 Dessert and Snack Recipes

| | | | |
|---|---|---|---|
| 88 | Pear and Pecan Crumble Pie | 91 | Healthy Raspberry-Chocolate Chia Pudding |
| 88 | Quick Chocolate Yogurt Granita | 91 | Tasty Herbed Yogurt Sauce |
| 88 | Homemade Vanilla Bean Ice Cream | 92 | Spiced Honey Roasted Almonds |
| 88 | No Bake Apple Pie Parfait | 92 | Tasty Blueberries with Sweet Cashew Cream |
| 88 | Simple Oatmeal-Cranberry Cookies | 92 | Chocolate Covered Strawberries |
| 88 | Healthy Berry Smoothie Pops | 92 | Classic Dark Chocolate Baking Drops |
| 89 | Roasted Peach and Coconut Yogurt Bowls | 92 | Simple Berry Sorbet |
| 89 | Frozen Chocolate Peanut Butter Freezer Bites | 92 | Easy Stuffed Dates |
| 89 | Healthy Dark Chocolate Almond Butter Cups | 93 | Homemade Carrot Cake |
| 89 | Low Calorie Carrot Cake Bites | 93 | Almond Energy Balls |
| 89 | Tasty Strawberry Cream Cheese Crepes | 93 | Perfect Mango Smoothie |
| 90 | Homemade Cream Cheese Swirl Brownies | 93 | Authentic Green Goddess Dressing |
| 90 | Soft Oatmeal Cookies | 93 | Tropical Fruit Salad with Coconut Milk and Lime |
| 90 | No-Bake Peanut Butter Energy Balls | 93 | Roasted Spiced Pears with Cinnamon and Pistachios |
| 90 | Easy Pecan Sandies | 94 | Easy Apple Crisp |
| 90 | Creamy Minty Hot Chocolate | 94 | Tasty Sweet Potato Cake |
| 91 | Homemade Strawberry Yogurt Pops | | |
| 91 | Classic Omega-3 Crackers | | |
| 91 | Low Carb Microwave Keto Bread | | |
| 91 | Low Calorie Avocado Chocolate Mousse | | |

## Pear and Pecan Crumble Pie

Prep time: 10 minutes | Cook time: 20 minutes | Serves: 6

2 teaspoons butter
4 pears, peeled, cored, and sliced
1 tablespoon cornstarch
½ teaspoon ground cinnamon
¼ teaspoon ground nutmeg
1 cup rolled oats
½ cup chopped pecans
¼ cup almond flour
2 tablespoons ground flaxseed
½ teaspoon ground cinnamon
¼ teaspoon ground cloves
¼ teaspoon sea salt
¼ cup melted butter
2 tablespoons maple syrup

1. Preheat the oven to 400°F temp setting. 2. In a medium ovenproof skillet, melt the butter over medium heat and sauté the pears for about 5 minutes, until tender-crisp and purged of juices. 3. Stir in the cornstarch, cinnamon, and nutmeg and set aside. 4. In a medium bowl, toss the oats, pecans, almond flour, flaxseed, cinnamon, cloves, and salt until well mixed. 5. Add the melted butter with maple syrup and mix until the mixture resembles coarse crumbs. 6. Top the fruit in the skillet evenly with the crumble mixture. 7. Put the skillet in the oven and bake for about 15 minutes, until golden. Serve warm.
**Per Serving:** Calories 348; Total Fat 18g; Saturated Fat 7g; Sodium 171mg; Carbs 40g; Fiber 11g; Sugar 15g; Protein 4g

## Quick Chocolate Yogurt Granita

Prep time: 5 minutes | Cook time: 0 minutes | Serves: 4

2 cups low-fat plain Greek yogurt
½ cup unsweetened almond milk
¼ cup unsweetened cocoa powder
2 tablespoons maple syrup
2 teaspoons pure vanilla extract

1. Place the yogurt, almond milk, cocoa powder, maple syrup, and vanilla in a blender and blend until very smooth. 2. Pour the mixture into a metal 9-inch square baking dish and place in the freezer. Stir with a fork every 30 minutes or so for about 3 hours, until frozen and the mixture resembles soft snow. Serve.
**Per Serving:** Calories 134; Total Fat 3g; Saturated Fat 2g; Sodium 93mg; Carbs 19g; Fiber 3g; Sugar 14g; Protein 8g

## Homemade Vanilla Bean Ice Cream

Prep time: 5 minutes | Cook time: 0 minutes | Serves: 4

3 overripe bananas, cut into chunks and frozen
¼ cup unsweetened vanilla almond milk
1 vanilla bean, seeds scraped out
Pinch salt

1. Place the bananas, almond milk, vanilla bean, and salt in a blender and blend until it is a soft-serve texture. 2. Serve immediately or freeze in a sealed container for up 2weeks
**Per Serving:** Calories 83; Total Fat 0g; Saturated Fat 0g; Sodium 47mg; Carbs 20g; Fiber 3g; Sugar 10g; Protein 1g

## No Bake Apple Pie Parfait

Prep time: 25 minutes | Cook time: 0 minutes | Serves: 2

1 apple, peeled, cored, and chopped
1 teaspoon maple syrup (optional)
½ teaspoon ground cinnamon
1 cup low-fat vanilla yogurt, divided
¼ cup chopped almonds or pecans, divided
¼ cup whipped coconut cream

1. In a bowl, toss the apple, maple syrup (if using), and cinnamon until well mixed. 2. Layer ¼ cup yogurt in the bottom of a tall, wide glass or small bowl. Then layer in ¼ of the apple and 1 tablespoon almonds. Repeat the layering and top the glass with 2 tablespoons of whipped coconut cream. 3. Repeat with a second glass or bowl and serve immediately.
**Per Serving:** Calories 311; Total Fat 20g; Saturated Fat 11g; Sodium 87mg; Carbs 23g; Fiber 4g; Sugar 15g; Protein 9g

## Simple Oatmeal-Cranberry Cookies

Prep time: 15 minutes | Cook time: 10 minutes | Serves: 18

½ cup melted butter
¼ cup honey
1 large egg
1 teaspoon pure vanilla extract
1 cup white whole-wheat flour
1 cup rolled oats
1 cup leftover cooked quinoa
½ cup dried cranberries
½ teaspoon baking soda
¼ teaspoon baking powder
¼ teaspoon ground nutmeg
¼ teaspoon sea salt
⅛ teaspoon ground allspice

1. Preheat the oven to 375°F. Manage a baking sheet with parchment paper. 2. In a large bowl, mix the butter, honey, egg, and vanilla. 3. In a bowl, add the flour with oats, quinoa, cranberries, baking soda, baking powder, nutmeg, salt, and allspice until well combined. 4. Mix all wet ingredients mix and dry ingredients mix together well. 5. Scoop the batter in heaped tablespoons onto the baking sheet and flatten out. 6. Bake for 10 minutes until golden brown. 7. Store the cookies in a sealed container at room temperature for 5 days or freeze for up to 1 month.
**Per Serving:** Calories 127; Total Fat 6g; Saturated Fat 3g; Sodium 98mg; Carbs 16g; Fiber 2g; Sugar 6g; Protein 2g

## Healthy Berry Smoothie Pops

Prep time: 5 minutes | Cook time: 0 minutes | Serves: 6

2 cups frozen mixed berries
½ cup unsweetened plain almond milk
1 cup plain nonfat Greek yogurt
2 tablespoons hemp seeds

1. In a blender, process all ingredients until finely blended. 2. Pour into 6 clean ice pop molds and insert sticks. 3. Freeze for few hours until firm.
**Per Serving:** Calories 70; Total Fat 2g; Saturated Fat 0.1g; Sodium 28mg; Carbs 9g; Fiber 3g; Sugar 2g; Protein 5g

## Roasted Peach and Coconut Yogurt Bowls

**Prep time: 5 minutes | Cook time: 10 minutes | Serves: 4**

2 peaches, halved and pitted
½ cup plain nonfat Greek yogurt
1 teaspoon pure vanilla extract
¼ cup unsweetened dried coconut flakes
2 tablespoons unsalted pistachios, shelled and broken into pieces

1. Preheat the broiler to high. Arrange the rack in the closest position to the broiler. 2. In a shallow pan, arrange the peach halves, cut-side up. Broil for 6 to 8 minutes until browned, tender, and hot. 3. In a small bowl, mix the yogurt and vanilla. 4. Spoon the yogurt into the cavity of each peach half. 5. Sprinkle 1 tablespoon of coconut flakes and 1½ teaspoons of pistachios over each peach half. Serve warm.
Per Serving: Calories 102; Total Fat 5g; Saturated Fat 0.3g; Sodium 12mg; Carbs 11g; Fiber 2g; Sugar 8g; Protein 5g

## Frozen Chocolate Peanut Butter Freezer Bites

**Prep time: 5 minutes | Cook time: 0 minutes | Serves: 32**

1 cup coconut oil, melted
¼ cup cocoa powder
¼ cup honey
¼ cup natural peanut butter

1. Pour the melted coconut oil into a medium bowl. Whisk in the cocoa powder, honey, and peanut butter. 2. Transfer the mixture to ice cube trays in portions about 1½ teaspoons each. 3. Freeze for 2 hours or until ready to serve.
Per Serving: Calories 80; Total Fat 8g; Saturated Fat 0.6g; Sodium 20mg; Carbs 3g; Fiber 0g; Sugar 2g; Protein 1g

## Healthy Dark Chocolate Almond Butter Cups

**Prep time: 15 minutes | Cook time: 0 minutes | Serves: 12**

½ cup natural almond butter
1 tablespoon pure maple syrup
1 cup dark chocolate chips
1 tablespoon coconut oil

1. Prepare a 12-cup muffin tin with liners. 2. In a bowl, mix the almond butter and maple syrup. If necessary, heat in the microwave to soften slightly. 3. Spoon about 2 teaspoons of the almond butter mixture into each muffin cup and press down to fill. 4. In a microwave, melt the chocolate chips. Add in the coconut oil, until well incorporate. 5. Drop 1 tablespoon of chocolate on top of each almond butter cup. 6. Freeze for at least 30 minutes to set. Thaw for 10 minutes before serving.
Per Serving: Calories 101; Total Fat 8g; Saturated Fat 0.2g; Sodium 32mg; Carbs 6g; Fiber 1g; Sugar 4g; Protein 3g

## Low Calorie Carrot Cake Bites

**Prep time: 15 minutes | Cook time: 15 minutes | Serves: 20**

½ cup old-fashioned oats
2 medium carrots, chopped
6 dates, pitted
½ cup chopped walnuts
½ cup coconut flour
2 tablespoons hemp seeds
2 teaspoons pure maple syrup
1 teaspoon ground cinnamon
½ teaspoon ground nutmeg

1. In a blender jar, combine the oats and carrots, and process until finely ground. Transfer to a bowl. 2. Add the dates along with walnuts in blender and process until coarsely chopped. Return the oat-carrot mixture to the blender and add the coconut flour, hemp seeds, maple syrup, cinnamon, and nutmeg. Process until well mixed. 3. Shape the dough into medium size balls. 4. Store in the refrigerator in an airtight container for up to 1 week.
Per Serving: Calories 68; Total Fat 3g; Saturated Fat 0.1g; Sodium 6mg; Carbs 10g; Fiber 2g; Sugar 6g; Protein 2g

## Tasty Strawberry Cream Cheese Crepes

**Prep time: 10 minutes | Cook time: 10 minutes | Serves: 4**

½ cup old-fashioned oats
1 cup unsweetened plain almond milk
1 egg
3 teaspoons honey, divided
Nonstick cooking spray
2 ounces low-fat cream cheese
¼ cup low-fat cottage cheese
2 cups sliced strawberries

1. In a blender jar, process the oats until they resemble flour. Add the almond milk, egg, and 1½ teaspoons honey, and process until smooth. 2. Heat a large skillet over medium heat. Spray with nonstick cooking spray to coat. 3. Add ¼ cup of oat batter to the pan and quickly swirl around to coat the bottom of the pan and let cook for 2 to 3 minutes. When the edges begin to turn brown, flip the crepe with a spatula and cook until lightly browned and firm, about 1 minute. Transfer to a plate. Continue with the remaining batter, spraying the skillet with nonstick cooking spray before adding more batter. Set the cooked crepes aside, loosely covered with aluminum foil, while you make the filling. 4. Clean the blender jar, then combine the cream cheese, cottage cheese, and remaining 1½ teaspoons honey, and process until smooth. 5. Fill crepe with the cream cheese mixture, topped with ¼ cup of strawberries. Serve.
Per Serving: Calories 149; Total Fat 6g; Saturated Fat 0.2g; Sodium 177mg; Carbs 20g; Fiber 3g; Sugar 10g; Protein 6g

## Homemade Cream Cheese Swirl Brownies

**Prep time: 10 minutes | Cook time: 20 minutes | Serves: 12**

2 eggs
¼ cup unsweetened applesauce
¼ cup coconut oil, melted
3 tablespoons pure maple syrup, divided
¼ cup unsweetened cocoa powder
¼ cup coconut flour
¼ teaspoon salt
1 teaspoon baking powder
2 tablespoons low-fat cream cheese

1. Preheat the oven to 350°F. Grease an 8-by-8-inch baking dish. 2. In a bowl, mix the eggs with the applesauce, coconut oil, and 2 tablespoons of maple syrup. 3. Stir in the cocoa powder and coconut flour, and mix well. Sprinkle the salt and baking powder evenly over the surface and mix well to incorporate. Place the mix to the baking dish. 4. In a small, microwave-safe bowl, microwave the cream cheese for 10 to 20 seconds until softened. Add the remaining 1 tablespoon of maple syrup and mix to combine. 5. Drop the cream cheese onto the batter, and use a toothpick or chopstick to swirl it on the surface. Bake for 20 minutes, until a toothpick inserted in the center comes out clean. Cool and cut into 12 squares. 6. Store refrigerated in a covered container for up to 5 days.

**Per Serving:** Calories 84; Total Fat 6g; Saturated Fat 0.3g; Sodium 93mg; Carbs 6g; Fiber 2g; Sugar 4g; Protein 2g

## Soft Oatmeal Cookies

**Prep time: 5 minutes | Cook time: 15 minutes | Serves: 16**

¾ cup almond flour
¾ cup old-fashioned oats
¼ cup shredded unsweetened coconut
1 teaspoon baking powder
1 teaspoon ground cinnamon
¼ teaspoon salt
¼ cup unsweetened applesauce
1 large egg
1 tablespoon pure maple syrup
2 tablespoons coconut oil, melted

1. Preheat the oven to 350°F temp setting. 2. In a medium mixing bowl, combine the almond flour, oats, coconut, baking powder, cinnamon, and salt, and mix well. 3. In another medium bowl, combine the applesauce, egg, maple syrup, and coconut oil, and mix. Stir the wet mixture into the dry mixture. 4. Form the dough into balls a little bigger than a tablespoon and place on a baking sheet, leaving at least 1 inch between them. Bake for 12 minutes until browned. Let cool for 5 minutes. 5. Using a spatula, remove the cookies and cool on a rack.

**Per Serving:** Calories 76; Total Fat 6g; Saturated Fat 0.2g; Sodium 57mg; Carbs 5g; Fiber 1g; Sugar 2g; Protein 2g

## No-Bake Peanut Butter Energy Balls

**Prep time: 20 minutes | Cook time: 0 minutes | Serves: 12**

1 cup unsweetened peanut or almond butter, stirred well
½ cup almond or coconut flour
¼ cup rolled quick-cooking oats
2 to 4 tablespoons granulated sugar-free sweetener
¼ cup unsweetened coconut flakes
¼ cup sugar-free chocolate chips, chopped
2 tablespoons chia seeds

1. In a bowl, add the peanut butter, almond flour, oats, sweetener to taste (if using), coconut flakes, chocolate chips, and chia seeds, mixing well with a fork or spoon. 2. Shape the mix into 12 balls, about 1 inch in diameter each. Transfer the energy balls to an airtight storage container, with a piece of parchment paper or waxed paper between each layer. The mixture will be sticky, but the balls will harden as they sit in the refrigerator. 3. Store covered in the refrigerator for up to 1week or the freezer for up to 3 months.

**Per Serving:** Calories 203; Total Fat 17g; Saturated Fat 4g; Sodium 5mg; Carbs 11g; Fiber 4g; Sugar 1g; Protein 7g

## Easy Pecan Sandies

**Prep time: 10 minutes | Cook time: 20 minutes | Serves: 12**

½ cup (1 stick) unsalted butter
½ cup granulated sugar-free sweetener, such as Swerve
1 large egg
1 teaspoon vanilla extract
2 cups almond flour
1 teaspoon xanthan gum
½ teaspoon baking powder
½ teaspoon ground cinnamon
1 cup chopped pecans

1. Preheat the oven to 350°F. Manage a baking sheet with parchment paper. 2. In a bowl, using an electric mixer on medium speed, cream together the butter and sweetener until smooth. Add the egg along with vanilla and beat well, scraping down the sides of the bowl as needed. 3. Add the almond flour, xanthan gum, baking powder, and cinnamon, and stir with a wooden spoon or spatula until well incorporated. Stir in the pecans. 4. Using a tablespoon, spoon 2-tablespoon mounds of dough, about 1 inch apart, on the prepared baking sheet. 5. Bake the cookies for 18 minutes, until set and lightly golden. Let sit on the baking sheet for 10 minutes before transferring to a cooling rack.

**Per Serving:** Calories 246; Total Fat 24g; Saturated Fat 6g; Sodium 31mg; Carbs 13g; Fiber 3g; Sugar 8g; Protein 5g

## Creamy Minty Hot Chocolate

**Prep time: 2 minutes | Cook time: 2 minutes | Serves: 1**

1 cup unsweetened almond milk
¼ cup heavy (whipping) cream
1 teaspoon peppermint extract
2 tablespoons sugar-free chocolate chips, such as Lily's
2 tablespoons unsweetened cocoa powder
1 tablespoon granulated sweetener (optional)

1. In a microwave-safe mug, combine the almond milk, heavy cream, peppermint extract, and chocolate chips. Microwave on high for 90 seconds. 2. Remove and stir to blend the melted chips into the liquid. Add the cocoa powder and sweetener to taste (if using), and whisk with a fork until smooth. 3. Microwave for another 15 to 20 seconds. Whisk again and serve.

**Per Serving:** Calories 383; Total Fat 34g; Saturated Fat 20g; Sodium 191mg; Carbs 27g; Fiber 13g; Sugar 6g; Protein 7g

## Homemade Strawberry Yogurt Pops

Prep time: 20 minutes | Cook time: 0 minutes | Serves: 5

12 ounces fresh or frozen (and thawed) strawberries, chopped
¼ cup plus 2 tablespoons granulated sugar-free sweetener, such as Swerve, divided
1½ cups full-fat plain Greek yogurt
2 teaspoons vanilla extract
1½ cups heavy (whipping) cream

1. Combine the strawberries and ¼ cup of sweetener in a blender or food processor and blend until pureed and smooth. 2. Place the mix to a bowl and mix in the yogurt and vanilla extract. 3. In bowl, using an electric mixer or by hand with a whisk, whip the cream with the remaining 2 tablespoons of sweetener until fluffy and stiff peaks have formed. 4. Fold the whipped cream into the yogurt-and-strawberry mixture until well combined. Freeze in ice-pop molds or transfer to a large airtight container and freeze until firm, 6 to 8 hours.

Per Serving: Calories 166; Total Fat 14g; Saturated Fat 9g; Sodium 24mg; Carbs 12g; Fiber 1g; Sugar 7g; Protein 5g

## Classic Omega-3 Crackers

Prep time: 20 minutes | Cook time: 15 minutes | Serves: 6-8

1 cup almond flour
1 tablespoon flaxseed
1 tablespoon chia seed
1 tablespoon cumin seed (optional)
½ teaspoon salt
¼ teaspoon baking soda
1 large egg, beaten
1 tablespoon extra-virgin olive oil

1. Preheat the oven to 350°F temp setting. 2. In a large bowl, combine the almond flour, flaxseed, chia seed, cumin seed (if using), salt, and baking soda, and stir well. 3. Add the egg and olive oil to the dry ingredients and stir well until the dough forms a ball. 4. Cover the dough with parchment papers, using a rolling pin, roll the dough to ⅛-inch thickness, aiming for a rectangular shape. 5. Remove the parchment and, using a knife, cut the dough into 1- to 2-inch-square crackers. Transfer the cut cracker dough to a baking sheet. 6. Bake for 15 minutes, until crispy and slightly golden.

Per Serving: Calories 159; Total Fat 14g; Saturated Fat 1g; Sodium 262mg; Carbs 5g; Fiber 3g; Sugar 0g; Protein 6g

## Low Carb Microwave Keto Bread

Prep time: 2 minutes | Cook time: 2 minutes | Serves: 1 or 2

1 large egg
3 tablespoons almond flour
1 tablespoon extra-virgin olive oil
¼ teaspoon baking powder
¼ teaspoon salt

1. In a microwave-safe ramekin, mug, or small bowl, beat the egg. Add the almond flour, olive oil, baking powder, and salt, and mix well with a fork. 2. Microwave on high for 90 seconds. 3. Loosen the edges with help of knife of the ramekin and flip onto a plate or cutting board to remove the bread. Allow to cool for 2 minutes. 4. Slice the bread in half with a serrated knife.

Per Serving: Calories 318; Total Fat 29g; Saturated Fat 4g; Sodium 776mg; Carbs 5g; Fiber 2g; Sugar 9g; Protein 11g

## Low Calorie Avocado Chocolate Mousse

Prep time: 10 minutes | Cook time: 0 minutes | Serves: 4

2 ripe avocados, pitted and peeled
¼ cup unsweetened cocoa powder
¼ cup full-fat coconut milk, plus extra as needed
2 to 4 tablespoons granulated sugar-free sweetener, such as Swerve (optional)
2 teaspoons vanilla extract
½ teaspoon cinnamon (optional)
¼ teaspoon salt

1. In a blender, combine the avocados, cocoa powder, heavy cream, sweetener to taste (if using), vanilla, cinnamon (if using), and salt, and blend until smooth and creamy. If the mixture is too thick, add additional cream, 1 tablespoon at a time. 2. Serve immediately or store in an airtight container in the refrigerator for up to 2 days.

Per Serving: Calories 183; Total Fat 17g; Saturated Fat 5g; Sodium 158mg; Carbs 10g; Fiber 7g; Sugar 0g; Protein 3g

## Healthy Raspberry-Chocolate Chia Pudding

Prep time: 10 minutes | Cook time: 15 minutes | Serves: 4

½ cup raspberries, fresh or frozen (thawed)
1 cup unsweetened almond milk
1 cup full-fat canned unsweetened coconut milk or heavy (whipping) cream
2 to 4 tablespoons granulated sugar-free sweetener, such as Swerve (optional)
½ cup chia seeds
¼ cup no-sugar-added chocolate protein powder

1. Put the raspberries in a large bowl and mash them well with a fork. Add the almond milk, coconut milk, and sweetener to taste (if using), and whisk until smooth. 2. Add the chia seeds along with protein powder, and whisk until well combined. 3. Divide the mixture evenly among 4 ramekins or small jars.

Per Serving: Calories 247; Total Fat 18g; Saturated Fat 10g; Sodium 95mg; Carbs 15g; Fiber 9g; Sugar 0g; Protein 11g

## Tasty Herbed Yogurt Sauce

Prep time: 10 minutes | Cook time: 0 minutes | Serves: 1½ cups

½ cup Italian parsley leaves
1 garlic clove
1 cup full-fat plain Greek yogurt
¼ cup extra-virgin olive oil
¼ cup freshly squeezed lemon juice
1 teaspoon salt
¼ teaspoon freshly ground black pepper

1. Combine the parsley with garlic in a blender or food processor and blend until well chopped. 2. Add the yogurt with olive oil, lemon juice, salt, and pepper, and pulse until smooth and creamy. 3. Store in an airtight container in the refrigerator for up to 1 week.

Per Serving: Calories 117; Total Fat 11g; Saturated Fat 2g; Sodium 411mg; Carbs 2g; Fiber 0.1g; Sugar 0g; Protein 4g

## Spiced Honey Roasted Almonds

**Prep time: 5 minutes | Cook time: 15 minutes | Serves: 8**

3 tablespoons honey
1 teaspoon ground cinnamon
½ teaspoon ground cayenne pepper
½ teaspoon salt
2 cups almonds

1. Preheat the oven to 325°F. Line a baking sheet with parchment paper. Set aside. 2. In a saucepan, warm the honey until softened. 3. Add the cinnamon, cayenne, and salt, and stir well to combine. 4. Add the almonds, and stir until coated. Place the almonds on the sheet, and bake for 15 minutes. 5. Let cool on the baking sheet, then serve or transfer to a serving bowl or airtight container. Store at room temperature.

**Per Serving:** Calories 162; Total Fat 12g; Saturated Fat 1g; Sodium 148mg; Carbs 12g; Fiber 3g; Sugar 8g; Protein 5g

## Tasty Blueberries with Sweet Cashew Cream

**Prep time: 10 minutes | Cook time: 0 minutes | Serves: 4**

1 cup raw cashews
2 tablespoons maple syrup
¼ to ½ cup unsweetened vanilla almond milk
2 tablespoons freshly squeezed lemon juice
½ teaspoon vanilla extract
Pinch salt
1 pint fresh blueberries

1. In a bowl, soak the cashews with enough hot water to cover. Soak for 30 minutes. 2. Drain the cashews, and place to a food processor. Add the maple syrup, ¼ cup of almond milk, and the lemon juice, vanilla, and salt. Process until smooth. 3. Serve the cashew cream with the blueberries. Refrigerate any unused cashew cream separately in an airtight container for 3 to 4 days.

**Per Serving:** Calories 265; Total Fat 14g; Saturated Fat 2g; Sodium 56mg; Carbs 30g; Fiber 4g; Sugar 16g; Protein 6g

## Chocolate Covered Strawberries

**Prep time: 15 minutes | Cook time: 1 minutes | Serves: 6**

1 pint fresh strawberries, rinsed individually and thoroughly dried with a towel
1½ ounces dark baking chocolate, chopped into small pieces

1. Manage a baking sheet with parchment paper. Set aside. 2. Set the dried strawberries on a clean, dry towel to continue to air dry while you prepare the chocolate. 3. Place the chocolate in a microwave-safe jar or bowl, and microwave on medium power for 30 seconds. Stir the chocolate in and continue to microwave at 20-second intervals, stirring after each, until melted. 4. Holding strawberry from top, dip the berries into the chocolate and place on the prepared baking sheet. Let rest at room temperature until hardened, or refrigerate for 30 minutes. Serve immediately or refrigerate in an airtight container for up to 3 days.

**Per Serving:** Calories 54; Total Fat 2g; Saturated Fat 1g; Sodium 3mg; Carbs 9g; Fiber 1g; Sugar 6g; Protein 1g

## Classic Dark Chocolate Baking Drops

**Prep time: 10 minutes | Cook time: 1 minute | Serves: 24**

8 ounces dark chocolate, chopped
3 tablespoons dried fruit, such as cranberries, blueberries, cherries, pineapple, or mango
3 tablespoons chopped nuts, such as almonds, walnuts, hazelnuts, pistachios, or peanuts
1 tablespoon seeds, such as sunflower, chia, hemp, or flaxseed

1. Manage a baking sheet with parchment paper. Set aside. 2. Place the chocolate in a microwave-safe bowl, and microwave on medium power for 30 seconds. Stir and continue to microwave in 20-second intervals, stirring after each, until melted. Drop teaspoon-size spoonfuls of chocolate onto the prepared baking sheet, making rounds that spread to about 2 inches in diameter. 3. Spread the fruit, nuts, and seeds to the chocolate. Let sit at room temperature until it hardens, or refrigerate for 30 minutes. Serve immediately or transfer to an airtight container and refrigerate for up to 2 weeks.

**Per Serving:** Calories 111; Total Fat 7g; Saturated Fat 3g; Sodium 7mg; Carbs 14g; Fiber 0g; Sugar 11g; Protein 1g

## Simple Berry Sorbet

**Prep time: 10 minutes | Cook time: 5 minutes | Serves: 6**

¼ cup sugar
1 thyme sprig
¼ cup water
1 pound fresh or frozen raspberries
8 ounces fresh or frozen blueberries

1. Manage a rimmed sheet with parchment paper. Set aside. 2. In a saucepan, mix the sugar with thyme, and water. Heat, stirring, until the sugar dissolves. Once cool, remove the thyme sprig. 3. In a high-speed blender, combine the raspberries, blueberries, and simple syrup. Process until smooth. Pour the mixture through a fine-mesh strainer or cheesecloth set over a bowl to remove the seeds. Transfer the purée to the prepared baking sheet, and freeze for 2 to 3 hours, or until solid. 4. Break the sorbet into pieces, place them in a blender, and process again to your desired texture. Serve immediately, or freeze again until ready to use.

**Per Serving:** Calories 131; Total Fat 0g; Saturated Fat 0g; Sodium 1mg; Carbs 34g; Fiber 4g; Sugar 29g; Protein 1g

## Easy Stuffed Dates

**Prep time: 15 minutes | Cook time: 0 minutes | Serves: 24**

24 Medjool dates
4 ounces low-fat cream cheese, at room temperature
¼ teaspoon ground nutmeg
¼ teaspoon dried ginger
24 raw almonds

1. Using a paring knife, slice each date lengthwise just enough to remove its pit. Set the dates aside. 2. In a bowl, stir the cream cheese, nutmeg, and ginger until well combined. Stuff each date with about 1 teaspoon of the cream cheese mixture, and top each with 1 almond. 3. Chill until ready to serve. Refrigerate in an airtight container for up to 1 week.

**Per Serving:** Calories 211; Total Fat 5g; Saturated Fat 2g; Sodium 40mg; Carbs 43g; Fiber 4g; Sugar 34g; Protein 2g

## Homemade Carrot Cake

**Prep time: 10 minutes | Cook time: 25 minutes | Serves: 12**

Nonstick cooking spray
1½ cups whole-wheat pastry flour
½ cup all-purpose flour
1½ cups grated carrot
½ cup sugar
2 teaspoons baking powder
1 teaspoon baking soda
½ teaspoon salt
4 large eggs, lightly beaten
¼ cup canola oil

1. Preheat the oven to 350°F temp setting. Grease a 9-inch baking pan. Set aside. 2. In a medium bowl, stir together the whole-wheat pastry and all-purpose flours, carrot, sugar, baking powder, baking soda, and salt. 3. Add the eggs and canola oil, and stir until the flour is completely mixed in. Transfer the thick batter to the prepared pan. Bake for 20-25 minutes, until browned. 4. Slice into 12 pieces and serve.

**Per Serving:** Calories 173; Total Fat 7g; Saturated Fat 1g; Sodium 235mg; Carbs 25g; Fiber 2g; Sugar 9g; Protein 4g

## Almond Energy Balls

**Prep time: 10 minutes | Cook time: 0 minutes | Serves: 6**

1½ cups raw almonds
½ cup tightly packed pitted Medjool dates
2 tablespoons almond or peanut butter
Pinch sea salt
¼ cup unsweetened shredded coconut

1. In a processor, pulse the almonds until crumbs. Add the dates and process until chopped. 2. Add the almond butter along with salt, and process until mixed. While processing, add water, 1 teaspoon at a time, until the dough comes together. Roll the dough into 1½-inch balls. 3. Place the coconut in a bowl, and roll the balls in it, pressing to coat. Refrigerate for about 1 hour before serving. Refrigerate in an airtight container for up to 2 weeks.

**Per Serving:** Calories 269; Total Fat 20g; Saturated Fat 6g; Sodium 67mg; Carbs 19g; Fiber 6g; Sugar 11g; Protein 8g

## Perfect Mango Smoothie

**Prep time: 5 minutes | Cook time: 0 minutes | Serves: 2**

2 cups frozen or fresh chopped mango
½ cup skim milk
½ cup plain nonfat Greek yogurt

1. In a high-speed blender, combine the mango, milk, and yogurt. Process until smooth, and serve.

**Per Serving:** Calories 154; Total Fat 1g; Saturated Fat 0g; Sodium 79mg; Carbs 33g; Fiber 3g; Sugar 30g; Protein 6g

## Authentic Green Goddess Dressing

**Prep time: 10 minutes | Cook time: 0 minutes | Serves: 1½ cups**

2 very ripe avocados, pitted and peeled
½ cup packed cilantro or parsley leaves
½ cup mayonnaise
Zest of 1 lemon
Juice of 1 lemon
1 teaspoon garlic powder
1 tablespoon dried chives or onion powder
1 teaspoon salt
¼ teaspoon freshly ground black pepper
Warm water, as needed

1. In a blender, blend the avocados, cilantro, mayonnaise, lemon zest and juice, garlic powder, dried chives, salt, and pepper until smooth. 2. The dressing will be thick. Add warm water, little at a time, blending after each addition to reach your desired consistency. A thicker dressing is great to use as a dipping sauce.

**Per Serving:** Calories 102; Total Fat 10g; Saturated Fat 2g; Sodium 257mg; Carbs 3g; Fiber 2g; Sugar 0g; Protein 1g

## Tropical Fruit Salad with Coconut Milk and Lime

**Prep time: 10 minutes | Cook time: 0 minutes | Serves: 8**

2 cups pineapple chunks
2 kiwi fruits, peeled and sliced
1 mango, peeled and chopped
¼ cup canned light coconut milk
1 tablespoon freshly squeezed lime juice
1 tablespoon honey

1. In a bowl, toss the pineapple, kiwi, and mango. 2. In a small bowl, combine the coconut milk, lime juice, and honey, stirring until the honey dissolves. Pour over the fruits, and coat. Serve immediately or refrigerate in an airtight container for up to 3 days

**Per Serving:** Calories 70; Total Fat 1g; Saturated Fat 0g; Sodium 2mg; Carbs 17g; Fiber 2g; Sugar 14g; Protein 1g

## Roasted Spiced Pears with Cinnamon and Pistachios

**Prep time: 5 minutes | Cook time: 30 minutes | Serves: 4**

2 pears, halved
¼ teaspoon ground cinnamon
1 tablespoon honey
¼ cup crushed pistachios

1. Preheat the oven to 350°F temp setting. 2. Using a spoon, scoop out and discard the pears' seeds. Sprinkle the pear halves with cinnamon, drizzle on the honey, and sprinkle the pistachios over the top. Place the pears on a sheet, and bake for 30 minutes, until tender. Let cool and serve.

**Per Serving:** Calories 136; Total Fat 5g; Saturated Fat 1g; Sodium 2mg; Carbs 23g; Fiber 4g; Sugar 15g; Protein 2g

## Easy Apple Crisp

Prep time: 15 minutes | Cook time: 45 minutes | Serves: 6

**For the Apple Filling**
Nonstick cooking spray
5 medium apples, peeled, cored, and sliced
2 tablespoons freshly squeezed lemon juice
2 tablespoons sugar
½ teaspoon ground cinnamon
1 tablespoon whole-wheat flour
1 tablespoon butter, melted
Pinch salt

**For the Crisp Topping**
1 cup quick-cooking oats
¼ cup whole-wheat flour
¼ cup sugar
½ teaspoon ground cinnamon
¼ teaspoon salt
4 tablespoons butter, cut into ¼-inch pieces

To make the apple filling
1. Preheat the oven to 350°F. Grease an 8-inch baking pan. Set aside. 2. In a bowl, toss the apples along with lemon juice, sugar, cinnamon, flour, butter, and salt. Transfer the mixture to the prepared dish.
To make the crisp topping
1. In a bowl, mix the oats along with flour, sugar, cinnamon, salt, and butter. Using a pastry blender or two forks, cut the butter into smaller pieces and mix well. 2. Crumble the topping over the apples. Bake for 45 minutes, until browned and the apples are tender. 3. Slice into 6 pieces and serve.
**Per Serving:** Calories 287; Total Fat 11g; Saturated Fat 6g; Sodium 169mg; Carbs 48g; Fiber 6g; Sugar 32g; Protein 3g

## Tasty Sweet Potato Cake

Prep time: 15 minutes | Cook time: 30 minutes | Serves: 10

**For the Cake**
Nonstick cooking spray
2 small sweet potatoes, peeled and shredded
1 cup whole-wheat flour
1 cup all-purpose flour
¼ cup sugar
2 teaspoons baking powder
2 teaspoons ground cinnamon
½ teaspoon ground ginger
½ teaspoon salt
1 cup unsweetened applesauce
¼ cup canola oil
2 large eggs

**For the Frosting**
1 (8-ounce) package low-fat cream cheese, at room temperature
¼ cup honey
1 teaspoon vanilla extract

To make the cake
1. Preheat the oven to 350°F. Grease a 9-inch baking dish. Set aside. 2. In a large bowl, stir together the sweet potatoes, whole-wheat and all-purpose flours, sugar, baking powder, cinnamon, ginger, and salt. 3. In a bowl, mix the applesauce, oil, and eggs. Pour the wet mix to the dry mix, and mix until combined. Transfer the mix to the baking dish. Bake for 25-30 minutes, until browned and a toothpick inserted into the middle comes out clean. 4. Let cool completely before frosting.
**Per Serving:** Calories 306; Total Fat 15g; Saturated Fat 6g; Sodium 214mg; Carbs 39g; Fiber 3g; Sugar 16g; Protein 6g

# Chapter 8 Sauces, Dips, and Dressings Recipes

- 96 Fresh Cranberry Orange Relish
- 96 Homemade Cranberry-Raisin Chutney
- 96 Easy Roasted Red Pepper and Plum Sauce
- 96 Homemade Vegan Worcestershire Sauce
- 96 Fresh Basil Pesto
- 96 Low Calorie Fat-Free Roux
- 97 Classic Hummus with Lemon
- 97 Homemade Raspberry Vinaigrette
- 97 Lemon Basil Pesto Sauce
- 97 Low Carb Whole Wheat Pizza Dough
- 97 Authentic Sweet-and-Sour Sauce
- 98 Easy Creamy Chipotle-Lime Dressing
- 98 Simple Lemon Vinaigrette Dressing
- 98 Chile-Lime Salad Dressing
- 98 Apple Cider Vinaigrette Dressing
- 98 Spicy Horseradish Mustard
- 98 Simple Mock Cream
- 98 Homemade Cherry Barbecue Sauce
- 99 Delicious Poppy Seed Dressing
- 99 Creamy Yogurt Dill Sauce
- 99 Classic Marinara Sauce
- 99 Lemon Tahini Dressing
- 99 Caesar Salad Dressing, Two Ways

## Fresh Cranberry Orange Relish

**Prep time: 5 minutes | Cook time: 2 minutes | Serves: 12**

16 ounces fresh cranberries
1½ cups orange sections
2 teaspoons orange zest
¼ cup brown sugar
⅓ cup Splenda Granular
1 teaspoon cinnamon

1. Place the cranberries and orange sections in a food processor and chop using the pulse setting until coarsely chopped. Transfer to a saucepan. 2. Bring cranberry mixture, orange zest, brown sugar, and Splenda to a boil over medium heat. Cook for 2 minutes. 3. Remove from heat, and stir in cinnamon. Chill before serving.
**Per Serving:** Calories 62; Total Fat 0g; Saturated Fat 0g; Sodium 3mg; Carbs 16g; Fiber 2g; Sugar 1g; Protein 0g

## Homemade Cranberry-Raisin Chutney

**Prep time: 10 minutes | Cook time: 1 hour | Serves: 3 cups**

1 cup diced onions
1 cup diced, peeled apples
1 cup diced bananas
1 cup diced peaches
¼ cup raisins
¼ cup dry white wine
¼ cup dried cranberries
¼ cup apple cider vinegar
1 teaspoon brown sugar
Salt and ground black pepper

1. In a saucepan, mix all the ingredients. Cook over low flame heat for about 1 hour, stirring occasionally. Cool completely. 2. Can be kept for a week in the refrigerator or in the freezer for 3 months, or canned using same sterilizing method you'd use to can mincemeat.
**Per Serving:** Calories 14; Total Fat 0g; Saturated Fat 0g; Sodium 1mg; Carbs 3g; Fiber 0g; Sugar 0g; Protein 0g

## Easy Roasted Red Pepper and Plum Sauce

**Prep time: 15 minutes | Cook time: 1 hour 30 minutes | Serves: 2 cups**

1 large roasted red pepper, pulp only
½ pound apricots, quartered and pitted
¾ pound plums, quartered and pitted
1⅓ cups apple cider vinegar
⅔ cup water
⅓ cup white sugar
½ cup brown sugar
2 tablespoons corn syrup
2 tablespoons fresh grated ginger
1 teaspoon salt
1 tablespoon toasted mustard seeds
4 scallions, chopped (white part only)
1 teaspoon minced garlic
½ teaspoon ground cinnamon

1. Place the ingredients in a stockpot and boil. Reduce heat and simmer, covered, for 30 minutes. 2. Uncover and simmer for 1 hour. 3. Place in a blender and process to desired consistency. Can be stored in refrigerator for 4–6 weeks.
**Per Serving:** Calories 38; Total Fat 1g; Saturated Fat 0g; Sodium 76mg; Carbs 10g; Fiber 1g; Sugar 1g; Protein 0g

## Homemade Vegan Worcestershire Sauce

**Prep time: 10 minutes | Cook time: 1 hour | Serves: 1 cup**

1½ cups cider vinegar
¼ cup plum jam
1 tablespoon blackstrap molasses
1 clove garlic, crushed
⅛ teaspoon chili powder
⅛ teaspoon ground cloves
Pinch of cayenne pepper
¼ cup chopped onion
½ teaspoon ground allspice
⅛ teaspoon dry mustard
1 teaspoon Bragg's Liquid Aminos

1. Mix all the ingredients in a saucepan. Stir until the mixture boils. Lower heat and manage to simmer uncovered for 1 hour, stirring occasionally. 2. Store in covered jar in refrigerator. Will last in refrigerator up to 3 weeks.
**Per Serving:** Calories 14; Total Fat 0g; Saturated Fat 0g; Sodium 15mg; Carbs 4g; Fiber 0g; Sugar 0g; Protein 0g

## Fresh Basil Pesto

**Prep time: 10 minutes | Cook time: 15 minutes | Serves: 3 cups**

¾ cup pine nuts
4 cups tightly packed fresh basil leaves
½ cup freshly grated Parmesan cheese
3 large garlic cloves, minced
¼ teaspoon salt
1 teaspoon freshly ground black pepper
½ cup extra-virgin olive oil

1. Preheat the oven to 350°F temp setting. 2. Place the pine nuts on a baking sheet. Bake for about 5 minutes and then stir. Continue to bake for 10 minutes until nuts are golden brown and highly aromatic, stirring occasionally. Let nuts cool completely and then chop finely. 3. In a blender or food processor, combine the basil, pine nuts, cheese, garlic, salt, pepper, and all but 1 tablespoon olive oil. Process until smooth and uniform. 4. Pour into an airtight container and add remaining olive oil on top to act as a protective barrier. To freeze pesto, place it in a tightly sealed container. 5. To freeze small amounts of pesto, pour into ice cube trays and freeze until solid. Once frozen, you can remove the pesto cubes and place them in sealed freezer bags.
**Per Serving:** Calories 37; Total Fat 4g; Saturated Fat 1g; Sodium 14mg; Carbs 1g; Fiber 0g; Sugar 0g; Protein 1g

## Low Calorie Fat-Free Roux

**Prep time: 5 minutes | Cook time: 15 minutes | Serves: ¼ cup**

1 tablespoon cornstarch
2 tablespoons wine

1. Whisk all the ingredients until well blended, making sure there are no lumps. 2. To use as thickener for 1 cup of broth, heat the broth until it reaches a boil. Slowly whisk cornstarch-wine mixture into broth and return to a boil. Reduce heat and manage to simmer, stirring constantly, until mix thickens enough to coat back of spoon.
**Per Serving:** Calories 13; Total Fat 0g; Saturated Fat 0g; Sodium 1mg; Carbs 2g; Fiber 0g; Sugar 0g; Protein 0g

## Quick and Easy Mock White Sauce

Prep time: 5 minutes | Cook time: 10 minutes | Serves: 1/2 cup

1 tablespoon unsalted butter
1 tablespoon flour
¼ teaspoon sea salt
Pinch of white pepper
1 cup Mock Cream

1. In a medium-sized heavy nonstick saucepan, melt the butter over very low heat. Butter should gently melt; you do not want it to bubble and turn brown. 2. While the butter melts, mix the flour, salt, and white pepper in a small bowl. 3. Add the flour mixture in butter, stirring constantly. 4. Once mixture thickens and starts to bubble, about 2 minutes, slowly pour in one-third of the mock cream; stir until blended with roux. Add another one-third mock cream; stir until blended. Add remaining mock cream and continue cooking, stirring constantly to make sure sauce doesn't stick to bottom of pan. Once sauce begins to steam and appears it's just about to boil, reduce heat and simmer until sauce thickens, or about 3 minutes.

Per Serving: Calories 61; Total Fat 3g; Saturated Fat 2g; Sodium 190mg; Carbs 6g; Fiber 0g; Sugar 0g; Protein 2g

## Classic Hummus with Lemon

Prep time: 15 minutes | Cook time: 0 minutes | Serves: 8

1 (15 ounce) can no-salt-added chickpeas, drained (liquid reserved) and rinsed
¼ cup ground flaxseed
2 tablespoons olive oil
2 tablespoons freshly squeezed lemon juice
3 garlic cloves, peeled
½ teaspoon ground cumin
½ teaspoon salt
½ teaspoon sesame oil

1. Place the chickpeas and ¼ cup of the reserved liquid, flaxseed, olive oil, lemon juice, garlic, cumin powder, salt, and sesame oil in a processor. Process until smooth and creamy. Pour in additional reserved bean liquid until it reaches your desired consistency. 2. Transfer the hummus to a bowl. Drizzle with additional olive oil and serve. 3. Store in an airtight container in the refrigerator for up to 7 days.

Per Serving: Calories 108; Total Fat 6g; Saturated Fat 1g; Sodium 149mg; Carbs 10g; Fiber 3g; Sugar 2g; Protein 4g

## Homemade Raspberry Vinaigrette

Prep time: 5 minutes | Cook time: 0 minutes | Serves: 1 cup

¾ cup avocado oil
¼ cup red wine vinegar
¼ cup fresh raspberries
1 tablespoon honey
¼ teaspoon paprika
⅛ teaspoon salt
⅛ teaspoon freshly ground black pepper

1. Put the oil, vinegar, raspberries, honey, paprika, salt, and pepper in a blender. Puree until it reaches a smooth consistency, 30 to 60 seconds. Serve. 2. Refrigerate in a sealed container for up to 7 days.

Per Serving: Calories 192; Total Fat 20g; Saturated Fat 3g; Sodium 40mg; Carbs 3g; Fiber 0g; Sugar 2g; Protein 0g

## Lemon Basil Pesto Sauce

Prep time: 5 minutes | Cook time: 0 minutes | Serves: 1 cup

2 cups fresh basil leaves
½ cup extra-virgin olive oil
½ cup finely shredded Parmesan cheese
¼ cup pine nuts
3 garlic cloves, peeled
2 tablespoons freshly squeezed lemon juice
¼ teaspoon salt
¼ freshly ground black pepper

1. Put the basil, olive oil, Parmesan, pine nuts, garlic, lemon juice, salt, and pepper in a food processor on high for 45 to 60 seconds or until it reaches a smooth consistency. Serve. 2. Store in an airtight container in the refrigerator for up to 5 day or in the freezer for 3 to 4 months.

Per Serving: Calories 178; Total Fat 18g; Saturated Fat 3g; Sodium 186mg; Carbs 2g; Fiber 0g; Sugar 0g; Protein 3g

## Low Carb Whole Wheat Pizza Dough

Prep time: 15 minutes | Cook time: 0 minutes | Serves: 1 crust

1 cup warm water
2¼ teaspoons active dry yeast
1 teaspoon sugar
2½ cups white whole wheat flour
2 tablespoons extra-virgin olive oil
1 teaspoon Italian seasoning
¾ teaspoon salt
½ teaspoon garlic powder

1. In a bowl, whisk the water, yeast, and sugar until the yeast is dissolved. Let the mix stand for 10 minutes, or until it is bubbly and creamy. 2. Stir in the flour, olive oil, Italian seasoning, salt, and garlic powder. Knead until smooth, about 5 minutes. 3. Roll the dough into a ball. Use immediately or store in an airtight container in the refrigerator for up to 3 days or in the freezer for up to 3 months.

Per Serving: Calories 138; Total Fat 4g; Saturated Fat 1g; Sodium 219mg; Carbs 23g; Fiber 4g; Sugar 1g; Protein 4g

## Authentic Sweet-and-Sour Sauce

Prep time: 5 minutes | Cook time: 10 minutes | Serves: 1 ¼ cups

½ cup 100% pineapple juice
⅓ cup apple cider vinegar
⅓ cup ketchup
3 Medjool dates, pitted
2 garlic cloves, peeled
2 tablespoons water
1 tablespoon reduced-sodium tamari
2 teaspoons cornstarch

1. Put the pineapple juice, apple cider vinegar, ketchup, dates, garlic, water, tamari, and cornstarch in a blender. Blend it for 2 minutes, or until it forms a smooth, uniform consistency. 2. Transfer the sauce to a saucepan over medium-high heat. Boil on low heat, stirring constantly, until the sauce has darkened and slightly thickened, about 10 minutes. Serve.

Per Serving: Calories 40; Total Fat 0g; Saturated Fat 0g; Sodium 124mg; Carbs 10g; Fiber 1g; Sugar 8g; Protein 0g

## Easy Creamy Chipotle-Lime Dressing

**Prep time: 5 minutes | Cook time: 0 minutes | Serves: 1 cup**

¾ cup plain nonfat Greek yogurt
1 chipotle pepper
1 to 2 teaspoons adobo sauce
1 tablespoon freshly squeezed lime juice
1 teaspoon grated lime zest
1 garlic clove, peeled
½ teaspoon smoked paprika
¼ teaspoon salt
¼ teaspoon freshly ground black pepper

1. Put the yogurt, chipotle pepper, adobo sauce, lime juice, lime zest, garlic, paprika, salt, and pepper in a blender or food processor. Blend for 30 seconds until creamy. Serve. 2. Use as a salad dressing, a topping for tacos, nachos, or power bowls, a condiment in your sandwich or wrap, or as a dip for chicken strips or baked sweet potatoes.
**Per Serving:** Calories 16; Total Fat 0g; Saturated Fat 0g; Sodium 81mg; Carbs 2g; Fiber 0g; Sugar 1g; Protein 2g

## Simple Lemon Vinaigrette Dressing

**Prep time: 5-10 minutes | Cook time: 0 minutes | Serves: 1 cup**

¼ cup freshly squeezed lemon juice
2 garlic cloves, minced
1 teaspoon Dijon mustard
½ teaspoon maple syrup (optional)
¼ cup extra-virgin olive oil
½ cup grapeseed oil
Kosher salt
Freshly ground black pepper

1. In a bowl, add the lemon juice, garlic, mustard, and maple syrup (if using). Slowly whisk in the extra-virgin olive oil, followed by the grapeseed oil, until the dressing is completely emulsified. Spice with salt and pepper. 2. Store the dressing in an airtight container for up to 1 week in the refrigerator or in the freezer for up to 3 months.
**Per Serving:** Calories 184; Total Fat 20g; Saturated Fat 0.8g; Sodium 122mg; Carbs 1g; Fiber 0.2g; Sugar 0.2g; Protein 0.9g

## Chile-Lime Salad Dressing

**Prep time: 5 minutes | Cook time: 0 minutes | Serves: 1 cup**

5 ounces grapeseed or safflower oil
Zest and juice of 4 limes
4 garlic cloves, minced
4-inch piece fresh ginger, minced
2½ tablespoons chile paste
2 teaspoons fish sauce (optional)
¼ teaspoon kosher salt

1. Combine the grapeseed oil, lime zest and juice, garlic, ginger, chile paste, fish sauce (if using), and salt in a jar or container with a tight-fitting lid. Close the lid and shake the mixture vigorously to combine. 2. Store the dressing in an airtight container for up to 1 week in the refrigerator or in the freezer for up to 3 months.
**Per Serving:** Calories 179; Total Fat 18g; Saturated Fat 0.6g; Sodium 159mg; Carbs 6g; Fiber 0.2g; Sugar 0.2g; Protein 0.9g

## Apple Cider Vinaigrette Dressing

**Prep time: 5 minutes | Cook time: 0 minutes | Serves: 2/3 cup**

⅓ cup extra-virgin olive oil
¼ cup apple cider vinegar
2 teaspoons honey
2 teaspoons Dijon mustard
1 garlic clove, minced
⅛ teaspoon freshly ground black pepper
⅛ teaspoon salt

1. Put the oil, vinegar, honey, mustard, garlic, pepper, and salt in a small jar, cover, and shake until well blended. Serve. 2. Refrigerate for up to 1 week. Shake the dressing well to recombine ingredients before using.
**Per Serving:** Calories 139; Total Fat 14g; Saturated Fat 2g; Sodium 85mg; Carbs 3g; Fiber 0g; Sugar 2g; Protein 0g

## Spicy Horseradish Mustard

**Prep time: 5 minutes | Cook time: 1 hour | Serves: 2/3 cups**

¼ cup dry mustard
2½ tablespoons prepared horseradish
1 teaspoon sea salt
¼ cup white wine vinegar
1 tablespoon olive oil
Cayenne pepper, to taste (optional)

1. Combine all the ingredients in a food processor or blender. Process until smooth. pour into a jar and store in refrigerator. Will last up to 3 weeks refrigerated.
**Per Serving:** Calories 10; Total Fat 1g; Saturated Fat 0g; Sodium 68mg; Carbs 1g; Fiber 0g; Sugar 0g; Protein 0g

## Simple Mock Cream

**Prep time: 5 minutes | Cook time: 0 minutes | Serves: 1 ¼ cup**

1 cup skim milk
¼ cup nonfat dry milk

1. Blend all the ingredients until mixed. Use as a substitute for heavy cream.
**Per Serving:** Calories 147; Total Fat 1g; Saturated Fat 1g; Sodium 221mg; Carbs 21g; Fiber 0g; Sugar 0g; Protein 14g

## Homemade Cherry Barbecue Sauce

**Prep time: 5 minutes | Cook time: 0 minutes | Serves: 2 cups**

10 ounces pitted fresh cherries
1 small onion, quartered
2 tablespoons Dijon mustard
2 tablespoons red wine vinegar
1 tablespoon ground fennel seeds
3 chipotle peppers in adobo sauce, plus 1 tablespoon sauce
Pinch freshly ground black pepper

1. In a blender, combine the cherries, onion, mustard, vinegar, fennel, chipotle peppers, adobo sauce, and black pepper. Puree until combined and adjust the seasonings as desired. 2. Store in an airtight container in the refrigerator for up to 1 week or in the freezer for up to 3 months.
**Per Serving:** Calories 39; Total Fat 1g; Saturated Fat 0.1g; Sodium 222mg; Carbs 8g; Fiber 2g; Sugar 3g; Protein 1g

## Delicious Poppy Seed Dressing

Prep time: 5 minutes | Cook time: 0 minutes | Serves: 1 cup

½ cup plain Greek yogurt
¼ cup white wine vinegar
3 tablespoons grapeseed oil
2 tablespoons Dijon mustard
1 tablespoon honey
1 small shallot, minced
1½ tablespoons poppy seeds

1. In a blender, puree the yogurt, vinegar, grapeseed oil, mustard, honey, and shallot. Transfer to a container or jar with a lid and stir in the poppy seeds. If you don't have a blender, mix by hand in a medium bowl using a whisk or add to a jar with a fitted lid and shake vigorously. 2. Store the dressing in an airtight container for up to 1 week in the refrigerator or in the freezer for up to 3 months.

Per Serving: Calories 83; Total Fat 7g; Saturated Fat 0.2g; Sodium 123mg; Carbs 5g; Fiber 1g; Sugar 1g; Protein 2g

## Creamy Yogurt Dill Sauce

Prep time: 5 minutes | Cook time: 0 minutes | Serves: 1 cup

1 cup plain nonfat Greek yogurt
1½ tablespoons freshly squeezed lemon juice
1 tablespoon dried dill weed or 2 tablespoons chopped fresh dill
¼ teaspoon salt
¼ teaspoon freshly ground black pepper

1. In a bowl, whisk the yogurt with the lemon juice, dill, salt, and pepper until well blended. Serve. 2. Refrigerate in a sealed jar or container for up to 1 week.

Per Serving: Calories 18; Total Fat 0g; Saturated Fat 0g; Sodium 84mg; Carbs 1g; Fiber 0g; Sugar 1g; Protein 3g

## Classic Marinara Sauce

Prep time: 5 minutes | Cook time: 25 minutes | Serves: 8 cups

¼ cup extra-virgin olive oil
1 small onion, minced
4 garlic cloves, thinly sliced
2 basil sprigs
1 teaspoon dried oregano
2 (28-ounce) cans diced or crushed tomatoes
Kosher salt
Freshly ground pepper

1. Heat the oil in a stockpot. Cook the onion, until very soft, 3 to 5 minutes. 2. Cook the garlic until soft, about 5 minutes. Add the oregano and basil. 3. Add in the tomatoes and manage to simmer. Lower the heat and manage to simmer, stirring occasionally, until the sauce is thick, about 15 minutes. 4. Season with salt and pepper. 5. Store in an airtight container in the refrigerator for up to 1 week or in the freezer for up to 3 months.

Per Serving: Calories 59; Total Fat 3g; Saturated Fat 0.1g; Sodium 213mg; Carbs 6g; Fiber 2g; Sugar 2g; Protein 1g

## Lemon Tahini Dressing

Prep time: 5 minutes | Cook time: 0 minutes | Serves: 1 cup

⅔ cup filtered water
⅓ cup tahini
¼ cup lemon juice
1 tablespoon extra-virgin olive oil
2 teaspoons maple syrup
Kosher salt
Freshly ground black pepper

1. In a bowl, whisk the water, tahini, lemon juice, extra-virgin olive oil, and maple syrup. Season to taste with salt and pepper. Maintain the consistency by adding extra-virgin olive oil. 2. Store the dressing in an airtight container for up to 1 week in the refrigerator or in the freezer for up to 3 months.

Per Serving: Calories 81; Total Fat 7g; Saturated Fat 0.3g; Sodium 236mg; Carbs 4g; Fiber 1g; Sugar 1g; Protein 2g

## Caesar Salad Dressing, Two Ways

Prep time: 5 minutes | Cook time: 0 minutes | Serves: 1 cup

1 cup plain Greek yogurt
¼ cup lemon juice
4 anchovy fillets, coarsely chopped
2 tablespoons Dijon mustard
2 tablespoons extra-virgin olive oil
3 garlic cloves, peeled
1 teaspoon Worcestershire sauce
Pinch freshly ground black pepper

1. Place the yogurt, lemon juice, anchovies, mustard, extra-virgin olive oil, garlic, Worcestershire, and pepper in a blender and puree until smooth. Adjust the seasonings as desired. 2. Store in an airtight container for 5 to 7 days, or in the freezer for up to 3 months.

Per Serving: Calories 44; Total Fat 3g; Saturated Fat 0g; Sodium 331mg; Carbs 2g; Fiber 0.1g; Sugar 0.2g; Protein 2g

**For the Vegan Version**

½ cup raw sunflower seeds, soaked in water for 2 hours or overnight
¼ cup extra-virgin olive oil
3 tablespoons freshly squeezed lemon juice
2 garlic cloves, minced
1 tablespoon nutritional yeast
1 tablespoon tahini
1 teaspoon Dijon mustard
1 teaspoon maple syrup
½ teaspoon tamari

1. Place sunflower seeds in a blender with the extra-virgin olive oil, lemon juice, garlic, nutritional yeast, tahini, mustard, maple syrup, and tamari. Blend until smooth. If the dressing is too thick, slowly stream in cold water as the machine is running and blend until smooth. Adjust the seasonings as desired. 2. Store in an airtight container in the refrigerator for 5 to 7 days or in the freezer for up to 3 months.

Per Serving: Calories 87; Total Fat 8g; Saturated Fat 0g; Sodium 231mg; Carbs 3g; Fiber 1g; Sugar 0.1g; Protein 2g

# Conclusion

The major aim of this cookbook was to provide an idea of managing a diabetic diet while using simple and easy-to-follow recipes. Life is tough, and cooking every other day makes it harder to manage time; easy recipes in this regard bring convenience. This cookbook, therefore, shares good food and delicious recipes for all diabetic patients or those who want to prevent the ills of this disorder. The extensive range of recipes, along with a meal plan, gives a wholesome package to all the readers. Divided into different segments, all the shared recipes can meet the daily needs of an individual as well as a whole family.

# Appendix 1 Measurement Conversion Chart

## WEIGHT EQUIVALENTS

| US STANDARD | METRIC (APPROXIMATE) |
|---|---|
| 1 ounce | 28 g |
| 2 ounces | 57 g |
| 5 ounces | 142 g |
| 10 ounces | 284 g |
| 15 ounces | 425 g |
| 16 ounces (1 pound) | 455 g |
| 1.5 pounds | 680 g |
| 2 pounds | 907 g |

## TEMPERATURES EQUIVALENTS

| FAHRENHEIT(F) | CELSIUS (C) (APPROXIMATE) |
|---|---|
| 225 °F | 107 °C |
| 250 °F | 120 °C |
| 275 °F | 135 °C |
| 300 °F | 150 °C |
| 325 °F | 160 °C |
| 350 °F | 180 °C |
| 375 °F | 190 °C |
| 400 °F | 205 °C |
| 425 °F | 220 °C |
| 450 °F | 235 °C |
| 475 °F | 245 °C |
| 500 °F | 260 °C |

## VOLUME EQUIVALENTS (DRY)

| US STANDARD | METRIC (APPROXIMATE) |
|---|---|
| ⅛ teaspoon | 0.5 mL |
| teaspoon | 1 mL |
| ½ teaspoon | 2 mL |
| teaspoon | 4 mL |
| 1 teaspoon | 5 mL |
| 1 tablespoon | 15 mL |
| cup | 59 mL |
| ½ cup | 118 mL |
| cup | 177 mL |
| 1 cup | 235 mL |
| 2 cups | 475 mL |
| 3 cups | 700 mL |
| 4 cups | 1 L |

## VOLUME EQUIVALENTS (LIQUID)

| US STANDARD | US STANDARD (OUNCES) | METRIC (APPROXIMATE) |
|---|---|---|
| 2 tablespoons | 1 fl.oz | 30 mL |
| cup | 2 fl.oz | 60 mL |
| ½ cup | 4 fl.oz | 120 mL |
| 1 cup | 8 fl.oz | 240 mL |
| 1½ cup | 12 fl.oz | 355 mL |
| 2 cups or 1 pint | 16 fl.oz | 475 mL |
| 4 cups or 1 quart | 32 fl.oz | 1 L |
| 1 gallon | 128 fl.oz | 4 L |

# Appendix 2 Recipes Index

## A

| | |
|---|---|
| 70 | All-Day Pot Roast |
| 93 | Almond Energy Balls |
| 79 | Apple and Bulgur Salad |
| 98 | Apple Cider Vinaigrette Dressing |
| 19 | Apple, Kale and Cheddar Omelet |
| 60 | Authentic Asian Pepper Steak |
| 64 | Authentic Beef Stew Bourguignonne |
| 67 | Authentic Chinese Pot Roast |
| 93 | Authentic Green Goddess Dressing |
| 72 | Authentic Mexican Tortilla Soup |
| 97 | Authentic Sweet-and-Sour Sauce |
| 26 | Avocado Toast with Egg and Black Pepper |

## B

| | |
|---|---|
| 77 | Baby Spinach Salad with Strawberries and Toasted Almonds |
| 72 | Bacon and Fruit Baked Bean Casserole |
| 40 | Baked Almond Shrimp with Grapefruit Salsa |
| 32 | Baked Beans with Raisin and Apple |
| 27 | Baked Berry-Oat Breakfast Bars |
| 46 | Baked Cajun Shrimp Casserole with Quinoa |
| 39 | Baked Caprese Fish and Bean |
| 20 | Baked Chocolate-Zucchini Muffins |
| 22 | Baked Egg and Veggie Quesadillas |
| 43 | Baked Ginger-Glazed Salmon and Broccoli |
| 62 | Baked Lamb Shanks and Vegetable |
| 23 | Baked Lemon-Poppyseed Muffins |
| 45 | Baked Oysters and Vegetable |
| 25 | Baked Ricotta with Strawberry and Mint |
| 42 | Baked Sesame Salmon with Bok Choy |
| 18 | Baked Spiced Seeds and Nuts Granola |
| 41 | Baked Tilapia and Quinoa |
| 35 | Barbecued Lima Beans |
| 22 | Basic Fruit Smoothie |
| 63 | Beef and Beans Stew |
| 69 | Beef and Lentil Stew |
| 70 | Beef and Vegetables Stew |
| 67 | Beef Braised with Mushroom Barley |
| 60 | Beef Noodles with Tomatoes |
| 60 | Beef Roast with Multiple Vegetables |
| 57 | Beef, Onion and Tomato Spaghetti Sauce |
| 45 | Blackened Tilapia with Mango Salsa |
| 31 | Black-Eyed Peas and Kale Salad |
| 63 | Braised Rump Roast and Vegetables |
| 22 | Breakfast Bruschetta with Cheese and Egg |
| 21 | Breakfast Egg Muffins |
| 29 | Breakfast Tostada with Salsa |
| 34 | Broccoli, Chard, and Cheddar Bread Pudding |
| 31 | Broccoli-Almond-Sesame Soba Noodles |
| 20 | Brussels Sprout Hash with Fried Eggs |
| 78 | Burger with Jicama Chips |
| 45 | Butter Scallops and Asparagus Skillet |

## C

| | |
|---|---|
| 99 | Caesar Salad Dressing, Two Ways |
| 56 | Calico Beans with Beef and Bacon |
| 85 | Cauliflower and Mushroom Soup |
| 42 | Ceviche with Vegetable |
| 24 | Cheesy Breakfast Casserole with Red Pepper and Mushroom |
| 68 | Cheesy Chili Rice |
| 37 | Cheesy Garlic Pasta Salad |
| 39 | Cheesy Herbed Potato Fish Bake |
| 20 | Cheesy Oat Pancakes with Carrot and Yogurt |
| 41 | Cheesy Tomato Tuna Melts |
| 75 | Chicken and Mushroom Soup |
| 51 | Chicken and Shrimp Jambalaya |
| 48 | Chicken Cacciatore with Red Wine Sauce |
| 53 | Chicken Lo Mein with Coleslaw |
| 85 | Chicken Noodle Soup |
| 81 | Chicken Salad with Apricots and Almonds |
| 83 | Chickpea and Spinach Soup |
| 50 | Chickpea Pasta with Turkey Meatballs in Pomodoro Sauce |
| 98 | Chile-Lime Salad Dressing |
| 92 | Chocolate Covered Strawberries |
| 67 | Chuck Wagon Beef Stew |
| 57 | Chunky Mushroom and Meat Spaghetti Sauce |
| 28 | Cinnamon Buckwheat Groats Breakfast Bowl |
| 23 | Cinnamon Quinoa Berry Breakfast |
| 62 | Classic Beef Pot Roast |
| 92 | Classic Dark Chocolate Baking Drops |
| 61 | Classic Ernestine's Beef Stew |
| 68 | Classic French Dip Roast |
| 97 | Classic Hummus with Lemon |
| 99 | Classic Marinara Sauce |
| 91 | Classic Omega-3 Crackers |
| 76 | Classic Pasta e Fagioli |
| 65 | Classic Stroganoff Steak |
| 85 | Classic Tuscan Pasta Fagioli |
| 27 | Coconut, Berry and Leafy Greens Sunrise Smoothie |
| 22 | Country-Style Cheesy Vegetables Omelet |
| 74 | Cowboy Beans with Sliced Bacon |
| 66 | Cowboy Casserole Stew |
| 23 | Creamed Egg Clouds on Toast |
| 21 | Creamy Almond Butter Pancakes |
| 24 | Creamy Blueberry Crêpes |
| 53 | Creamy Chicken Saltimbocca with Prosciutto |
| 39 | Creamy Curried Shrimp |
| 90 | Creamy Minty Hot Chocolate |
| 52 | Creamy Mushroom and Kale Sliced Chicken |
| 37 | Creamy Pesto Zoodles |
| 39 | Creamy Seafood Pasta |
| 86 | Creamy Smoked Salmon on Toast |
| 86 | Creamy White Bean and Collard Green Soup |
| 78 | Creamy White Bean Soup |
| 99 | Creamy Yogurt Dill Sauce |
| 74 | Creole Black Beans with Celery and Green Pepper |
| 31 | Crisp Vegetable and Quinoa Bowl |
| 21 | Crispy Breakfast Pita with Egg and Bacon |
| 31 | Crispy Sage-Roasted Root Vegetables |
| 68 | Crock Pot Dripped Beef |
| 68 | Crock Pot Swedish Cabbage Rolls |
| 64 | Crock Pot Three-Bean Burrito Bake |
| 34 | Crock-O-Beans |

## D

| | |
|---|---|
| 76 | Daily Lentil Soup |
| 58 | Daily Slow-Cooker Stew |
| 99 | Delicious Poppy Seed Dressing |

## E

| | |
|---|---|
| 94 | Easy Apple Crisp |
| 18 | Easy Avocado and Goat Cheese Toast |
| 36 | Easy Barbecued Lentils |
| 19 | Easy Buttermilk Pancakes |
| 79 | Easy Chickpea Fattoush Salad |
| 98 | Easy Creamy Chipotle-Lime Dressing |
| 25 | Easy Herby Egg Salad with Capers |
| 48 | Easy Hoisin Chicken Lettuce Wraps |
| 64 | Easy Homemade Beef Stew |

| | |
|---|---|
| 48 | Easy Lemon Chicken Piccata |
| 73 | Easy Low Cooker Beans with Sausage |
| 69 | Easy Meal-in-One-Casserole |
| 35 | Easy Party-Time Beans |
| 90 | Easy Pecan Sandies |
| 58 | Easy Pot Roast |
| 63 | Easy Roast |
| 96 | Easy Roasted Red Pepper and Plum Sauce |
| 18 | Easy Shakshuka Eggs |
| 84 | Easy Smoked Turkey Chili |
| 77 | Easy Spanish Black Bean Soup |
| 92 | Easy Stuffed Dates |
| 48 | Easy Turkey Bolognese with Mushroom and Cheese |
| 82 | Easy Turkey Taco Soup |
| 25 | Easy Yogurt Parfait with Nuts and Berries |
| 33 | Easy, Cheesy Quinoa Fritters |
| 23 | Egg and Ham Slice Breakfast "Burritos" |
| 21 | Egg White and Oatmeal Pancakes |

**F**

| | |
|---|---|
| 34 | Famous Baked Beans |
| 42 | Fish Tacos with Avocado Salsa and Lettuce |
| 50 | Flavored Roast Chicken with Collards |
| 96 | Fresh Basil Pesto |
| 75 | Fresh Chickpea and Salmon Salad Dijon |
| 96 | Fresh Cranberry Orange Relish |
| 75 | Fresh Fish Chowder Soup |
| 76 | Fresh Herbed Tomato Salad |
| 89 | Frozen Chocolate Peanut Butter Freezer Bites |
| 28 | Frozen Tofu and Fruit Smoothie |

**G**

| | |
|---|---|
| 85 | Garden Fresh Tomato Soup |
| 44 | Ginger-Garlic Cod with Bell Pepper |
| 61 | Gone-All-Day Low Calorie Casserole |
| 58 | Gourmet Spaghetti Sauce with Red Wine |
| 27 | Greek Yogurt Sundae with Mixed Berries |
| 52 | Greek-Inspired Turkey Sauté with vegetables |
| 69 | Green Chili Stew with Pork |
| 81 | Green Tofu Soup |
| 79 | Grilled Romaine with White Beans Salad |

**H**

| | |
|---|---|
| 88 | Healthy Berry Smoothie Pops |
| 77 | Healthy Citrus Avocado Salad |
| 75 | Healthy Cream of Carrot Soup |
| 89 | Healthy Dark Chocolate Almond Butter Cups |
| 28 | Healthy Egg and Veggie Breakfast Cups |
| 86 | Healthy Low-Cal Garden Soup |
| 26 | Healthy Overnight Oatmeal |
| 91 | Healthy Raspberry-Chocolate Chia Pudding |
| 66 | Healthy Swedish Meatballs |
| 25 | Healthy Tuna Salad Stuffed Avocado |
| 63 | Hearty and Nutritious New England Dinner |
| 76 | Hearty Italian Minestrone Soup |
| 37 | Hearty Vegan Slow Cooker Chili with Yogurt |
| 36 | Herbed Chickpea Pasta |
| 56 | Herbed Lamb Stew with Peas |
| 93 | Homemade Carrot Cake |
| 98 | Homemade Cherry Barbecue Sauce |
| 52 | Homemade Chicken Satay with Peach Fennel Salad |
| 96 | Homemade Cranberry-Raisin Chutney |
| 90 | Homemade Cream Cheese Swirl Brownies |
| 82 | Homemade Egg Drop Soup |
| 43 | Homemade Fish Stock |
| 53 | Homemade Juicy Turkey Burgers |
| 65 | Homemade Machaca Beef |
| 69 | Homemade Mary Ellen's Barbecued Meatballs |
| 97 | Homemade Raspberry Vinaigrette |
| 49 | Homemade Shirataki Noodles with Vegetables and Turkey |
| 59 | Homemade Sour Beef |
| 91 | Homemade Strawberry Yogurt Pops |
| 59 | Homemade Swiss Steak |
| 20 | Homemade Turkey Breakfast Sausage Patties |

| | |
|---|---|
| 81 | Homemade Turkey Pastrami and Pimento Cheese Sandwich |
| 88 | Homemade Vanilla Bean Ice Cream |
| 96 | Homemade Vegan Worcestershire Sauce |
| 64 | Home-Style Pot Roast with Gravy and Vegetables |

**I**

| | |
|---|---|
| 58 | Italian-Style Stew |

**J**

| | |
|---|---|
| 85 | Jalapeño Lime Chicken Soup |
| 62 | Judy's Slow Cooker Beef Stew |
| 59 | Juicy Nadine & Hazel's Swiss Steak |

**L**

| | |
|---|---|
| 57 | Lamb Stew with Carrot and Potato |
| 62 | Lazy Day Beef Stew |
| 97 | Lemon Basil Pesto Sauce |
| 99 | Lemon Tahini Dressing |
| 41 | Lemon Trout with Potato Hash Browns |
| 81 | Lentil Sloppy Joes with Roasted Asparagus |
| 91 | Low Calorie Avocado Chocolate Mousse |
| 60 | Low Calorie Big Beef Stew |
| 89 | Low Calorie Carrot Cake Bites |
| 96 | Low Calorie Fat-Free Roux |
| 59 | Low Calorie Margaret's Swiss Steak |
| 68 | Low calorie Old World Sauerbraten |
| 91 | Low Carb Microwave Keto Bread |
| 97 | Low Carb Whole Wheat Pizza Dough |
| 62 | Low Carb, Full-Flavored Beef Stew |
| 70 | Low Fat Cranberry Meatballs |
| 76 | Low Fat Manhattan Clam Chowder |
| 73 | Low-Fat Cajun Sausage and Beans |

**M**

| | |
|---|---|
| 34 | Macaroni and Cheese with Mixed Vegetables |
| 55 | Main Dish Baked Beans and Beef |
| 82 | Manhattan-Style Seafood Chowder |
| 32 | Mashed Cauliflower and Potatoes |
| 32 | Mediterranean Oven-Roasted Potatoes and Vegetables with Herbs |
| 80 | Miso Baked Tempeh and Carrot Wraps |
| 24 | Mixed Berry Vanilla Baked Oatmeal |
| 57 | Mom's Meatballs with Tomato Sauce |
| 37 | Mushroom Burgers |
| 28 | Mushroom, Zucchini, and Onion Frittata with Feta Cheese |

**N**

| | |
|---|---|
| 57 | Nancy's Beef and Mushroom Spaghetti Sauce |
| 34 | New England Baked Beans |
| 74 | New Mexico - Style Pinto Beans |
| 73 | New Orleans Red Beans with Sausage |
| 88 | No Bake Apple Pie Parfait |
| 90 | No-Bake Peanut Butter Energy Balls |
| 79 | Nutritional Sweet Beet Grain Bowl |

**O**

| | |
|---|---|
| 19 | Oat and Walnut Granola with Dried Cherries |
| 32 | Old-Fashioned Sweet Potato Bake with Pecans |
| 48 | One-Pot Chicken and Brown Rice |
| 80 | Oven Roasted Carrot and Quinoa with Goat Cheese |

**P**

| | |
|---|---|
| 31 | Pasta with Sun-Dried Tomatoes, Feta Cheese, and Arugula |
| 61 | Pat's Meat Slow Stew |
| 88 | Pear and Pecan Crumble Pie |
| 41 | Peppercorn-Crusted Baked Spiced Salmon |
| 93 | Perfect Mango Smoothie |
| 58 | Pheasant a la Elizabeth with Mushroom |
| 73 | Pizza Beans with Tomato and Sausage |
| 25 | Potato, Zucchini and Sausage Breakfast Hash |

| | | | | |
|---|---|---|---|---|
| 55 | Pot-Roasted Spiced Rabbit | | 90 | Soft Oatmeal Cookies |
| 19 | Puff Pancakes with Berry Topping | | 35 | Soft Pioneer Beans |
| 26 | Pumpkin Pie Smoothie with Pecans | | 44 | Spaghetti with Shrimp Marinara |
| | | | 60 | Spanish Delicious Round Steak |
| **Q** | | | 44 | Speedy Vegetable Broth and Tomato Fish Stew |
| 77 | Quick and Easy Minestrone Soup | | 92 | Spiced Honey Roasted Almonds |
| 97 | Quick and Easy Mock White Sauce | | 72 | Spiced Lamb Chops |
| 76 | Quick Chicken and Shrimp Gumbo | | 74 | Spicy Asian-Style Tofu Salad |
| 88 | Quick Chocolate Yogurt Granita | | 98 | Spicy Horseradish Mustard |
| 84 | Quick Moroccan Style Chicken Stew | | 77 | Spicy Slow Cooker Turkey Chili |
| 79 | Quinoa and Cucumber Feta Salad | | 39 | Spicy Tuna Barbecue |
| 33 | Quinoa and Vegetable Pilau | | 86 | Spicy Vegetable and Bean Chili Soup |
| | | | 20 | Spinach Artichoke Breakfast Bake with Cheese |
| **R** | | | 23 | Spinach Potato Cheese Quiche |
| 19 | Raspberry, Ricotta, and Banana Smoothie | | 26 | Steel-Cut Oatmeal with Fruit and Nuts |
| 35 | Red Beans and Pasta | | 18 | Strawberry, Spinach and Avocado Smoothie |
| 35 | Red Beans and Sausage | | 51 | Sun-Dried Tomato Stuffed Grilled Chicken Breasts |
| 67 | Red Wine Tender Roast | | 82 | Super Easy Minted Sweet Pea Soup |
| 35 | Refried Beans with Bacon | | 72 | Sweet and Sour Beans with Bacon Drippings |
| 18 | Refrigerated Lemon-Blueberry Overnight Oats | | 21 | Sweet Potato and Turkey Sausage Hash with Onion |
| 33 | Roasted Broccoli and Parmesan Millet Bake | | 32 | Sweet Potato Fries |
| 84 | Roasted Butternut Squash and Pear Soup | | 22 | Sweet Potato Pancakes with Apple Sauce |
| 45 | Roasted Halibut with Red Peppers and Green Beans | | | |
| 89 | Roasted Peach and Coconut Yogurt Bowls | | **T** | |
| 43 | Roasted Salmon with Honey-Mustard Sauce | | 50 | Tandoori, Chicken with Cauliflower Rice |
| 93 | Roasted Spiced Pears with Cinnamon and Pistachios | | 50 | Tandoori-Style Grilled Chicken |
| 43 | Roasted Spiced Salmon with Salsa Verde | | 92 | Tasty Blueberries with Sweet Cashew Cream |
| 80 | Roasted Tomato Tartine with Ricotta Cheese | | 21 | Tasty Buckwheat Pancakes |
| 83 | Roasted Tomato-Basil Soup with Grilled Cheese Croutons | | 65 | Tasty Garlic Beef Stroganoff |
| | | | 75 | Tasty Herbed Chicken Stew with Noodles |
| 44 | Roasted Whole Veggie-Stuffed Trout | | 91 | Tasty Herbed Yogurt Sauce |
| | | | 49 | Tasty Manhattan Chicken Salad |
| **S** | | | 61 | Tasty Santa Fe Stew |
| 41 | Salmon and Vegetables Po'boy | | 18 | Tasty Strawberry and Ricotta Pancakes |
| 41 | Salmon Cheese Mushroom Casserole | | 89 | Tasty Strawberry Cream Cheese Crepes |
| 56 | Sausage Beef and Tomato Spaghetti Sauce | | 94 | Tasty Sweet Potato Cake |
| 26 | Savory Cherry Tomato Cheese Salad | | 36 | Tempeh-Stuffed Peppers with Cheddar |
| 66 | Savory Sweet Crock Pot Roast | | 67 | Tender Beef Burgundy |
| 40 | Seafood and Vegetable Gumbo | | 53 | Tender Spiced Butter Chicken |
| 39 | Seafood Medley with Milk Butter Soup | | 59 | Tender Venison or Beef Stew |
| 29 | Shakshuka Eggs | | 65 | Three-Pepper Steak Stew |
| 82 | Shaved Asparagus Salad with Chile-Lime Dressing | | 63 | Traditional "Smothered" Steak |
| 77 | Shaved Brussels Sprouts and Kale Salad with Poppy Seed Dressing | | 75 | Traditional English Beef Stew |
| | | | 84 | Traditional Golden Chicken Soup |
| 81 | Shortcut Wonton Soup | | 67 | Traditional Hungarian Goulash |
| 42 | Shrimp and Ham Jambalaya | | 49 | Tropical Chicken Salad Sandwiches |
| 40 | Shrimp and Vegetable Creole | | 93 | Tropical Fruit Salad with Coconut Milk and Lime |
| 46 | Shrimp Burgers with Fruity Salsa and Salad | | 40 | Tropical Shrimp Cocktail with Sweet and Sour Sauce |
| 92 | Simple Berry Sorbet | | 74 | Tuna Noodle Casserole with Almonds Topping |
| 74 | Simple Broccoli Slaw Crab Salad | | 51 | Turkey Cutlets with Zucchini |
| 80 | Simple Cauli-Lettuce Wraps | | | |
| 98 | Simple Lemon Vinaigrette Dressing | | **V** | |
| 98 | Simple Mock Cream | | 55 | Veal and Green Peppers |
| 88 | Simple Oatmeal-Cranberry Cookies | | 78 | Vegan Kale Caesar Salad |
| 78 | Simple Pomegranate "Tabbouleh" with Cauliflower | | 56 | Venison in Onion Sauce |
| 55 | Simple Pot Roast and Veggies | | 56 | Venison Steak with Tomato Juice |
| 68 | Simple Spanish Rice | | 59 | Venison Swiss Steak Slow Stew |
| 19 | Simple Stir Fry Tofu | | | |
| 65 | Simple Succulent Steak | | **W** | |
| 55 | Six-Bean Barbecued Beans with Pork | | 83 | West African Peanut Soup |
| 28 | Sliced Peach Muesli Bake | | 51 | West African–Style Chicken Stew with Potatoes |
| 72 | Slow Cooker Apple Bean Bake | | 32 | Wheat Berry and Tabbouleh Salad |
| 61 | Slow Cooker Becky's Beef Stew | | 49 | Whole Spatchcock Chicken with Roasted Vegetable Medley |
| 36 | Slow Cooker Butter Macaroni with Cheese | | | |
| 66 | Slow Cooker Dilled Pot Roast | | 27 | Whole-Grain Breakfast Cookies with Cherries and Chocolate |
| 73 | Slow Cooker Four-Bean Medley | | | |
| 73 | Slow Cooker Kidney Beans with Apple | | 26 | Whole-Grain Dutch Baby Pancake with Cinnamon |
| 36 | Slow Cooker Red Beans | | 27 | Whole-Grain Pancakes with Fresh Fruit |
| 66 | Slow Cooker Roast Beef with Apple and Onion | | 24 | Whole-Wheat Blueberry Breakfast Cake |
| 36 | Slow Cooker Scandinavian Beans | | 33 | Wild Rice Pilaf with Broccoli and Carrots |
| 61 | Slow Cooker Steak San Morco | | 86 | Winter White Turkey Chili Soup |
| 70 | Slow Cooker Sweet and Sour Meatballs | | | |
| 55 | Slow Cooker Venison Roast | | **Y** | |
| 60 | Slow-Cooked Low Fat Pepper Steak | | 23 | Yogurt and Fruit Smoothie |

Made in the USA
Coppell, TX
29 August 2024